THE
TUSCAN
COOKBOOK

The Province of Tuscany

THE
TUSCAN
COOKBOOK

Wilma Pezzini

ATHENEUM

New York

1978

Library of Congress Cataloging in Publication Data
Pezzini, Wilma.
  The Tuscan cookbook.
  Includes index.
  1. Cookery, Italian. I. Title.
TX723.P44   641.59'45'5   77–15809
ISBN 0–689–10866–4

Text copyright © 1978 by Wilma Pezzini
Map copyright © 1978 by Anita Karl
All rights reserved
Published simultaneously in Canada by
McClelland and Stewart Ltd.
Manufactured in the United States of America by
American Book–Stratford Press
Saddle Brook, New Jersey
Designed by Kathleen Carey
First Edition

To my mother,
who did most of the cooking

I want to thank Siegmund and Norma Levarie for having suggested this book to me, Mr. J. Philip O'Hara for having believed in it and Howard Greenfeld for having made it possible. Furthermore, my sincere gratitude to all the friends, and friends of friends, who helped in many ways, large and small. And to all those who gave me recipes, told tales, offered advice, brought books on Tuscan customs and traditions and history, or just showed interest, thanks again.

CONTENTS

THE
TUSCAN
COOKBOOK

INTRODUCTION

IT's AN OLD Tuscan tradition that when a bride enters the house of her husband's parents for the first time she asks her mother-in-law, who is standing on the threshold: "Are you pleased to have me enter this house?" and as soon as that formidable lady answers "Do come in" the father-in-law hands the young woman a glass of *Vin Santo,* symbol of affection and hospitality. It's a simple little ceremony, but significant, because it points up two fundamental aspects of Tuscan life. First, it underlines the importance attached to wine; second, it illustrates the ageless good sense of the Tuscans, for with this little pantomime tension is created and immediately relieved, and family relationships are established, understood and accepted for what they are.

Ten years ago I came here, the foreign wife of a young Italian doctor. Since I had lived most of my adult life either in Brazil or in the United States, my knowledge of Italy was limited and superficial. Tuscany to me was the leaning tower of Pisa, the famous art works that fill the Florentine galleries, or the Sienese *Palio*. In the years that followed I've had time to learn more, but I still feel as if I'd only scratched the surface.

A couple of years ago, however, I came across a comment that gave me something of a clue to the quiet self-satisfaction that pervades this land. The writer of the comment simply pointed out that this part of Italy, called Etruria or Tuscia by the Romans two thousand years ago and Toscana by modern Italians, had been, at two entirely different points in European history, the cradle of civilization. The first time was during the Etruscan period, approximately the 9th to 5th centuries before Christ. The mysterious Etruscans who inhabited the Italian peninsula in an area that can be roughly described as lying between the Arno and Tiber rivers were a highly civilized nation. They knew how to build bridges, roads, sewage systems and waterworks; they made lovely, delicate gold jewelry—Florence is still known for its artisanship in that field, but no one has been able to equal the perfect workmanship of the Etruscan goldsmiths—they manufactured fine linen cloth and made good leather shoes, and they exported their products, for Etruscan shoes and pottery have been found beyond the Alps and all over the Mediterranean. Their religion was highly developed, they had an efficient navy, and their socio-political structure was complex and extremely functional at the same time. And all of this was going on at a time when England, Germany and France were still inhabited by men at the iron weapon stage, and when in all of Europe only Greece was beginning to establish its first cities on the Ionian sea. Later, the beautiful Etruscan cities were destroyed by the Romans, those same Romans who, according to some authoritative historians, had been taught the art of civilization by this very nation, a nation they not only later defeated in a long and bloody war, but tried to cancel from the annals of history. This may be one explanation for the fact that we know so little about the Etruscans. Roman power was present for a long time and did a thorough job. Now, modern archeology has been analyzing what is left of Etruscan culture, and the tombs and ruins that have been found prove that this nation was peace loving and highly artistic, civilized and downright sophisticated, and its golden age was around the 7th century B.C., before any other on the European continent.

The second period of Tuscan greatness is much closer to our time, when Europe was awakening from the Middle Ages. Beginning in the 12th century, through the 13th, 14th and 15th centuries, it was this same small strip of land that led Europe on the way to the Renaissance.

The feudal system was breaking down and men were beginning to flock to the cities, to organize themselves into what were then called corporations (and which are closer to our concept of labor unions) and to shake off the burdens of servitude and bondage. The middle class or *bourgeoisie* was being born—in fact the word *bourgeoisie* is French for town or city dweller, from the Latin *borgus*, town, as in the German *burg* or English 'borough.' With the advent of the city and of the middle class came a major cultural shift, the old classical languages (Latin, Greek and Hebrew) began to lose ground in favor of the dialects spoken by the common people, the so-called 'vulgar' tongues. Italian as we know it today is based on 13th century Florentine, just as modern French is based on the dialect spoken in Paris at about that time and, to a lesser extent, English recalls the language of 14th century London. In Italy, however, the men who helped popularize the 'vulgar' language of 13th century Florence were the three Tuscan geniuses who gave the world some of its best and most famous literary works—Dante, Petrarch and Boccaccio.

But Tuscan leadership wasn't limited to writing. Dante Alighieri, the father of modern literature ('modern' as opposed to 'classical,' since up to Dante's *Divine Comedy* all good writing had been done in the classical languages), was born in 1265 and Giotto, the first painter to use perspective, in 1266. This ugly man of simple birth gave life to the gilded, flat-faced Madonnas of Byzantine tradition. He did it by using depth and with him we have the beginning of realism in painting. A charming little anecdote tells of how Giotto won the competition for the projection of the *campanile*, or belltower, of the Florence cathedral, Santa Maria del Fiore. It seems that Giotto, who by 1334 was tired and sick, and whose disposition apparently matched his appearance, told the emissaries of the city fathers that he had no intention of submitting a project for the tower. "Let it be done by a younger man," he said. But the emissaries insisted: "Please, Maestro, give us something, anything, we can't go back empty handed . . ." so the old man turned from his easel, took a sheet of parchment, angrily drew something, and gave it to them, saying he hoped that now they would leave him alone. The city fathers carefully examined all the projects submitted, and after lengthy deliberation declared Giotto the winner of the competition. Freehand, he had drawn a perfect circle.

But Giotto was only the first—and not even the first, for before him came his great teacher, Cimabue—in a long line of extraordinary Tuscan painters that, through Masaccio and Botticelli, Beato Angelico and Fra' Filippo Lippi, arrives at Michelangelo Buonarrotti.

All of this wasn't accidental, of course. The city of Florence was one of the most active centers of that time, rich and powerful, strong and bursting with energy, and men such as the ones mentioned above, as well as many others—Leonardo da Vinci and Nicolò Macchiavelli, for instance—drew strength from and were stimulated by this heady atmosphere. The Renaissance Florentines were merchants and bankers, and what they did for their city at the height of its wealth and power has proven as wise as any banker could wish. They invested in art, and the investment has really paid for itself. Throughout the centuries Italian and foreign visitors alike have been flocking to Florence to see its art galleries, museums and churches, its palaces, gardens and bridges, paying just homage to taste, beauty, and the Tuscan genius.

Let's take a look at Tuscany. It lies on the central part of Italy's Western or Thyrrenian coast, has a Mediterranean climate, rolling hills, and a well-tended soil where vines, rosemary and sage, myrtle, lavendar and eucalyptus, olives, chestnuts and walnuts, oaks, cypresses and firs have been growing side by side for the past thirty centuries, and maybe more. The best beef in Italy comes from the Val di Chiana, a valley that lies between Florence and Arezzo. A large flat region on the Southern end of Tuscany, the Maremma, is famous for being one of the last places in Europe where the wild boar roams. Herds of small sheep graze in the hills and pigs are raised with loving care, because hams and other pork by-products are greatly appreciated. The local rivers are full of sweet water crabs, trout, eels and frogs, tench and pike, and the coastal sea harbors fish and shellfish of all kinds. Prawns, shrimp and crawfish; squid, tiny cuttlefish, clams and mussels; bass, bream, mullet and mackerel are brought in daily by the little fishing boats that are still characteristic of this part of the Mediterranean. The local farmers raise chickens, ducks, pigeons, rabbits, and hare. The woods and fields are aflutter with pheasant, partridge, woodcock and thrush, and while the main feature of the countryside is the olive tree and the neatly tended vine, most fruit and vegetables of the temperate climate grow in Tuscany, and specialties such as mushrooms, truffles and snails are easily found. In short, it is a gourmet's paradise.

And yet, the geography of the region isn't responsible for all this. Tuscany is mostly a land of hills, often a land of beaches and moun-tains, and its soil is not of the richest kind. The quality of what is available here is, to a large extent, the result of the effort of man. For countless generations the Tuscan peasant has worked intelligently and well, getting as much as possible out of his beloved, beautiful and rugged country.

This labor of love seems the more remarkable when we study the history of the land. Italy has been, for twenty centuries, the most in-vaded and the most desired of countries. Tuscany, placed in the very heart of the country and, for anyone coming from the north, one of the most tempting byways to Rome, has been the target for a large portion of the attacks, invasions and plunder directed at Italy. Over and above this, there were the local wars and squabbles, fought for reasons which range from the sublime desire for independence and freedom to the simple materialistic wish for commercial supremacy.

Italian cooking originates mainly in the old Mediterranean cul-tures, Egypt, Greece and Rome, but this broad base has been modified and enlarged upon throughout the years. As mentioned above, many peoples have ravaged the peninsula in the past two thousand years. The Goths, the Arabs, the Normans, the Spaniards, the Austrians and the French, to list but a few, and not even in chronological order, have all either invaded or occupied Italy, or both. Each time these strangers came they not only took away but also left something behind, and as a result Italy's is a heterogeneous culture. From the gastronomical point of view this means that while it isn't always easy to trace the exact origin of a particular dish, we can make educated guesses, and say with a reasonable margin of safety that the "Sienese Cabbage," recipe No. 191, still popular in Siena today, dates back to the Austrian occupation of the 19th century, while something like the "Sweet and Pungent Sauce" (recipe No. 79) was served to the citizens of ancient Rome as an accompaniment to wild boar, hare, elephant and whatever other meats they ate.

In addition to the influences described above, Tuscany boasts, as we have already seen, the heritage of the Etruscans. A highly civilized nation of uncertain origin, they inhabited this part of the Italian peninsula when Rome was only a small village, the last wading point on the Tiber river before it reached the sea. Tradition has it that the Etruscans improved the local wine by mixing several types of grapes, and paintings found on the walls of Etruscan tombs show banquet scenes where small animals roasted on sticks are being served. It could be just a coincidence, but Tuscany is the land of Chianti wine, and the most fragrant roasts in all of Italy are eaten here.

Nowadays Tuscany leads a perfectly modern life. Well designed highways cut it from one end to another, powerful cars fill the air with noise, industrial buildings of all kinds pollute the air and water and spoil the view. On closer inspection, however, the industrial buildings are small; the average Tuscan factory employs less than one hundred workers. The modern highways are crisscrossed by lovely little country roads which lead to lovely little villages which usually house a lovely little *trattoria* where one can have a lovely big meal. And the powerful cars are often carting a typical, numerous Tuscan family to just such a *trattoria*, where they will noisily settle themselves around a large, solid walnut, *fratino* style table, and start their meal by ordering wine (usually red), mineral water, a basket of fragrant Tuscan bread, and *antipasti*.

Antipasti translates as "appetizers," but literally it means "before the meal" from the Latin *ante*, before and *prandium*, meal. *Antipasto* is identical to the German *vorspeise*, before the meal, similar to the French *hors d'oeuvre*, outside the main piece of work, but different from the Russian *zakuska*, snack, all of which are words used to indicate that which in English is called "appetizer." A Tuscan *antipasto*—as served in a *trattoria*, not in a restaurant or private home—consists of a trayful of *prosciutto*, *salame*, *mortadella nostrana* and other *insaccati*, cold cuts, various bowls of *sott'olii*, which literally means "under oil" and are actually vegetables, such as mushrooms, artichokes, onions, peppers, etc., marinated in vinegar and then kept under oil, and the excellent Tuscan *crostini*, small pieces of fried bread with a liver spread, of which there are as many variations as there are cooks in Tuscany.

When all this has been eaten, the meal will continue with a substantial *primo*, or first course, which is also called *minestra*. There are two basic types of *minestra: asciutta*, dry, and *in brodo*, in broth. Personally, I would add a third variety, the semi-liquid *zuppe*. *Zuppa* does not mean soup in the Northern European sense, because it is dense to begin with and furthermore has slices of toasted or slightly stale bread that soak in it to produce a consistency that resembles a gruel. To the *minestra asciutta* variety belong all the *pasta* dishes, the *risotti*, the *gnocchi* and the *tortelli*. To the *in brodo* belong all the broths, with small *pastina* or *tortellini* added, or in the form of clear *consommé*. The various forms of *polenta* belong to the semi-liquid group when they are prepared soft and have to be eaten with a spoon, and to the *asciutta* type when they are hard enough to be eaten with a fork.

After the first course comes the second, *secondo*, which is sub-divided into two parts: the *secondo* proper, consisting of meat or fish, and the *contorno*, literally "contour," actually a side dish of vegetables. After that, if the occasion requires, there will be a *dolce*, sweet dessert, and always *frutta di stagione*, fruit in season. The meal is then concluded with a strong demi-tasse of coffee, to which the men will add brandy, *grappa*, rum, or anise-flavored liqueur, making it into a *corretto*, which in Tuscany means a corrected cup of coffee.

I live in a small town called Camaiore, where my husband's ancestors settled way back in the 15th century. It nestles cozily in a bright valley named, with a touch of the Tuscan genius for visual accuracy, La Valle della Luce, the valley of light, about halfway between the sea and the walled city of Lucca, which is the capital of one of the nine provinces that make up the Tuscan region.

Life in Camaiore is traditional. Women are expected to cook two meals each day, men are expected to come home and eat them. Morning coffee is often taken at the bar, because homemade coffee isn't as good as that made by the *espresso* machine. But that's just as well; there's enough to do with two meals to prepare. The average family meal here, while not as elaborate as the one described above, is composed of a cooked *minestra*, a *secondo* of either meat or fish with a *contorno*, and fruit. Shopping for each day's cooking is done in the morning, and in some cases the food for dinner is bought again in the afternoon. Even though the basic staples are kept in the *dispensa*, or pantry, items such as meat, eggs, butter, vegetables, fruit, cheese, milk and so on are bought fresh each day. This is one reason why shopping for food in Camaiore (and, I dare say, in most small Italian towns) is a lengthy business. There are many stores to choose from— *alimentari*, grocery stores, *verduraie*, vegetable stalls, *macellai*, butcher shops. But no matter how many, they are always crowded.

In the beginning of my life here I shopped once a week, the way

I always had. Stoically, my husband said nothing and ate what I prepared. Slowly, however, experience and observation taught me that it was wiser to shop more often. There are fresh things to be had at the vegetable store every day. Sometimes, at the turn of a season, a new item, *una primizia*, will show up unexpectedly. This year the asparagus were out in April instead of May, and nothing is quite as good as the first fresh asparagus. The first tender peas can be had in early June, sweet as sugar, and I start keeping an eye out for them as early as May 20th. In the fall, the early, small cauliflowers taste better. And the aroma and flavor of the first wild strawberries (early June) borders on the divine. No wonder then that, according to an old tradition, one says a small prayer of thanksgiving before eating them.

The butcher should be seen often, too. Milk-fed veal is killed only once a week, sometimes not even as often as that, and if I want the special cuts I like it's a good idea to be there on the day the meat arrives. Fresh liver is available on Tuesday, the best chickens arrive on Thursday, and Saturday is the day to buy beef roast, stewing beef, and steaks. In hunting season, one never knows when a hunter will bring a good hare, a freshly-killed pheasant or a side of venison, and as soon as they are seen they are bought, so if you're not there, you miss these special treats.

By now I'm a good Italian wife and I shop almost every day. It does use up a bit more time but the food on our table is much more varied and better!

But there are other reasons that explain the complications of shopping in Camaiore. They go under the general heading of "Italian character traits" and include such things as the national tendency to talk a lot, individuality, and the fact that the principle "the customer is always right" has never been heard of.

The owner of the milk store is never there. She casually leaves the key stuck on the outside of her locked door, which means she isn't far, and if you want milk all you have to do is go looking for her. Once you find her, however, you'll be rewarded not only by her good (and inexpensive) milk, but also by the latest news on who has been hospitalized, born, married or deceased—and how and why. The butcher who sells the best pork in town should be left alone in the morning. By mid-afternoon, after his plump, attractive wife has given him his lunch and his *fiasco* of Chianti, he becomes pleasant, almost jolly, and the customer gets his money's worth. And if buying a piece of bread takes at least ten minutes, it's only because you exchange with the shopkeeper comments about the weather, the latest political news item, your mother's health, and the local football team. At first, these conversations irritated me, I couldn't understand the reason for them, they were a waste of time. I've since learned that they are a form of social intercourse, the relaxed moment of an otherwise busy day. I'm so used to them by now that I often participate, and actually feel neglected if, on Monday morning, the grocer doesn't ask me how my Sunday lunch turned out.

This book is about cooking and eating in Tuscany. In order to appreciate the effort put into the organization and planning of meals, the work and effort that go into the making of food here, it should be kept in mind that Italians in general and Tuscans in particular like to eat well. There's an old local proverb that says A tavola non s'invecchia, one doesn't age at the table, and in keeping with this philosophy Tuscans try to spend as much time as possible at the table. With this in mind, I've tried to include, as often as possible, comments on how things are eaten, served, enjoyed—not just how to cook them.

This is not a collection of old-fashioned Tuscan recipes. It hopes to be a compendium of the best in Tuscan cooking as it is now, in 1977. It was put together by a combination of research, leg work, and the trial-and-error method. Spurred on by both our love of good food and our curiosity, my husband and I have driven all over the region, searching out restaurants and trattorie, country inns—big and small— poking around in their kitchens whenever possible, trying to find out how they prepare this sauce or that roast. I've taken notes on scraps of paper and tried to make sense out of the vague explanations given to me. I've talked to relatives, friends, and friends of friends. I've tested recipes and double-checked them, sometimes adding an item, sometimes discarding something, mainly enjoying the results and adding pounds to what used to be my slim figure. The result is this book, a list of the everyday dishes eaten in Tuscany today, with a few comments on where they come from, how they became the way they are, and anything else I thought might be of interest. I've also included some of the traditional, old Tuscan recipes, because they're delicious and even if you don't have the time to make them, they are worth reading. Some of these recipes are easy to make, others take effort and time; some are inexpensive, others require costly ingredients; some are very digestible, others call for healthy stomachs, but they're all genuine, hearty fare.

An English newspaperman who has recently written a book about this country says that "Cooking in Italy fundamentally consists of serving something exquisitely fresh with the least amount of modification in the process of preparation." He goes on to say that this applies mainly to central Italy, and in fact a large portion of Tuscan cooking is practically summed up in that statement.

At this point it should be noted that French cooking originates in Tuscany. When Catherine de Medici went to France in 1533 to marry the Dauphin—later King Henry II—part of her dowry was a household of Tuscan servants. Her cook's excellent meals started the French on the way to their famous *cuisine*. Now, these two forms of cooking are very different, because in Tuscany cooking has retained its basic simplicity while the French have added refinement and formality to the original base.

But to say that Tuscan cooking is simple doesn't necessarily mean it's easy. There are dishes that take almost two days to prepare, such as *Zuppa alla Frantoiana*, not so much because of the amount of work involved but because the cooking required is lengthy and the taste improves on the second day. Most of the wild boar, venison and hare dishes have to be started a few days in advance, because they need marinating, the longer the better. There are other difficulties as well. It's important to have the right ingredients, and to have them of the right quality. When a recipe calls for mushrooms, they should be either fresh mushrooms or good-quality dried mushrooms, but not the cultivated variety known as *champignons*. When grated Parmesan cheese is used, it should be grated in your kitchen, better still at the table, just before eating, but never, never bought in grated form. One gourmet I know grates it with a knife, slowly, claiming that heat alters the flavor and that quick grating generates heat. Butter should be fresh and of excellent quality, and it shouldn't be replaced by margarine unless the recipe says so. Olive oil *must*, and I wish to underline this emphatically, be genuine olive oil. When a recipe calls for Chianti wine, or good dry white wine, it means just that. And pepper is much better when fresh ground—a well equipped kitchen should have two pepper grinders, one for black and one for white pepper. But to go back to what I was saying before, many Tuscan dishes are simple because they require few ingredients, because they are served as they come, sometimes in the very container in which they were cooked, and their goodness is often the result of a happy marriage between two items that have complementary flavors, such as the spicy aroma of fresh basil and the tartness of tomatoes, rather than the result of a complex mixture of many ingredients.

In my search for original, local recipes, I found a few of them cropping up again and again. I tried them all, excluded some, but still ended up with more than one recipe for the same dish. Where more than one recipe for a dish is given it means that to me they were equally valid. Often the first one listed is my personal favorite, but I would like to suggest that you read through the ingredients in all of them, and pick the one that has your favorites listed—our tastes may be different. I say all this for a reason. Not only is individual taste different, but the results obtained by the same person using the same ingredients to make the same dish may also be different. No two saucepans cook alike. The same cut of meat, coming from two different animals, may produce different results. Potatoes grown in Germany are not like potatoes grown in Argentina, and California oranges are not Florida oranges. As far as cooking is concerned, the difference in outcome widens as we cook in different kitchens, in different cities and in different countries. I've had a *Soufflé au Grand Marnier* cooked for me by a friend in Paris, and it was delicious, while the same soufflé cooked by the same friend in New York was just tolerable. Once, in Rio de Janeiro, I made an Italian lunch, and served *Tagliatelle al Ragù Bolognese*. They were hardly edible, yet when I make the same dish in Italy it's excellent.

The reasons for this are countless—water changes from place to place, vegetation grows in different ways because of soil composition, exposure to the sun, wind, rain, and humidity. The taste of meat is influenced by what the animal eats. Furthermore, no two brands of olive oil, butter, or cheese are alike. There are other factors as well. If a frying pan is used for fish, meat and eggs, it will have a different undertaste than a frying pan that is used for only one of these items. A baking dish used for both sweet and salted food will produce flavor that is unlike the flavor produced by a baking dish used only for sweet or only for salted food. And even a cutting board can alter the taste of what you're cooking. Hasn't it happened that you have found a roast chicken smelling of onion when it had no onion in it, only to discover that you'd carved it on a cutting board that had been used for chopping the onions for the salad?

To me, a cookbook should not be a scientific text. Cooking instructions are meant to guide, to point the way, to give information, but they are not a formula. For example, the European tablespoon holds two or three more drops than the U.S. standard measuring tablespoon, but it makes little or no difference to the final taste of a *zuppa* or a *risotto*. I find it equally difficult to give exact information on portions. A recipe may serve four in my house but only three in yours. Not only that, but it may serve four in my house provided they are Mother, our friend Helen, my husband and I, and only three if our friend Gianni comes to dinner. Keep the guests in mind when calculating portions!

Good cooks don't always weigh and measure. Rather than the gift of precision a good cook needs the gift of patience, the intuition for knowing when to cover a stew and when to let a sauce boil uncovered, the knack for choosing the right pot for the right piece of meat, the curiosity to taste what's in the pot while it's cooking, the courage to correct when necessary. But over and above all of these things, one of the most important attributes of a good cook is simply the appreciation of good food.

I hope all of this hasn't discouraged you, for it shouldn't. The other side of the coin is that cooking is also a game and should be accepted as such. As someone once said, cooking is the only sport that doesn't have a season. So, when you least expect it, the dinner turns out splendidly. When at the last minute you find that there are no lemons in the house and add vinegar instead, the sauce tastes better than ever. And, when unexpected guests show up on Sunday evening and in desperation you throw together all the leftovers and make a big salad, that's when everyone asks you for the recipe!

As a last word, don't be surprised at the diversity of recipes in this book. It can be seen from what I have said that the food cooked in Tuscany today is the final product of the interaction among ancient traditions and foreign influences, as interpreted by Tuscan taste and imagination and made feasible by the variety of ingredients available here. The recipe for *"Thin Spaghetti with Cream and Whisky Sauce"* is just a reminder that during World War II the U.S. occupation forces were here.

THE TUSCAN PANTRY

From the elegant *villa signorile* to the simple *rustico di campagna*, from the sophisticated Florentine apartment on the Lungarno to the humble house of the Garfagnana peasant, there is hardly a Tuscan home without a pantry. The modest ones contain only a few *fiaschi* of neighborhood wine, a bottle or two of olive oil, bunches of onions and garlic hanging from large iron nails, a piece of Italian raw ham, *prosciutto*, on the bone, a string of sausages, possibly a *salame*, a can of anchovies, a few jars of homemade *sott'olii* and *sottaceti*, a handful of dried *peperoncini* and a few bunches of bay leaves and fennel stalks. There is no limit to what a better stocked Tuscan pantry may hold.

It seems a contradiction, at first. If the Tuscan housewife shops for food once or even twice each day, can't she buy everything she needs as she goes along? Why store anything? The main reason is simple, and it can be reduced to the practical aspect of food purchasing and consumption. In Tuscany (and, I dare say, in most of Italy as well), a large part of the average household budget goes into food and drink. Naturally, it follows that money saved on food and drink is of major importance. Thus, large quantities of wine are bought when wine is least expensive. The same goes for olive oil. Pork products like ham, sausage and salami are bought wholesale and stored for future use. Seasonal vegetables are also a source of savings. Artichokes are cheap at the end of May–early June, so they are bought by the hundreds, cleaned, boiled in vinegar, dried accurately and stored in clean glass jars, under olive oil, *sott'olio*, to be eaten all winter as part of the *antipasti* or as a *contorno*. Mushrooms are available from July to October, provided the season alternates periods of heavy rains with periods of sunshine. Some years bring an abundant mushroom harvest—a metaphoric expression, since picking mushrooms is a very special hobby in Tuscany, and bears little resemblance to an actual harvest—other years don't have enough rain, or enough sunshine, and the mushrooms are few, far between and very expensive. But no matter what quantities are available, almost every Tuscan eats mushrooms at least once every year; it's the biggest possible treat, as mushrooms are probably the most highly valued of all foods here. In a good mushroom year the smaller specimens are treated like the artichokes: cleaned, boiled in vinegar, dried and stored under olive oil in sterile glass jars. The larger ones are sliced and dried, then stored on strings or in airtight containers.

The tomato, available from July to October, is at present a very basic staple of Tuscan cooking. I say at present because tomatoes were not part of the old-fashioned Tuscan kitchen, and arrived rather late on the cooking scene. It was Garibaldi and his Thousand who brought the tomato back from Sicily in the mid-19th century, but by now it is so much a part of the local eating habits that most households store large quantities of *pelati*, peeled plum tomatoes, or *conserva*, tomato sauce, both of which are made at home during the tomato season.

At this point I would like to digress. In many recipes you will find either "peeled Italian plum tomatoes," "tomato sauce" or "tomato paste." There is a difference, of course, but in an emergency the tomato sauce and the peeled plum tomatoes are interchangeable. Not so the tomato paste, which has a stronger, more concentrated flavor and if used in place of either of the other two will produce a change in the end result. The tomato sauce (see recipe No. 86) is basically the plum tomato put through a food mill, flavored by the addition of a few items, and cooked for an hour or two. It is therefore more concentrated than the plain, peeled, plum tomato and if used instead of it we can consider one tablespoon of sauce plus one tablespoon of water equivalent to one plum tomato. The recipe will not suffer greatly from the substitution. If, on the other hand, you use the peeled plum tomato instead of the sauce, keep in mind that it contains more liquid and will make the resulting sauce a bit more watery.

I'd also like to mention the possible methods for reducing peeled plum tomatoes into usable pieces. Some recipes say "chop the tomatoes, discarding seeds and hard parts," other say "squeeze the tomatoes in your hand, discarding the hard parts," a few suggest putting the tomatoes through a food mill. Obviously, the second is the easiest method for the Tuscan housewife who is, more often than not, a woman used to cooking and to using her hands in the kitchen. The first method is my solution, both because I don't like to see tomato seeds in my sauces and stews and because I find it equally easy and more hygienic to chop the tomatoes on a board. The last method is the solution of a few modern Italian cooks I know, who find it easiest to put everything through the food mill or chopper. But all methods are equally valid and each one to his own taste.

To get back to the *dispensa*, the Tuscan pantry, there is one more aspect of Italian life that explains it, besides the obvious economic and seasonal reasons listed above. Italy is a country that has known many wars, invasions, famines and shortages. These are things that leave a deep impression on the mind of a nation, and even if modern agricultural methods and 20th century food production and distribution systems have practically removed the threat of these ancient evils, some of the fear still lurks in the national subconscious and many a pantry contains large quantities of such staple goods as salt, sugar, coffee, tea, flour, rice and dried beans.

Let's take a closer look at an imaginary Tuscan *dispensa*. We've already seen the wine, the olive oil (sometimes two kinds of olive oil, the heavy, greenish virgin oil, *olio di prima spremitura*, for seasoning the *zuppe*, the beans and winter salads, and for making the *pinzimonio* (see recipe No. 210), and the cheaper, more refined oil used for cooking and frying), the onions and garlic, the bay leaves and fennel stalks, the jars and bottles of tomato in various forms, the *sott'olii*, the *sottaceti*, the *insaccati*, the staples. What else is there? Jams and marmalades, not only of the well-known Mediterranean fruit such as cherries, peaches, apricots or pears but also chestnut jam, grape marmalade, fig and persimmon preserves. Then, there are several boxes of *dadi*, bouillon cubes, a basic item in Tuscan cooking. The more sophisticated will also have *estratto di carne*, meat extract, which is more expensive but very flavorful. *Capperi*, capers, are indispensable, whether they be in small commercial jars or homemade, often picked by someone in the family when out on a picnic—the plant grows out of old stone walls, usually in high places—then boiled and stored under vinegar.

Ventresca or *tonno*, tuna fish, is always present, often next to other cans of fish, such as salmon, anchovies, sardines. Containers of *pinoli* nuts, *uvetta sultanina*, raisins, candied fruit, almonds and walnuts, for baking. During the winter, chestnuts and chestnut flour for making *mondine*, home-roasted chestnuts, which are baked in a special pan on the fireplace and flavored with a dash of good red wine, and for the *castagnaccio*, a chestnut flour cake that was once a staple among the mountaineers of Garfagnana.

Before moving on to the spices and herbs two additional items catch the eye on the shelf: the jar of *pane grattugiato*, bread crumbs, and the jar of *zucchero a velo vanigliato*, confectioners' sugar with a vanilla stick in it.

If at all possible, the herbs used in cooking should be fresh. Parsley, basil, thyme, tarragon, mint, sage and rosemary all grow in flower pots and in window boxes, in gardens and on small corners of land. Only basil is delicate and seasonal; the others, if well tended, can be nurtured through the winter. And basil can be picked when ready and prepared for the winter—personally, I wipe each leaf with a damp cloth and freeze it in a plastic bag. I find that it retains its aroma almost without change—but it can also be dried, or stored under oil or under salt.

But to go back to the pantry shelf. If fresh herbs are absolutely unavailable, buy them dried, but buy them in small quantities, of the best possible quality; don't store them for more than one year, and check them frequently for freshness of smell and appearance. There is nothing worse than a sauce or roast seasoned with sage that smells of dust or a tomato salad with basil that tastes of dried grass. Much wiser to add no herbs at all.

The situation is different for spices. Oriental spices are potent enough to be used in dried form without losing their aroma, and can be stored for reasonable lengths of time without changing their characteristics too much. So the *dispensa* can contain a small jar of black pepper, another one of white pepper (which is just black pepper with its outer shell removed, and is used mainly in pale sauces, to avoid the little black spots that would result from the use of black pepper); one or two nutmegs and their little grater; a small container of cloves and a few sticks of cinnamon—or for those who prefer it, cinnamon powder, but it loses its aroma faster than the stick. For those who are really interested in the flavor and aroma of spices I would also suggest a small jar of *coriandolo*, coriander seeds, a pleasant, pungent spice that adds zest to stews and roasts. Coriander is used in curry powder, but few people use it by itself.

There are other spices used in Italian cooking—which would therefore be present on the pantry shelf—that are not Oriental but grown nearby. Saffron, *zafferano*, which is the pistil of the autumn-flowering crocus, is sold in small envelopes, each containing ten to twelve pistils. It adds a strong, typical flavor to fish stews and *risotti*, and gives a golden color that would be hard to imitate. Juniper berries, *bacche di ginepro*, are needed during the game season, for they add a special taste to marinades and roasts. And then there could be a jar of that red powder known the world over as *paprika*, which is nothing but our very Italian *pereroncino* reduced to powder form.

Near the spices and the dried herbs a well stocked *dispensa* might have containers of *pistachio* nuts, dried figs and apricots, and a small can of dry mustard. The list could become embarrassingly long; many modern Tuscan pantries have cans of good Russian caviar, French *paté de foie gras*, American ketchup or Chinese soy sauce. But these are of little interest to us as they are seldom used in Tuscan cooking. So the last thing I would like to mention is that a good pantry should be cool—not cold or hot—dry, and not too exposed to the sunshine. The shelves, ideally, should be made of wood, lined with paper or plastic, and cleaned frequently. If all these conditions are met, and there is additional space in the room, it could be used for a small, home-style *cantina*, or wine cellar. But I won't go into that here because in Tuscany the subject of wine is very serious and requires very special treatment.

THE TUSCAN CELLAR

Three things characterize the Tuscan table and, because of their simplicity, or in spite of it, are responsible for the fact that Tuscan fare is so genuine, so hearty, and so delicious. These three things are bread, olive oil and wine. Of the three, wine is undeniably the most varied, the most delicate and the most discussed. Every Tuscan has an opinion about wine, almost every Tuscan drinks wine at his meals, practically all Tuscans know something about making wine and most of them know a lot.

It should therefore come as no surprise that the most famous wine in the world is Tuscan. Who hasn't heard of Chianti? It is one of the best known alcoholic beverages in the world, its fame equalled only by Scotch whisky and French Champagne. Its dry, tannic, full-bodied flavor, its slightly flowery, acrid perfume, its brilliant, dark, ruby-red are a perfect match for all roasts, steaks or grilled meats and make it a world-wide favorite, from Norway to Japan.

This chapter will describe a few Tuscan wines, and suggest a small, well-stocked Tuscan cellar. The cellar will be limited by the choices available in the United States—all wines listed are excellent, but some excellent wines are missing because they do not reach the American market.

The oldest red wine in Tuscany is made in the province of Siena and bears the name of Brunello di Montalcino. The first documents about it date back to the 8th century, when the Lombards were masters of the region. This wine must be aged in special wooden barrels for at least four years; otherwise it cannot be bottled as Brunello. One of its exceptional features is that it continues to age indefinitely in the bottle, and its flavor becomes better and more velvety as the years pass. It is made with only one type of grape, the *brunello*, is produced in limited quantities in a very restricted zone and is bottled by very few producers. In the United States, Brunello di Montalcino can be bought with the Poggio alle Mura label. If in Italy, try the Biondi e Santi. The Brunello is an austere and expensive wine, and should be enjoyed at room temperature with first class red meats or very good game.

In years when the grape harvest is particularly good, some of the *mosto*, must, is separated out and aged longer. The resulting wine is then labeled "Riserva" and should be tasted with special reverence. In the case of the above described Brunello the aging required for "Riserva" is five years; for Chianti it's three years. In the recent past only the 1964, 1967, 1970, 1971 and 1974 harvests have deserved this privilege. The 1976 grape harvest was so poor that, in most of Tuscany, it will be bottled only for local consumption. It is therefore probable that no Brunello or well-known Chianti brand will reach the international market with 1976 on its label.

Another well-known Sienese red is the Nobile di Montepulciano, a good, full-bodied wine which tends to get browner with age, has a dry flavor and a delicate, slightly flowery perfume. Like the Brunello, it should also be enjoyed at room temperature with red meats and game. This wine is made by mixing the grapes of several vines, namely: the *prugnolo*, black *canaiolo*, *malvasia del Chianti*, and *trebbiano*. Its name, Nobile, noble, is a reminder of the fact that in times past the grapes used to make it were carefully selected.

The province of Lucca produces a good table red that goes under the name of Rosso delle Colline Lucchesi. It's a bright, pleasant wine that can be drunk with either first or second courses, and it reaches its perfect aging point after two or three years.

The area that produces the wine known as Chianti Classico lies between the cities of Florence and Siena. It is the oldest of the Chianti zones, and its traditional trademark is a black cock on a field of yellow-gold, a symbol taken from an *affresco* painted by Vasari on a ceiling of the Palazzo Vecchio in Florence. The producers who have a right to use this trademark are limited by geographic position and by the severe standards of the *Consorzio del Gallo Nero,* established in 1924.

Chianti characteristics are, as mentioned above, a dry, slightly tannic, slightly acid flavor which becomes softer with age—Chianti is perfect when 3 years old—a winey perfume with undertones of iris and a bright, ruby-red which tends to become darker, more bricklike with time. While the proportions are, of course, the well-guarded secret of each individual producer, Chianti wine is a cocktail of several grapes: *sangiovese, trebbiano toscano,* black *canaiolo, malvasia del Chianti.* Its alcoholic content is between 24 and 27 proof and it should be served at room temperature with everything but fish and sweets. Chianti is one of the most universal red table wines.

In 1932, a few years after the Chianti Classico area was established by law, the wine producers who were left immediately outside the small area complained, and a small wine squabble followed. The resulting compromise gave six other areas the right to bottle wine using the Chianti name, provided it was not followed by the word Classico. These six areas are attached to the Gallo Nero zone, and the names of the wines produced are:

> Chianti dei Colli Senesi
>   "   dei Colli Aretini
>   "   dei Colli Fiorentini
>   "   Rufina
>   "   Montalbano
>   "   delle Colline Pisane

The difference between Chianti Classico and the other Chianti wines is confined to the neck label. Most of the producers belong to the *Consorzio del Chianti Putto,* which uses the statuette of a naked Renaissance child, the *putto,* as its symbol. These producers can be from the Colli Senesi, Aretini and Fiorentini, from the Rufina and Montalbano zones, and some from the Colline Pisane. About 150 of the latter have formed a separate group, which uses a centaur as its symbol, so there is also some Chianti to be had which has the *centauro* neck label. Finally, there is some Chianti bottled which has no neck label. Some of the largest producers, such as Baron Ricasoli, who makes Brolio, or the Antinori vineyards, with their very good Sta. Cristina Chianti, have chosen to leave the *consorzi* in an attempt to make their own name the major attraction. Still, they use the words Chianti Classico on their label, because it indicates the geographic location of their vineyards and is a guarantee of quality and taste.

The characteristics of the other Chianti wines are similar to the ones described above for Chianti Classico; only experts dwell on the minor details that distinguish one Chianti from another. All Chianti is a delightful, highly drinkable wine—the Montalbano is just a touch sweeter than the others, the Colli Aretini lighter in color and flavor than the Classico, the Colli Senesi better suited to everyday drinking.

The subject of rosé and white wine brings on a few considerations. It was once said—making things easy for everyone—that red wine was served with red meats, rosé wine with pink meats and white wine with white meats (fish or domestic fowl). In my experience this is no longer the case.

Since white wines—and most rosés—are good when served chilled, they have become a sort of universal summer wine. Thus I find that often, in the summer, we find ourselves drinking a rosé with our steak and a good, chilled white with our spaghetti.

And there is a reverse side to this coin. In Tuscany, *baccalà* and *stoccafisso* are often served with red wine. Personally, though, I tend to be very careful of what wine I drink with fish, because tannic or aromatic wines do not mix well with the flavor of seafood, and one can be left with an unpleasant aftertaste. In other words, drink what you like with meat, but be careful when choosing wine for a fish recipe. It should be light, dry and neutral, with a slightly bitter aftertaste. Unless you are a real connoisseur, it should be white and with a reasonably low alcoholic content.

The subject of what wine should be had with what dish can be argued endlessly. There are also a few general rules, such as: white wines should always precede rosé in a meal, rosé should precede red. Younger wines should precede older ones; robust ones should follow light ones; the dry should precede the aromatic and the aromatic come before the sweet. All of this must be taken with a grain of salt. My suggestion to a beginner is to plan a meal that can be washed down with one wine, at most two. But there are a few other little things about wine that I would like to pass on, for they have come to me with experience and make wine drinking more worthwhile. Only a dry, chilled, neutral white wine with as little aroma as possible is adequate drinking with a dish whose main ingredient is mushrooms—otherwise one aroma cancels the other. Cooked artichokes and raw fennel enhance the flavor of any good red wine. Try it, the surprise is pleasant. And one of the greatest treats I know of is to drink good red wine while eating fresh-picked walnuts and Tuscan bread. Make sure you peel the walnuts of their thin inner skin because it's very bitter when the fruit is fresh.

Chianti, by law, must be a red wine. Thus, the whites in Tuscany are not Chianti and while they are good, and made in several places, most of them are produced in small quantities and are used up locally. Of the few that get exported only one famous wine, the Vernaccia di S. Gemignano, is included in my cellar. The other two whites I include rely more on their brand names than on their areas of production. In the next few paragraphs I would like to mention some of the better known Tuscan white wines, even if they don't reach the American market.

One of the better known Tuscan whites is made near Lucca, in a small town called Montecarlo (not to be confused with the one on the sea). The wine made in Montecarlo is one of the most ancient in Tuscany and is known to have been a favorite at the Medici court. But in those days the praise went to the Montecarlo red (which still exists and can be had locally, in small quantities); now the area has become more specialized and makes a very good white wine. Pale in color, with a very faint, flowery perfume and a creamy, robust taste, the Montecarlo white has an alcoholic content of 22 to 24 proof, and is very suitable for drinking with stews, *umidi*, and with the excellent Tuscan fried dishes. It is made by mixing *trebbiano, semillon, pinot, vermentino* and *sauvignon* grapes.

Another great Tuscan white is made in the southernmost Tuscan province, Grosseto. It's called Bianco di Pitigliano, is a cocktail of *Trebbiano toscano, greco, malvasia bianca* and *verdello* grapes, has a dry, slightly bitter flavor, a delicate, almost nonexistent perfume, a very pale, yellow color and a low alcoholic content—22 to 24 proof. It is one of my choices for all fish recipes and is also good with fowl or egg dishes.

The Vernaccia di S. Gemignano is a good white wine, slightly more aromatic than the one mentioned previously, therefore more suit-able for veal or chicken than fish. Some like the Vernaccia with shrimp and lobster; personally I find a glass of it, well chilled, makes a very good summer cocktail.

Tuscany has two very exceptional dessert wines. The Aleatico is produced in most provinces, but the best comes from the Isle of Elba. Its color is a dark, blueish red, its flavor is sweet, soft and generous, its perfume is flowery and fruity and its alcoholic content is between 24 and 30 proof. It is very good with pies and cakes and, in summer, poured over vanilla ice cream.

The famous Tuscan Vin Santo is one of the oldest wines known. It is spiced and sweet, produced in very limited quantities, and I find its taste similar to that of good, sweet sherry. There is no official listing of the grapes that go into the making of Vin Santo because each manu-facturer has his own method and it's a well-guarded secret. It is an excellent, universal dessert wine and must be tasted to be appreciated. The famous Emilio Pucci, known for his beautiful clothes, also makes a good Vin Santo which can be bought in the United States. If in Italy, try the one made by Brolio.

Listed below are my choices for a 24-bottle cellar. It is a very small collection, but it covers every recipe in this book and lists Tuscan wines available in the U.S.

REDS

> 2 bottles of Chianti Classico—Castello di Gabbiano Riserva
> 2 bottles of Chianti Classico—Melini Riserva
> 2 bottles of Chianti Classico—Brolio Riserva
> 2 bottles of Chianti Classico—Serristori
> 2 bottles of Chianti Classico—Olivieri
> 2 bottles of Chianti Classico—La Quercia (Giovanni Cappelli)
> 2 bottles of Rosso delle Colline Lucchesi
> 1 bottle of Brunello di Montalcino—Poggio alle Mura
> 1 bottle of Nobile di Montepulciano—Fassati

WHITES

> 2 bottles of Vernaccia di S. Gemignano di Cuzona
> 2 bottles of Melini Lacrima d'Arno
> 2 bottles of Antinori Bianco Secco
>
> 2 bottles of Vin Santo—Marchese Pucci

ANTIPASTI

(*Appetizers*)

1. CROSTINI DI FEGATINI
(*Chicken Liver Crostini*)

SERVES 5 OR 6

To say *crostini* in Tuscany is to say appetizer. No matter what other preparations are served as *antipasto*, these little warm canapés are included every time. There are as many versions of *crostini* as there are homes in Tuscany. The following is my own adaptation of the simplest of them all, the chicken liver *crostino*.

1 small onion
1 small carrot
½ stalk celery
A few leaves of parsley
3 tablespoons olive oil
6 tablespoons butter
4 or 5 chicken livers

¼ cup white wine
1 teaspoon tomato paste
⅓ cup hot water
Salt and pepper
2 tablespoons capers
10 slices white bread

1. Clean, wash and chop fine the onion, carrot, celery and parsley. In a small saucepan put oil and 2 tablespoons of butter, add chopped vegetables and allow to color slightly.

2. Clean the chicken livers, wash and dry well, add to the simmering vegetables. After 2 or 3 minutes add the wine, lower the flame, allow the wine to evaporate slowly.

3. Dissolve the tomato paste in ⅓ cup hot water. Add to the saucepan. Add salt and a little fresh-ground pepper; cook for about 20 minutes. At this point take the livers out, chop, put back into the saucepan. Wash the capers and dry on paper towels, chop, add to saucepan. Stir, allow to warm through, remove from fire.

4. Cut each slice of bread in half, making 20 triangles. Fry in 3 tablespoons of butter—see recipe No. 179, step 4—add the remaining tablespoon of butter to the sauce, stir well to blend, then spread the chicken liver mixture on the fried bread. Serve warm.

2. CROSTINI AL FORMAGGIO
(*Cheese Crostini*)

It's hard to specify portions in appetizer recipes because so much depends on what else is being served. In this case there are 8 small toasts, which could be enough for 4 people (provided there are other toasts or cold cuts), for 8 (if more than two other kinds of appetizer are served) or for 2, if this is the only appetizer. In any case, these are very tasty and very easy to make.

1 egg
3 tablespoons grated Parmesan cheese
4 slices slightly stale white bread
Butter, as needed

1. Put the egg and grated Parmesan in a bowl and whip with a fork until a light cream is formed.

2. Preheat the oven to 350° F. Cut the crusts off the bread slices, then cut each slice in half.

3. Spread a thin layer of soft butter on each piece of bread, then

cover with the egg-cheese mixture. Put on a dry baking sheet and bake for about 10 minutes, or until golden. Serve hot or warm.

3. CROSTINI DELLA BONA
(*Bona's Chicken Liver Crostini*)

SERVES 5 TO 8

Casoli is a little Tuscan village that clings to the side of a hill and looks down on the sea. It was "discovered" by several painters, sculptors, art critics and photographers, all of clear fame and established reputation, who have either made it their home or who come to Casoli for long vacations. Their houses are tucked into the mountainside, far from the eyes of curious tourists but well exposed to the light and view which, in Casoli, are both exceptional.

There are only two restaurants in this small center, and one is particularly well liked by the foreign guests—so much so that the walls are covered with their paintings, sketches, poems and what-not. It's owned by a pleasant couple who like to chat with their guests and know how to insure their right to privacy, but its reputation derives mainly from the wife's cooking. Her name is Bona and this is her version of the Tuscan *crostini*.

10 to 16 small slices bread
Olive oil, as needed
5 large chicken livers
Butter, as needed

5 leaves fresh sage or ½ teaspoon dried
3 anchovy fillets
1 tablespoon drained capers

1. Fry the small slices of bread (preferably rounds of a French-type loaf) in hot olive oil (see recipe No. 179, step 4). Dry on paper towels.

2. Clean, wash and dry the chicken livers. Put 3 tablespoons of olive oil and 2 tablespoons of butter in a clean frying pan. When just heated add the sage and livers, fry for 5 minutes or until the livers are cooked.

3. Remove the frying pan from the stove and allow its contents to cool. Then put everything through the meat grinder: sage, chicken

livers and pan juices, the anchovy fillets and the capers. Repeat the operation in order to obtain a very smooth purée. Mix it with a wooden spoon and, if not creamy enough, add 1 or 2 tablespoons of softened butter, always making sure that everything is thoroughly blended.

4. Spread this cream on the fried bread and serve at once, preferably while it's still lukewarm.

4. CROSTINI SPECIALI
(*Special Crostini*)

SERVES 4, SEE RECIPE NO. 2

3 chicken livers
½ breast of chicken
Butter, as needed
2 tablespoons chopped onion
Salt
¼ cup Vin Santo or sweet sherry
1 slice white bread
Wine vinegar, as needed

1 egg yolk
½ bouillon cube dissolved in ½
　cup warm water
1 tablespoon capers
1 small sour gherkin
8 slices whole wheat or Tuscan
　bread (see recipe No. 220)

1. Dice the chicken livers and chicken breast. Put 2 tablespoons butter in frying pan, add chopped onion, let it wilt, then add pieces of livers and chicken, very little salt, and fry for a few minutes. When the meat is no longer red, add the Vin Santo or sherry, lower the flame, cover and cook for about 10 minutes.

2. Meanwhile, cut the crust off the white bread, tear up the rest into little pieces and soak in a little vinegar. Dissolve the egg yolk in 2 tablespoons of the bouillon. Chop the drained capers and gherkin fine.

3. When the Vin Santo or sherry has almost evaporated take out the pieces of meat (both livers and breast) and chop fine, put back into the frying pan, add the dissolved egg yolk and chopped capers and gherkin, add the remaining bouillon, and heat. Squeeze the vinegar out of the white bread crumbs and add crumbs to frying pan. Stir to blend well and continue to cook for a few minutes. Take off the flame and allow to cool slightly. The mixture should thicken somewhat as it cools.

4. Fry the whole wheat or Tuscan bread in butter (see recipe No. 179, step 4). As soon as the chicken liver mixture thickens to the right consistency (it should be like a thick jam), spread it on the fried bread and serve warm.

Note: If this recipe is used as one of several appetizers, the slices of bread can be cut into triangles, and it will serve more than 4.

5. FAGIOLI CON TONNO E POMODORI
(*Beans with Tuna Fish and Tomatoes*)

SERVES 4 OR 5

This is a hearty *antipasto* which in our house is also a favorite summer luncheon dish. For those who like them, thin-sliced onion rings can be added. The beans used in Tuscany are the white *cannellini*, but most good quality white or brown beans will do. If made with big, fat Spanish beans this recipe is really exquisite.

8 ounces dried beans	*One 7-ounce can tuna fish*
3 tomatoes	*¼ cup olive oil*
½ onion (optional)	*Salt and pepper*

1. Soak beans overnight in water to cover. Rinse, cover with fresh water, and cook until tender, about 1 to 1½ hours. Drain.
2. Slice tomatoes and onion, if desired. Drain the tuna fish and break into bite-size pieces.
3. Mix all ingredients. Season with oil, salt and fresh-ground pepper to taste. Serve with lemon wedges and vinegar on the side.

6. LA FETTA UNTA
(*Toasted Tuscan Bread with Garlic and Olive Oil*)

SERVES 4

Also known as *bruschetta*, this is the simplest, most popular appetizer in Tuscany. For the hearty Tuscan bread see recipe No. 220. This appetizer, served with a big green salad, makes an excellent, economical, spicy lunch.

> *8 slices of slightly stale Tuscan bread*
> *About 5 cloves garlic*
> *Salt and pepper*
> *⅓ cup olive oil, as needed*

1. Toast the bread, either in a hot oven or in a toaster.
2. Clean a few cloves of garlic, rub on the bread while still hot. For those who like garlic, rub on both sides. Sprinkle with salt and fresh-ground pepper.
3. Put on a large platter, pour oil generously over the bread and serve at once, while still warm.

7. FRITTATINA DI CIPOLLE
(*Little Onion Omelet*)

SERVES 4 OR 5

Frittata means omelet in Italian. It's not eaten as a main course, but a wedge of it is often included among the *antipasti*. If used as a luncheon dish, the recipe below will serve two.

> *1 large or 2 small onions*
> *4 eggs*
> *½ teaspoon salt*
> *¼ cup olive oil*

1. Clean onion and slice thin. Put the eggs and salt into a bowl and beat lightly.
2. Heat 3 tablespoons of oil in a medium to large skillet, add the onions, allow to wilt on medium flame.
3. When the onions are cooked but not browned pour the eggs on top of them and allow to set. Once the bottom has formed a crust, slide the omelet onto a plate, add the remaining oil to the skillet, allow to get hot and fry the other side of the omelet. The outside should have a

crust on both sides, the inside should be lighter in color and softer. Cut into wedges and serve hot, warm or cold.

Note: This omelet is equally good made with zucchini, artichokes, spinach or potatoes. Cooking time varies with each vegetable. The spinach should be boiled, drained and chopped, then cooked in the oil, etc.; the zucchini, artichokes and potatoes should be sliced thin and fried slowly, allowing the time necessary for each vegetable to cook through. The onions cook in 5 to 8 minutes, the zucchini, artichokes and potatoes in 10 to 15. Keep the flame low to medium, turn the vegetables often while cooking (before adding the eggs, of course), scrape the bottom of the pan gently to avoid sticking.

8. FRITTATA AFFOGATA
(*Drowned Omelet*)

SERVES 3

An omelet drowned in tomato sauce, the Tuscan omelet by definition. A good appetizer or, with a salad and cake, a quick, tasty lunch.

A small handful of parsley	*5 eggs*
3 leaves fresh basil or ½ teaspoon	*1 teaspoon flour*
dried	*1 teaspoon bread crumbs*
1 small onion	*Salt and white pepper*
1 stalk celery	*5 tablespoons olive oil*
6 or 7 peeled Italian plum	
tomatoes	

1. Clean and wash parsley and basil, onion and celery. Chop fine. Chop tomatoes, discarding seeds and hard parts.

2. Break the eggs into a bowl, add flour and bread crumbs, ½ teaspoon of salt and a few twists of the white pepper grinder. Beat well in order to blend thoroughly.

3. Pour oil into frying pan and, when hot, pour in eggs, allow to set, turn, allow to set on the other side, remove to a plate lined with a paper towel.

4. Remove half of the oil, add chopped vegetables, except the tomatoes, to the remaining oil, let them wilt. When wilted, add tomatoes, stir, allow to cook until the sauce thickens, about 15 to 20 minutes. Add salt and white pepper to taste.

5. Cut the omelet into 6 wedges, put back into the frying pan, allow to cook for another 5 minutes. Serve hot, with abundant sauce poured over each piece.

9. GNOCCHI DI PARMIGIANO
(*Parmesan Gnocchi*)

SERVES 4 TO 8

Rather than an appetizer, this is a snack to be served along with the potato chips, the olives and the peanuts. Guests who are fond of cheese will rave!

½ cup grated Parmesan cheese
¾ cup butter or margarine
1 tablespoon peanut or corn oil

1. Mix all ingredients, work into a dough. Preheat the oven to 400° F.

2. Divide the dough into several pieces, roll each piece into a long, sausage-like roll, the thickness of a finger. Cut each roll into pieces about 1-inch thick.

3. Arrange the *gnocchi* on a greased baking sheet, put into the oven for 15 minutes, check; they are ready when golden to golden brown. Some ovens bake faster, others more slowly; if necessary leave another 5 minutes. Serve warm or store in an airtight container.

10. INSALATA DI MARE
(*Seafood Salad*)

SERVES 4 OR 5

Don't let the name mislead you; this is a warm dish, suitable as an appetizer to an elegant meal.

1 pound mussels and warty
    venus, tartufi di mare
1 pound small shrimp, squid,
    cuttlefish and octopus. A
    few prawns, if available
Olive oil, as needed

1 clove garlic, cleaned
White pepper
3 tablespoons chopped parsley
1 tablespoon butter
3 tablespoons milk

1. Wash and scrub the mussels and warty venus; wash the small shrimp; wash and carefully clean the squid, cuttlefish, octopus and prawns, if used (if you're not familiar with this last operation have it done at the fish market).

2. Put 3 tablespoons of oil, the garlic, a little fresh-ground white pepper and half of the parsley in a frying pan. Allow to simmer for a couple of minutes on a medium flame, then add the mussels and the warty venus and, after a minute or two, the small shrimp. Cook for 5 more minutes, moving the pan back and forth, until the shells are opened wide. Remove the garlic.

3. Remove the frying pan from the stove. When cool enough to handle take the mussels and venus out of the pan and remove the meat from the shells. Then take out the shrimp and peel.

4. Reserve the mussels and *tartufi*. Chop the shrimp very fine and put back into the frying pan; stir well to incorporate the sauce left in the pan with the shrimp purée. Cut the cleaned squid, cuttlefish and octopus into very small pieces and add to the frying pan. Add the butter and 3 tablespoons of milk. Sprinkle with additional white pepper and cook on a low flame for 10 more minutes, stirring often.

5. When the milk has almost evaporated and the octopus (which needs more cooking than the rest) is soft, add the mussels and venus, sprinkle with the remaining parsley, and heat through. Serve on individual plates, surrounded by triangles of warm toast and pass a spicy sauce (which could be recipe No. 83).

Note: If prawns used, cook separately. Serve 2 or 3 on each dish.

11. INVOLTINI DI PROSCIUTTO
(*Prosciutto Rolls*)

SERVES 3 TO 4

Simple, delicious, refreshing—the best appetizer for a summer meal. The sweetness of figs and the saltiness of raw ham, a combination of sweet and salty tastes that the sacrament of baptism renders familiar to all Italians at a very early age.

12 ripe figs
6 large slices of prosciutto (*Italian raw ham*)

1. If figs were kept in the refrigerator, remove at least 1 hour before serving; they should be served at room temperature. Peel figs carefully. Cut each slice of *prosciutto* in half.
2. Wrap each fig in half a slice of *prosciutto*, fasten with a toothpick, and serve.

12. PANZANELLA
(*Panzanella*)

SERVES 4

This has been, across the years, a classic dish of both city Florentines and its country folk. The peasants use their fresh vegetables in the summer and add the good stale bread and the seasoning. The more sophisticated citizens add capers and anchovies to dress up the simple dish, but the real core of this preparation is Tuscan bread, the fresh vegetables and the olive oil.

8 slices of stale Tuscan bread
   (*see recipe No. 220.*)
4 ripe tomatoes
1 large white onion
1 cucumber
10 leaves fresh basil or 1
   teaspoon dried

2 anchovy fillets
5 tablespoons olive oil,
   approximately
2 tablespoons wine vinegar,
   approximately
Salt and pepper
2 tablespoons capers

1. Soak the bread in cold water for a few minutes, then squeeze out the excess water and put the bread in a salad bowl. Wash and dry the tomatoes; clean the onion and cut into thin slices; peel and slice the cucumber. Wash and dry the basil leaves.

2. Put the onion and cucumber slices into the salad bowl. Cut the anchovies into several pieces each. Slice the tomatoes and cut up the basil with scissors; add both to the salad bowl. Season with about 5 tablespoons of olive oil, 2 tablespoons of vinegar, salt and pepper to taste, then toss well. Sprinkle with the capers and anchovies and serve.

Note: In the proportions given above this is more of a salad than an appetizer. It's perfect for a cold summer buffet.

13. PASTICCIO DI FEGATO DI MAIALE
(*Pork Liver Pâté*)

SERVES 6 TO 8

This is not a strictly Tuscan dish, but it's a great favorite in my husband's family and deserves to be included in this cookbook because it is both easy to make and delicious to eat.

1 ½ *cups soft white bread crumbs*
Milk, as needed
12 *ounces pork liver*
3 *eggs*
¾ *cup grated Parmesan cheese*
½ *teaspoon salt*

¼ *teaspoon allspice*
5 *ounces Tuscan sausage*
1 *large piece of caul fat or* rete di maiale (*see recipe No. 151*) *or thin slices of lard*

1. Cover the soft bread crumbs with milk. Cut the liver into cubes and put through the meat grinder. Drain the bread and put that also through the meat grinder. Put everything in a bowl.

2. Preheat oven to 400° F. Add the eggs, cheese, salt and allspice. Mash the Tuscan sausage with a fork and add to the bowl—if not available blanch an equal amount of bacon, put through the meat grinder and add 2 fine-chopped garlic cloves and ¼ teaspoon coarse-ground black pepper.

3. Mix everything well. The result should be homogeneous and rather creamy.

4. Line a loaf-shaped pyrex or baking dish with aluminum foil, then cover the foil with the lard or *rete* (a thin and irregular web of pork fat that lines the animal's peritoneum or stomach cavity, and that in Tuscany is used in several pork dishes because the fat, as it melts, renders the meat tender and flavorful).

5. Pour the mixture into this dish, even it out with a spatula, cover with the remaining *rete*, or lard, and bake for about 15 minutes. Then turn the oven to 325° F. and bake for another 30 to 45 minutes, or until dry in the center.

6. Allow to cool, remove from the pyrex or baking dish, serve cold, sliced, with raw vegetables or *sott'olii* and other cold cuts.

14. PEPERONI SOTT'OLIO
(*Peppers in Oil*)

SERVES 6

A very tasty antipasto, this recipe can also double as a salad if the anchovies are omitted. Use only yellow peppers; green peppers won't peel well and aren't as sweet; red peppers are too spicy.

> *3 large, sweet yellow peppers*
> *2 anchovies*
> *⅓ cup olive oil*
> *1 tablespoon capers*

1. Wash and dry the peppers. Put in preheated oven or under grill for about 15 to 20 minutes. Turn once or twice. Remove and, while still warm, peel, open and remove seeds and inside filaments. Cut each anchovy into several pieces.

2. Cut each pepper lengthwise into 4 or 6 large pieces, lay flat on a dish. Pour olive oil over peppers. Dot with pieces of anchovy and capers. Serve cold.

15. POLPETTONE DI TONNO
(*Tuna Fish Loaf*)

SERVES 4 TO 6

½ teaspoon salt	3 tablespoons bread crumbs
One 7-ounce can tuna fish	2 eggs
5 tablespoons grated Parmesan cheese	¼ cup milk

1. Fill an oblong pan with water, add ½ teaspoon of salt, bring to the boiling point.

2. Put the tuna fish through a fine sieve. Add the other ingredients and mix everything well.

3. Shape this mixture into a loaf, wrap in several layers of cheesecloth, and tie the ends with a string like a *salame*.

4. Put the tied loaf into the boiling water, lower the flame, cover and allow to simmer for 15 minutes.

5. Remove loaf from water, put on a wooden board, weigh down with another board, allow to cool. When cold remove string and cheesecloth, serve sliced with mayonnaise or the sauce in recipe No. 77.

16. POMODORI DI MARE
(*Tomatoes Stuffed with Seafood*)

SERVES 4

This is an excellent way of using leftover fish. If, however, you cook the fish especially for this dish, use one that has solid flesh. Otherwise, any good baked or boiled fish will do very well. The shrimp and mussels add extra flavor but can be omitted.

For boiling fish and shrimp, prepare the following broth: to 1 quart of water add ⅓ cup vinegar, 1 small peeled onion, 1 cleaned carrot cut into quarters, 1 cleaned celery stalk, 1 bay leaf, a few grains of black pepper and ½ teaspoon salt. Put the fish and shellfish into the boiling broth, return to boiling point, cook for 10 minutes, drain, cool slightly, clean and peel the shellfish and flake the fish. The mussels should be well scrubbed and cooked for about 10 minutes in a hot covered frying pan with 2 tablespoons olive oil, 1 tablespoon chopped parsley and 1 jigger of dry white wine.

4 hard tomatoes, as even and round as possible
¾ cup mayonnaise
1 teaspoon strong prepared mustard
1 tablespoon ketchup
3 drops garlic juice (optional)

¾ cup cold boiled or baked fish, cleaned of skin and bones and flaked (see above)
24 mussels, cooked and removed from shell (see above)
16 cold shrimp, boiled and peeled (see above)

1. Wash and dry the tomatoes, cut in half horizontally and remove the seeds, the liquid and the inside membranes, leaving a hollow shell.

2. Mix the mayonnaise with the mustard, ketchup and garlic juice (which can be obtained by crushing a clove of garlic on a plate). Stir the flaked fish and the mussels into this mayonnaise.

3. Fill each tomato half with the fish mixture (each tomato half should be filled to overflowing), decorate with 2 shrimp and serve 2 halves per person. If you want it to look pretty, serve on a bed of chopped lettuce. In Tuscany, it's served as is.

17. TONNO E PATATE
(*Tuna Fish and Potatoes*)

SERVES 4

4 medium-size potatoes
¼ cup olive oil
Salt and pepper
1 onion

One 7-ounce can tuna fish
1 tablespoon capers
3 tablespoons vinegar

1. Boil potatoes in their skins. Cool to lukewarm, peel and slice into rounds. Season with oil and salt and pepper to taste.

2. Slice the onion into thin rounds, add to the potatoes. Drain the tuna fish, break into bite-size pieces, add to the potatoes and onions.

3. Add capers and vinegar, toss and serve.

18. UOVA AL TONNO
(*Eggs and Tuna Fish*)

Again this is an appetizer that can serve more people if included in a tray of assorted appetizers, and fewer people if served with only one or two other things, such as *prosciutto* and *crostini*, for example.

5 eggs, hard boiled	*3 tablespoons mayonnaise*
3 ounces tuna fish	*¼ teaspoon salt*
2 teaspoons drained capers	*Pepper*
1 tablespoon chopped parsley	

1. Shell the eggs, cut in half lengthwise.
2. Remove the yolks, put through a sieve. Put the tuna fish through a sieve. Chop capers fine.
3. Put yolks, tuna, capers, parsley, mayonnaise, salt and a little fresh-ground pepper into a bowl; mix well.
4. Fill the egg-white halves with this mixture. They should be filled to overflowing. Decorate each half with a leaf of parsley or 1 whole caper, if desired.

19. UOVA IN CAMICIA AL VINO
(*Poached Eggs in Wine Sauce*)

The following is a delicious recipe given to me by a friend from Siena. I find that it's easier to poach the eggs in acidulated water and use the wine brew to make the sauce while the eggs are poaching. But I give it the way it was given to me, for the purists and for those who are faster in the kitchen than I am.

2 cups good dry white wine	*6 eggs*
2 medium onions	*6 slices white bread*
2 cloves garlic, crushed	*4 tablespoons butter*
1 bay leaf	*2 tablespoons flour*
Salt and pepper	

1. Put the wine in a wide saucepan, add onions, peeled and quartered, crushed garlic, bay leaf, salt and pepper to taste, and bring to a boil. Allow to simmer gently for 10 minutes.

2. Break an egg carefully into a small saucer and let it slip gently into the simmering wine. Do the same with 2 more eggs and let cook for 3 to 4 minutes (depending on whether you like your egg white more or less solid). Remove with a slotted spoon, keep warm, and repeat with next 3 eggs.

3. Meanwhile, trim the crust off the slices of bread. Melt 2 tablespoons of butter in a frying pan, fry the bread quickly, remove onto absorbent paper, keep warm (see recipe No. 179).

4. Add the remaining butter to the frying pan, melt, add flour and stir. Let it darken to a golden color, then strain the hot wine into this *roux*. Squeeze the solids well in order to get the most flavor into the sauce. Stir and allow to thicken.

5. Serve the poached eggs on the fried bread, and cover with the wine sauce.

20. UOVA IN TEGAMINO AL POMODORO
(*Fried Eggs with Tomato Sauce*)

SERVES 2

2 tablespoons butter
8 tablespoons pomarola (*see recipe No. 86*)
4 eggs

1. In a small frying pan put 1 tablespoon of butter and 4 tablespoons of tomato sauce. Allow to heat through, stir.

2. Break 2 eggs into the skillet, cook for about 5 minutes, or as long as necessary to set the egg white the way you want it.

3. Repeat steps 1 and 2 for the second portion. Serve hot.

MINESTRE
(First Courses)

21. BRODO DI CARNE
(Meat Broth)

SERVES 8 TO 10

Brodo is almost always present in a Tuscan kitchen. It's needed as a base for sauces; a cup of it improves all meats and vegetables made *in umido*; it's indispensable for *risotto* and useful by itself, or with small *pasta* cooked in it, as the lightest and most digestible of soups. Furthermore, the meat used to make the *brodo* is perfectly edible: in our house on the day we make it the meat is served as a second course. The basic difference between good *lesso*, boiled meat, and *brodo di carne*, is that when the intention is to make good boiled meat it should be added to the water when it's already boiling, thereby sealing the good juices in the meat, whereas to make a good broth, the meat, water and other ingredients are put together while cold and brought to the boiling point together, so that the good meat juices are released into the water and make a good *brodo*.

The ingredients below are for a fairly large portion of broth, enough for a few plates of soup and a good *risotto* later (by the way, broth keeps well in a good refrigerator provided it's reboiled every 3 or 4 days). Smaller amounts of meat can be used if all you require is soup for one evening. But it's important to remember that at least two different cuts of beef plus one bone and a piece of stewing chicken are necessary to make a really tasty broth.

1 onion
2 carrots
3 sprigs parsley
1 stalk celery with leaves
3 leaves fresh basil
*2 pounds stewing beef, mixed
   (shank, chuck, short ribs,
   breast, etc.)*

*Beef bones, preferably joint
   (adding a piece of the foot
   will make the broth more
   gelatinous)*
1 stewing hen
2 bouillon cubes
Salt

1. Clean onion and carrots, leave onion whole, slice carrots in half. Wash parsley, celery and basil, tie with white string, forming a *bouquet garni*. Wash meats and bones. Clean and wash chicken, tie down wings and thighs.

2. Put the vegetables, meat and chicken in a large pot, add 3 quarts water. Turn flame high; as water starts to simmer a grayish foam will form on top. Skim off as much of it as you can. Lower flame to minimum and allow to simmer for at least 2 hours or until all meat is tender. After about 1 hour add bouillon cubes. Water should be reduced to ⅔ of original amount. Taste for seasoning, add salt if necessary.

3. Allow to cool slightly, remove meats. Take out the onion, carrots and *bouquet garni*. Strain the broth. When cold, put in refrigerator. After about 8 hours the fat will form a crust on top. Remove that crust before using the broth.

22. STRACCIATELLA

One of the lightest soups eaten in Italy, this broth is so well known that no cookbook dealing with this country would be complete without it. In Tuscany, the *stracciatella* (a word that comes from *stracciare*, to tear up), is eaten mostly in restaurants. But I've also had it at elegant dinners and in homes where the cooking tends to be on the light side.

5 cups good quality meat broth
  (see recipe No. 21)
2 eggs
6 tablespoons fresh-grated
  Parmesan cheese

White pepper
Salt
Nutmeg (optional)

1. Bring the broth to the boiling point.
2. Separate the egg whites from the yolks. Beat the whites until they lose transparency, then beat the yolks slightly.
3. Put whites, yolks, Parmesan, a little fresh-ground white pepper, a little salt and, if you like it, a few gratings of nutmeg into a bowl. Mix well.
4. Add the contents of the bowl to the boiling broth, stirring briskly with a wooden spoon. Allow to boil again for 3 minutes, serve hot.

23. CINESTRATA
(*Spiced Broth*)

In the Renaissance period, broth was often served with sugar and spices, as this recipe demonstrates. I find this broth-egg-spice soup very tasty, and its creamy appearance makes it a fit opening for an elegant meal.

2½ cups good quality meat broth
  (see recipe No. 21)
4 egg yolks
⅓ cup dry Marsala wine

¼ teaspoon powdered cinnamon
3 tablespoons butter
Nutmeg
Sugar

1. Put the cold broth (all fat removed, see recipe No. 21), the egg yolks, the Marsala and the powdered cinnamon into a bowl. Whip together, then filter through a fine sieve into a saucepan.

2. Put the saucepan on a medium flame and after a minute or two start adding the butter, a little piece at a time. Stir with a wooden spoon and allow to cook until the soup reaches the consistency of cream.

3. Prepare 4 hot consommé cups, ladle the hot soup into them, sprinkle each with a few gratings of nutmeg and a tiny pinch of sugar, and serve at once.

24. ACQUACOTTA SENESE
(*Sienese Cooked Water*)

SERVES 4

1 *pound fresh* porcini
    mushrooms or 3 ounces
    good quality dried
    mushrooms
6 *peeled Italian plum tomatoes*
4 *tablespoons olive oil*
1 *clove garlic, cleaned*
Salt and pepper

6 *cups good quality meat broth,*
    homemade (see recipe No.
    21) *or canned*
8 *slices toasted, stale Tuscan*
    bread (see recipe No. 220)
4 *eggs*
6 *tablespoons fresh-grated*
    Parmesan cheese

1. Clean and wash mushrooms if fresh; soak in lukewarm water for 30 minutes if dried, then wash well. Cut into slices. Chop the tomatoes, discarding seeds and hard parts.

2. Put oil and garlic into large saucepan, allow the garlic to brown, add mushrooms, stir. Lower the flame, add salt and pepper to taste, cook for a few minutes.

3. Add the tomatoes, stir, cover, cook for 20 minutes. Add broth, stir and cover again, cook for another 10 minutes or until mushrooms are soft.

4. Meanwhile, put 2 slices of bread into each individual soup bowl, then put the eggs and cheese into a large soup bowl and whip them slightly. Pour the boiling mushroom broth over the egg and cheese mixture, stir well and serve at once, ladling the soup into the individual bowls over the bread.

25. CIPOLLATA
(*Tuscan Onion Soup*)

SERVES 4 TO 6

2 pounds white onions
1 carrot
1 stalk celery
A few sprigs of parsley
1 pound pork spareribs
Salt
5 slices bacon
2 Tuscan sausages, if available

2 tablespoons olive oil
8 slices stale Tuscan bread (see
 recipe No. 220)
2 cloves garlic, cleaned and split
 lengthwise
Grated Parmesan cheese, as
 needed
Black pepper

1. Peel onions, slice into rounds, put in large bowl and keep under cold running water for 10 to 15 minutes. Meanwhile, wash carrot, celery and parsley, peel carrot and cut in two, put these 3 ingredients in a pot with about 2 quarts water, add spareribs, a piece of the onion, and 1 teaspoon salt and allow to cook for at least 1 hour or until the meat comes away from the bones.

2. When the meat is ready take it out of its broth and separate from the bones, then cut into small pieces and reserve. Strain the broth and reserve that, too.

3. Cut the bacon into squares, loosen up the sausage with a fork. If sausage is unavailable, double the amount of bacon. Put both in a large saucepan and cook slowly to render fat. When bacon is crisp add the olive oil, heat through, then add the drained onions and cook, uncovered, on a medium-to-low flame, until they are dry. As the water evaporates the onions will start simmering. Let them simmer for just 1 minute, *don't allow to brown*, add 2 ladles of the broth, cover, and lower the flame to the minimum. Continue to cook very slowly, for at least 1 hour, uncovering occasionally to check liquid level (there should be approximately 6 cups at all times) and adding more broth if necessary.

4. Toast the stale bread and rub with garlic. Add the rest of the broth and the meat to the onions. Cook for another 30 minutes. Line a soup tureen with the garlic-flavored bread, pour in the onion soup, allow to stand for a few minutes, then serve with fresh-grated Parmesan cheese and black pepper.

26. MINESTRA DI PORRI
(*Leek Soup*)

SERVES 4

In the quiet little village of San Macario in Piano, just outside Lucca, there's a simple restaurant. *Solferino* was founded by Solferino Gemignani and is now run by his two sons, Gianfranco in the kitchen and Sauro in the dining room. We go there often, not only because Sauro went to school with my husband but also because the food is always excellent. Eight years ago I took some friends there. They were traveling through Europe and stopping here and there—the lunch they had was a simple Tuscan lunch, but they're still talking about it. The recipe below is one of the restaurant's not–so–Tuscan dishes, but I thought it was worth including because it's an excellent soup. I also give their filling for *tortelli* because in my opinion it's one of the best.

½ *stewing chicken*
2 *pounds beef for broth (muscle,*
    breast)
A *few good beef bones, cracked*
1 *small onion*
1 *carrot*
Bouquet garni—*parsley, celery,*
    thyme
7 *cups water*

4 *leeks*
½ *cup butter*
Salt and pepper
2 *tablespoons brandy*
1 *bouillon cube*
8 *slices Italian bread, toasted and*
    rubbed with garlic
Parmesan cheese, as needed

1. Clean and wash the chicken, meat and bones. Clean and wash the onion and carrot. Put them in a pan with the *bouquet garni* and add 7 cups water. Make a broth, allowing it to cook for about 2 hours and *do not* add any more water. The broth should be very strong.

2. Clean and wash leeks, slice into rounds. Melt butter in a large frying pan, add the leeks and simmer for at least 20 minutes or until cooked through. Add salt, a good amount of fresh-ground pepper and the brandy. Stir, turn off flame and cover.

3. When the broth is ready add bouillon cube, allow to dissolve, taste; if necessary, add a little more salt. Remove all meat, strain the broth and reserve it. At this point there should be about 5 cups of liquid.

4. Remove all bones from the chicken, cut meat into small pieces, put back into the broth. Blend the cooked leeks and their butter into the broth mixture, stir, taste, correct seasoning if necessary.

5. Put 2 slices of garlic-flavored bread into each soup bowl, cover with 1 cup of hot soup and serve at once. Pass fresh-grated Parmesan.

27. SPAGHETTINI AL WHISKY E PANNA
(*Thin Spaghetti with Cream and Whisky Sauce*)

SERVES 4 OR 5

Here's a slightly different *spaghetti* dish that originates, it seems, with the Second World War. Use Scotch if you can, otherwise Rye, but no Bourbon.

2 ounces dried mushrooms
¾ cup whisky
Salt
A handful of parsley
1 clove garlic, cleaned
3 tablespoons butter

Pepper
1 pound thin spaghetti
1½ cups heavy cream
¼ cup grated Parmesan cheese
  (optional)

1. Soak the mushrooms in warm water for ½ hour. Clean well, carefully removing all sand and dirt, and put into the whisky. Allow to soak for at least 1 hour, more if possible.

2. Put a large pot of water on to boil. Salt to taste.

3. Wash and chop the parsley and the garlic. Melt the butter in a saucepan and, when bubbly, add the chopped vegetables. Let cook for a minute or two (no more or the garlic will burn).

4. Take the mushrooms out of the whisky, drain well, cut into small pieces, add to the simmering vegetables. Add salt and pepper to taste. Allow the mushrooms to cook in the butter for a minute or two, add the whisky, lower the flame, then let simmer, uncovered, until most of the whisky has evaporated.

5. Put the *spaghetti* into the boiling water, let it come to a boil again, stir well with a fork to separate each piece of *pasta* and cook for a few minutes. Taste one piece to see if it's ready and drain when

al dente, cooked but still firm. Put in a preheated bowl with 2 tablespoons of its hot water.

6. When most of the whisky has evaporated, taste the mushrooms. They should be soft. If not, add small amounts of hot water until they are cooked through. Add the cream, allow it to heat through, and pour over the *spaghetti*. Toss well.

7. Add the grated Parmesan if you like. I prefer it as is, but Tuscans use grated Parmesan over all *pasta*, except when made with a fish sauce.

28. SPAGHETTI AGLIO E OLIO, ALLA MANIERA DI GROSSETO
(*Garlic and Oil Spaghetti, Grosseto Style*)

SERVES 4 OR 5

Grosseto is the southernmost province in Tuscany. It's close to Rome and to the sea, and most of its cooking reflects this neighborhood. But in the case of *Spaghetti Aglio e Olio* the south gets even closer, and Tuscany seems to be moving over and making room for Naples.

Salt	*½ cup olive oil*
A handful of parsley	*Pepper*
4 large cloves garlic	Pecorino or *Parmesan cheese,*
1 pound spaghetti	*fresh-grated*

1. Fill a large pot with at least 5 quarts of water, add 2 teaspoons salt and put on high flame. Wash parsley and chop fine. Peel and chop the garlic.

2. When water is boiling add the *spaghetti*. Wait for it to wilt and for the water to bubble again, then stir with a kitchen fork, separating the strands carefully. Set timer for about 10 minutes, or according to directions on package. Allow to boil on high flame, partially covered. When cooked *al dente*, drain.

3. Put oil in large frying pan, add chopped garlic, salt and black pepper to taste, heat through. As soon as garlic turns gold add parsley and turn off flame. Add drained *spaghetti* to frying pan, mix well, serve with cheese.

29. PENNE ALLA CARMEN
(*Carmen's Penne*)

SERVES 4

Penne means feathers or pens (pens, as most people will remember, were once made of feathers) but in Tuscany it's a type of *pasta*. It's short and round and comes in several sizes, but the one used most frequently is about the length of half a cigarette, and slightly thicker. The outside is usually ridged (there is a smooth variety, but it's not as popular), the inside is hollow, and the ends are cut on a slant, which probably justifies the name. It's a *pasta* that doesn't overcook easily and that takes well to a thick sauce (some gets into the hole in the middle).

Carmen, who is an aesthetician and a friend, is also a very good cook. We often trade recipes, and this one is included because it's both simple and delicious. It's also spicy and garlicky, so have lots of good, cool wine on hand.

2 teaspoons *salt*
3 *cloves garlic*
6 ozs. mozzarella *cheese*
One 16-ounce can peeled Italian
    plum tomatoes

1 peperoncino (*Italian hot*
    pepper)
⅓ cup olive oil
1 pound penne

1. Put 4 quarts water in a large pot, add 2 teaspoons salt, cover, put on a high flame. Clean and wash garlic, chop fine. Chop the *mozzarella* cheese coarse. Drain the tomatoes, break up with your hands, discarding hard pieces. Cut *peperoncino* into 3 or 4 pieces.

2. Heat oil in a large skillet. Add the *peperoncino*, garlic and tomatoes, stir, allow to cook for about 5 minutes, or until most of the water from the tomatoes has evaporated.

3. When the water in the pot boils add the *penne*. Wait until the water bubbles again, then stir with a slotted spoon, separating the *pasta*. After 15 minutes, taste the *pasta*. When it has lost the floury taste, drain.

4. Add the *mozzarella* cheese to the tomato sauce in the skillet. Lower the flame and stir often. The cheese will melt and combine with the tomatoes. When all the cheese has turned to strings add the drained

penne to the skillet and stir with a wooden spoon. The sauce should coat each and every one of the *penne,* and some of it should get inside them. Keep the flame low while doing this and take your time. It's important that the sauce and *pasta* are completely blended. Serve in deep plates, putting a bit of extra sauce over each portion.

Note: This recipe has to be made in small quantities because a larger amount of *pasta* will not fit into the skillet. If you wish to make it for more people double the amounts of tomatoes, *mozzarella,* oil and garlic, make proportionately more *pasta,* and use two skillets.

30. PENNE ALLA GIOVANNI
(*Giovanni's Penne*)

SERVES 4

Giovanni owns a little *pizzeria* near Montecatini but his cooking is so good that many people go there for full meals, not just a *pizza.* These simple *penne* are especially good during the summer, when the basil is fragrant and abundant.

Salt
1 pound small penne
8 tablespoons butter
16 tablespoons pomarola (*see recipe No. 86*)

4 tablespoons chopped fresh basil
Parmesan cheese, as needed

1. Put 5 quarts of water into a large pot, add 2 tablespoons salt, bring to the boiling point.
2. Add the *penne,* allow to boil again, stir well with a slotted spoon, cook for about 15 minutes or until *al dente,* drain.
3. Put 2 tablespoons of butter and 4 tablespoons of *pomarola* into a frying pan, heat on medium flame. Stir, then add about ¼ of the drained *penne.* Take the handle of the pan into both hands and, with a short forward jerk, toss the *penne* into the air and catch them back again. This mixes *penne* and sauce much better than ordinary stirring, but if you can't do it just stir them around in the pan until they're covered with sauce.

4. Turn into a preheated individual bowl, sprinkle with ¼ of the chopped basil. Repeat 3 more times with the remaining ingredients. Pass the fresh-grated Parmesan separately.

31. PASTASCIUTTA ALLA FORNAIA
(*Baker's Pasta*)

SERVES 5 OR 6

Of all Italian seasonings for pasta one of the most famous is the Ligurian *pesto*. This fragrant mixture of garlic, pinoli, basil, olive oil and cheese cannot be considered Tuscan, as every child in Italy knows that the *pesto* is *genovese*, from Genoa. Nonetheless, the recipe for the *pesto* is included in the sauce section, because the Tuscan province of Massa is close to Liguira both geographically and gastronomically. But the recipe described below is a Tuscan variation of a nut–basil–olive oil–cheese seasoning, using the excellent local walnuts instead of the pinoli. Combined with *spaghetti* this turns into a very substantial dish.

Salt
7 ounces walnuts
30 to 35 leaves fresh basil, wiped
    clean

½ cup grated Parmesan cheese
⅓ cup olive oil
1 pound medium spaghetti

1. Put 5 quarts of water into a large pot, add 2 teaspoons salt, heat to boiling point. Crack the nuts and remove nut meats. Make sure they are all wholesome, fresh walnuts.

2. Put basil, cheese, ½ teaspoon salt and nut meats into a mortar and pound them to a pulp. Slowly add the olive oil, stirring.

3. When the water boils, add the *spaghetti*. Wait until it boils again, then stir, separating the *spaghetti* strand by strand. Allow to cook until *al dente*, drain, put into a large bowl and season with the sauce. Mix well and serve at once.

TORTELLI OR TORDELLI

Tortelli are the Tuscan version of a dish which exists in almost every country. In Yiddish they're called *kreplach*, in Russian *piroushki*, in Chinese *wonton*, in other parts of Italy *ravioli*. They are made with dough and various fillings which can be all meat, meat and vegetables, cheese and vegetables or meat, cheese and vegetables. Unlike the small *tortellini* for which Bologna is famous, and which are very good eaten *in brodo*, the Tuscan *tortello* or *tordello* is eaten with a sauce, *asciutto*. Following are two types of dough, the classic egg dough which can be used for noodles, *lasagne*, *pappardelle* and *tortelli*, and a lighter, softer dough which is the one used here. Then there are several suggestions for fillings: from cheese and vegetables (the lightest) to all meat (the most substantial). The sauce, which is the other indispensable item, can be melted butter and cheese—ideal with the spinach and *ricotta tortelli*—or a good *ragù* the meat and tomato sauce described in recipe No. 88.

32. PASTA ALL'UOVO
(*Egg and Flour Dough*)

SERVES 7 OR 8 AS PASTA,
MORE IF ADDED TO SOUP OR
USED WITH STUFFING

This dough can be used for *tagliatelle*, *pappardelle*, *lasagne*, *cannelloni*, *tortelli* or *tordelli*, and simply as *pasta all'uovo*, added to bean broth.

3 or more cups flour
4 eggs

1. Put 3 cups sifted flour into a large bowl, add the eggs, mix with a fork until all egg has been absorbed.
2. Gather dough with your hands and knead against a smooth surface that has been sprinkled with flour—in Tuscany most kitchens have a marble surface—working in all the little crumbly pieces. The dough should be hard and elastic. If necessary, add more flour.

3. Divide the dough into 3 or 4 parts and roll out one at a time, using a floured rolling pin. Work the sheet of dough until it's as thin as possible. If making *tortelli* a thickness that is between $\frac{1}{16}$ and $\frac{1}{8}$ inch is enough, but if making *tagliatelle* or *pappardelle* roll it out even thinner.

4. If making *tortelli* put little balls of filling at about 1-inch distance from one another on the sheet of dough, cover with another sheet of dough and cut with a crimper, that special wheel that makes a ragged edge. Be sure the edges stick together. For *tagliatelle*, etc., roll the sheet like a jelly roll and cut into strips of the desired width. Open each strip and allow to dry. Use at once or store for future use.

33. PASTA FATTA IN CASA
(*Homemade Dough*)

SERVES 3 OR 4 AS PLAIN
PASTA AND 5 OR 6 IF
STUFFED OR ADDED TO SOUP

This dough uses less egg than the preceding recipe, and is therefore softer. It's particularly suited for Tuscan *tortelli*, but can also be made as plain pasta, or pasta to be added to bean soup.

> 1¼ *cups flour, or more*
> 1 *egg*
> ¼ *cup milk*
> 1 *teaspoon salt*

1. Put 1¼ cups flour into a bowl, add the egg, milk and salt, mix with a fork until all egg and milk have been absorbed.

2. Gather dough with your hands and knead against a hard surface that has been sprinkled with flour. The dough should be elastic. If necessary, add more flour and keep the surface floured. Dough is ready when it comes easily away from the board without sticking.

3. Continue as in steps 3 and 4 of previous recipe.

34. RIPIENO DI RICOTTA E SPINACI
(*Spinach and Ricotta Filling*)

SERVES 4 OR 5

1½ cups drained, cooked spinach
1½ cups ricotta cheese, well
    drained
2 eggs

⅓ cup grated Parmesan cheese
Nutmeg (*optional*)
½ teaspoon salt

1. Drain spinach well, squeeze out excess water, chop fine.
2. Mix with all other ingredients and blend thoroughly.
3. Cut dough (see previous recipe) into pieces measuring about 2 inches square. Put 1 teaspoon of the filling in the center of each square, cover with another square, seal the edges with a fork or with a special pastry wheel and discard extra dough. Allow to stand for at least ½ hour.
4. Meanwhile, bring to the boil a large pot of lightly salted water.
5. When ready to serve, add several *tortelli*, allow to boil for a few minutes and when they come to the surface remove them with a slotted spoon. Put into a warm pyrex dish, pour in some melted butter, add some grated Parmesan cheese, continue until all dumplings are cooked. Serve hot.

35. TORTELLI CON RIPIENO DI CARNE, FORMAGGIO E VERDURA
(*Meat, Cheese and Vegetable Filling*)

SERVES 6 TO 8

1 onion
1 clove garlic
5 ounces blanched bacon
Approximately 1½ cups cooked
    spinach or Swiss chard
⅓ cup olive oil
1 pound cubed raw meat, some
    pork and some beef

Salt and pepper
1 cup hot water
¾ cup ricotta or other creamy
    white cheese
½ cup grated Pecorino or
    Parmesan cheese
2 eggs
Nutmeg (*optional*)

1. Clean the onion and garlic, and chop fine. Chop bacon. Drain cooked spinach or Swiss chard well, chop fine.

2. Put oil into a saucepan, add onion, garlic, bacon and meat. Simmer for 10 to 15 minutes, until meat is browned on all sides. Stir often in order to avoid burning the onion.

3. Add salt and pepper to taste and 1 cup of hot water. Cover, lower the flame and cook for another 40 minutes, until meat is soft.

4. Take the cooked meat out of the saucepan and put it through the meat grinder. If the remaining sauce is too liquid, boil, uncovered, until the liquid is reduced to ¼ cup. Allow to cool.

5. Put the meat back into the saucepan, add chopped spinach or Swiss chard, the white cheese, the grated cheese, the eggs and a little grated nutmeg, if desired. Blend well. Proceed as in previous recipe, from step 3.

36. TORTELLI CON RIPIENO DI CARNE— RISTORANTE SOLFERINO
(*Meat Filling—Solferino Restaurant*)

SERVES 6

2 cloves garlic
1 onion
5 leaves fresh sage or 1 teaspoon dried
1 small sprig fresh rosemary or 1 teaspoon dried
⅓ cup olive oil
2 tablespoons chopped parsley
1 pound raw meat, some pork and some beef, cut into large cubes

½ cup dry red wine
Salt and pepper
2 large slices mortadella di Bologna or cooked ham
2 eggs
7 tablespoons grated Parmesan cheese
Nutmeg

1. Clean and wash garlic and onion, chop fine. Chop the sage and the rosemary leaves. Put oil in a saucepan, add onion, garlic, rosemary, sage and parsley and simmer on medium flame for 2 or 3 minutes.

2. Add meat to saucepan, allow to brown slightly on all sides— about 10 to 15 minutes—then pour in wine, add salt and pepper, cover, lower flame and cook until all wine has evaporated.

3. Continue to cook for at least another hour, adding hot water in small quantities whenever necessary. Meat should be soft and have very little sauce.

4. Remove all meat from saucepan, allow to cool, put it through the meat grinder. Put the *mortadella* through the meat grinder as well. Add the eggs and cheese, taste for seasoning, add more salt and pepper if necessary, plus a few gratings of nutmeg. Blend thoroughly.

5. Have dough ready and proceed as in recipe No. 34.

37. PAPPARDELLE ALLA LEPRE I
(*Pappardelle with Hare Sauce I*)

SERVES 4 TO 5

Pappardelle are a wider version of *tagliatelle*, which are flat ribbons of *pasta* made with flour and eggs. In other words, egg noodles. They are exquisite when homemade (see recipe No. 32) but many of the existing commercial brands are equally satisfying.

The hare sauce is extremely popular in Tuscany, but the ways of making it vary from place to place. In one restaurant I was told they cooked the whole hare, then ground everything in a special machine, strained the pieces of bone out and used the remainder to season the *pasta*. Needless to say, that was a recipe I discarded without regrets. The two recipes that follow are the final result of extensive sampling and tasting, a sort of cross-section of the simplest and the best. One is plain, and is perhaps the most typical, the other uses tomato, and is the one I like best.

1 small onion
1 stalk celery
1 pound boned hare meat,
    usually from the legs
3 tablespoons olive oil
2 tablespoons butter
5 slices bacon, blanched and
    chopped
Salt and pepper
1 sprig fresh thyme or ½
    teaspoon dried

1 tablespoon flour
1 cup dry white wine
2 bouillon cubes dissolved in
    1½ cups hot water
1 pound commercial pappardelle
    (if homemade increase the
    amount by half)
Grated Parmesan cheese, as
    needed

1. Clean, wash and chop onion and celery. Cut hare meat into cubes. Put oil and butter in a saucepan, add chopped bacon, onion and celery, allow to simmer on medium flame for a few minutes, add the hare, a little salt, plenty of fresh-ground black pepper and the thyme, and continue to simmer until the hare is browned well—stir often so that the onion does not stick.

2. Sprinkle the hare with the flour, and when flour darkens, add the wine; stir well, continue to cook uncovered until most of the wine has evaporated.

3. When the meat and vegetables are surrounded by a thick sauce, add the hot water and bouillon cubes, stir, cover and cook on a low flame for 1½ to 2 hours.

4. At this point, remove the pieces of hare from the sauce, chop fine, and return the meat to the pan. Meanwhile, bring a large pot of salted water—1 teaspoon salt for each quart of water—to the boil and add the *pappardelle*. Cook *al dente*, drain, season with the hare sauce, sprinkle generously with fresh-grated Parmesan cheese and serve at once.

38. PAPPARDELLE ALLA LEPRE II
(*Pappardelle with Hare Sauce II*)

SERVES 4 OR 5

2 cups Chianti wine
1 cup wine vinegar
1 cup water
8 or 10 juniper berries
3 bay leaves
1 sprig fresh rosemary or ½
    teaspoon dried
Salt and pepper
1 pound boned hare meat,
    preferably legs, and liver
    (the saddle can be used for
    a roast)

5 peeled Italian plum tomatoes
1 clove garlic
1 stalk celery
1 onion
½ cup olive oil
1 bouillon cube
1 tablespoon butter
1 pound commercial pappardelle
    (if homemade increase the
    amount by half)
Grated Parmesan cheese, as
    needed

1. Make a marinade with 1 cup each wine, vinegar and water, the juniper berries, bay leaves, rosemary, salt, and fresh-ground black pep-

per. Put the hare meat (but not the liver) into this liquid and leave overnight. Be sure all meat is immersed.

2. Put the tomatoes through a food mill. Clean and wash the garlic, celery and onion and chop fine. Take the hare out of the marinade, dry well with paper towels. Put meat into a casserole, sprinkle with ½ teaspoon of salt, cover and cook on medium flame for 10 to 15 minutes. At the end of this time the hare meat will have rendered its liquid. Remove and transfer to another casserole.

3. Add the garlic, celery, onion and oil. Allow to simmer, browning the meat on all sides. Add the juniper berries and bay leaves used in the marinade. At this point, add the liver (this is not essential, as the liver adds a special flavor to the sauce that isn't congenial to everyone; in Tuscany liver is added to many sauces but personally I prefer this sauce without it). When the meat is well browned pour in the remaining wine, stir, and make sure you scrape up the coagulated juices that stick to the bottom of the casserole; they give the sauce that bit of extra flavor. Boil briskly until most of the wine has evaporated.

4. When the wine has evaporated almost completely lower the flame and remove the meat. Chop it fine and put back into the casserole. Add the tomatoes, stir, cover and allow to cook for at least 1 hour. If during this time the sauce starts getting thick, dissolve the bouillon cube in a cup of hot water and add some of this liquid to the saucepan. The final consistency of the sauce should be similar to the consistency of jam. Remove from fire and stir in the butter.

5. Cook the *pasta* as indicated in the previous recipe, season with the sauce, serve at once, with fresh-grated Parmesan cheese on the side.

39. PAPPARDELLE ALL'ARETINA
(*Egg Noodles with Duck and Tomato Sauce*)

SERVES 4

Salt
1 *pound* pappardelle (*wide egg noodles*)
4 *tablespoons butter*
Duck and tomato sauce, *from recipe No. 170*

½ *cup grated Parmesan cheese*
One 2-*ounce package cream cheese, broken into small pieces*
2 *tablespoons bread crumbs*

1. In a large pot bring to the boil at least 4 quarts of water seasoned with 2 teaspoons salt. Add the *pappardelle* and as soon as the water boils again stir, separating the noodles in order to avoid sticking. Allow to boil about 5 minutes, or until *al dente*, drain, then rinse quickly with cold water. Preheat the oven to 400° F.

2. Butter the bottom and sides of a large pyrex dish. Line the bottom with a quarter of the *pasta*, cover with ⅓ of the sauce, then sprinkle with ⅓ of the grated Parmesan and dot with ¼ of the cream cheese. Repeat these three layers, then finish with the remaining *pasta*. Cover with bread crumbs and dot with the remaining butter and cream cheese.

3. Bake in the hot oven for about 10 minutes, or until the top is browned and bubbling; serve at once.

40. TAGLIATELLE AL DOPPIO BURRO
(*Twice Buttered Noodles*)

SERVES 4 OR 5

Quick and rich, this is a delicious, easy first course. Perfect with a chicken, rabbit or veal stew because the white smoothness of the noodles is an ideal complement to the spicy meat and sauce.

> *1 pound egg noodles*
> *Salt*
> *½ cup butter*
> *Grated Parmesan cheese, as needed*
> *¼ cup heavy cream*

1. Boil noodles in abundant salted water, taste one after about 5 minutes, and drain when *al dente*. Preheat oven to 350° F.

2. Meanwhile, on low flame, melt about ⅔ of the butter, add ½ cup grated Parmesan. Season drained noodles with this mixture, add cream, toss well, put into buttered baking dish, sprinkle top with remaining butter cut up into little pieces and additional Parmesan.

3. Bake in preheated oven for about 10 to 15 minutes, serve hot.

41. PAGLIA E FIENO
(*Straw and Hay*)

SERVES 6

This excellent *pasta* dish is named for the two colors of egg noodles used: yellow and green. In order to be perfect, the dough should be homemade, so, if you can, use recipe No. 32. To make dough green add ½ cup cooked, puréed spinach. But if you don't have the time, there are very good commercial green and yellow egg noodles available. Be sure to get them the same width and brand so cooking time will be identical.

Here, the sauce is what makes this dish so special. It originates in Siena, and is particularly well made in the *contrada* of the Bruco* because their colors are yellow and green, with a dash of blue which, for the sake of this recipe, is overlooked.

There are many versions of *Paglia e Fieno*, and some use a great deal of cream in the sauce, but I've chosen this one because it's the most Tuscan. Cooking with butter and cream is closer to the *Bolognese* conception.

2 ounces dried mushrooms (if good fresh mushrooms are available use 3 to 4 times the amount)
1 medium onion
1 small carrot
1 stalk celery
4 ounces prosciutto (*Italian raw ham*)
4 ounces sliced bacon

⅓ cup olive oil
One 16-ounce can peeled Italian plum tomatoes
Salt or 1 bouillon cube
¾ cup dry white wine
7 ounces tender peas (shelled, fresh or frozen)
1¼ pounds green and yellow egg noodles, combined

1. Soak dried mushrooms in warm water for 30 minutes. Chop onion, carrot and celery fine. Dice ham and bacon.

2. Heat diced bacon in medium saucepan, allow to crisp, add ham, after a few minutes add the oil; when it's heated through add the chopped vegetables. Stirring, allow the vegetables to wilt and the onion

* A *contrada* is a section of the city. When the *palio* is run several of these *contrade* compete for the victory and each displays its own vivid colors.

to acquire a golden color. Meanwhile, clean soaked mushrooms carefully, removing all sand, and chop coarse.

3. Add mushrooms to saucepan, let simmer for another few minutes, stirring constantly in order to avoid sticking. Squash each tomato in your hand, remove hard parts, add to the saucepan. Stir, lower flame, and cook uncovered for about 20 minutes.

4. Bring to the boil a large pot of lightly salted water.

5. Taste the sauce, add salt or a bouillon cube if necessary, and pour in the wine. Allow to come to the boiling point, add the peas, stir, lower the flame, cover and cook for another 10 minutes.

6. Check to be sure peas are cooked and sauce is thick enough. If too liquid cook, uncovered, for another 10 minutes. It's ready when it has the consistency of marmalade.

7. Put the green and yellow noodles into the boiling water, cook until *al dente*, drain.

8. Pour sauce over cooked *pasta*, mix well and serve with fresh-grated Parmesan cheese and pass a black-pepper grinder.

42. TAGLIATELLE CON FEGATINI
(*Egg Noodles with Chicken Liver Sauce*)

SERVES 4 TO 5

The following is another Sienese recipe for egg noodles.

1 *pound egg noodles*
Salt
⅓ *cup heavy cream*
Double portion of sauce No. 85,
  Cibreo di Fegatini

2 *tablespoons butter*
½ *cup fresh-grated Parmesan*
  cheese

1. Cook the noodles in 5 quarts of lighlty salted water, drain when still *al dente*.

2. Add the heavy cream to the *cibreo*, allow to heat through.

3. Put the noodles, butter, sauce and grated Parmesan cheese into a warm bowl, toss well, serve at once.

43. CANNELLONI AL SUGO ANTICO
(*Cannelloni Filled with Old-fashioned Sauce*)

SERVES 4 TO 6

Cannelloni are large squares of *pasta* stuffed with a meat or vegetable filling. They are not exactly a Tuscan dish, but made with this particular sauce they couldn't be had anywhere else. Normally they are covered with a light béchamel sauce, but considering the richness of this filling I cover them with grated Parmesan and a little butter. A little plain *pomarola* (see recipe No. 86) is all right too.

Salt
3 tablespoons olive oil
About 12 squares of pasta for
  cannelloni, homemade or
  commercial

1 portion of Old-fashioned
  Sauce (see recipe No. 89)
Butter, as needed
Grated Parmesan cheese, as
  needed

1. If making *cannelloni* at home use recipe No. 32. Fill a large pot with water, add ½ teaspoon of salt per quart of water and the olive oil and bring to the boiling point.

2. Cook the squares of *pasta* in the boiling water; when ready remove with slotted spoon and drain well. Put one square on a plate, put 2 tablespoons of filling in the middle, fold both ends over filling. Repeat with all squares.

3. Butter an oblong baking dish, put the *cannelloni* in it side by side, sprinkle with the grated Parmesan and dot with butter. Bake in a preheated 325° F. oven for about 15 minutes or until heated through, serve at once.

44. PASTA TORDELLATA
(*Pasta Seasoned with Meat Filling and Tomato Sauce*)

SERVES 8

This is one of those substantial Tuscan dishes that to me is almost a whole meal. Instead of making *tordelli*, a dough envelope with a meat, cheese and vegetable filling which is then cooked and seasoned with a meat and tomato sauce, some efficient Tuscan housewife thought up the *pasta tordellata*, which makes filling and sauce into one, and seasoned the straight *pasta* with it, getting almost the same result in taste with considerably less effort.

1 *large carrot*	One *5-ounce can tomato paste*
1 *large onion*	2 *cups hot water*
1 *stalk celery*	1 *bouillon cube*
2 *cloves garlic*	*Pepper*
5 *ounces blanched bacon*	*Nutmeg* (*optional*)
5 *leaves fresh basil or* ½	¾ *cup* ricotta *cheese*
teaspoon dried	3 *tablespoons butter or*
Salt	*margarine*
2 *cups cleaned spinach*	2 *eggs*
½ *cup olive oil*	26 *ounces wide egg noodles*
About ¾ *cup each cubed raw*	*Parmesan cheese, as needed*
pork and raw beef	

1. Clean and wash carrot, onion, celery and garlic; cut into large pieces. Cut bacon into pieces. Put vegetables, basil and bacon through the meat grinder.

2. Boil spinach for 5 minutes in 1 cup lightly salted water. Drain, chop fine, and reserve.

3. Put oil into large saucepan, add ground bacon and vegetables and the meat, simmer for at least 20 minutes, until meat is no longer red. Stir often in order to avoid sticking.

4. Dissolve tomato paste in 2 cups hot water. Pour over the meat, lower the flame, add bouillon cube, a little salt and fresh-ground pepper, the nutmeg, if desired, then cover and cook for about 1 hour, or until meat is tender.

5. Put at least 5 quarts of water into a large pot, add 2 teaspoons of salt, bring to the boiling point. Meanwhile, take the cooked meat out of its sauce and run it through the meat grinder twice. Put in a bowl and allow to cool, then add the chopped spinach, *ricotta*, butter and eggs. Mix thoroughly and put back into the sauce, continue to cook on a very low flame, stirring often.

6. When the water boils add the *pasta* and cover partially. When it boils again stir the *pasta* well and continue to cook until ready, about 5 to 8 minutes. Then drain, put into a large bowl, or two medium

bowls, and season with the sauce. Serve hot, with fresh-grated Parmesan cheese on the side.

45. RAVIOLI DI SPINACI E RICOTTA
(*Spinach and Ricotta Dumplings*)

SERVES 4 TO 6

Also known as *gnocchi del Casentino*, these dumplings are among the lightest, most delicious items in Tuscan, Italian or international cooking. The word *ravioli* comes from the 13th century Latin *rabiola*, diminutive for *rapa*, turnip. Thus *ravioli*, small turnips. Or else dumplings made with turnips, which in those days was entirely possible.

1½ cups cooked spinach, well
    drained and chopped fine
2 cups drained ricotta cheese
1 egg
2½ teaspoons salt

Nutmeg (optional)
Grated Parmesan cheese, as
    needed
Flour, as needed
¼ cup melted butter

1. Mix chopped spinach with the *ricotta*, egg, ½ teaspoon salt, a little nutmeg, if desired, and 4 tablespoons Parmesan cheese. Make sure the mixture is well blended.

2. In a large pot, bring about 4 quarts of water and 2 teaspoons of salt to the boiling point.

3. Take a spoonful of the spinach mixture and shape it into a small dumpling, about the size of a walnut. Roll lightly in the flour. Continue until all materials are used up. Toss several dumplings at a time in a fine sieve in order to remove the excess flour. Repeat with all dumplings.

4. Take a few dumplings at a time and add gently to the pot of boiling water. They will come to the surface in 1 or 2 minutes. Remove with a slotted spoon, drain well, put into a pyrex dish with some of the melted butter, sprinkle with some grated Parmesan cheese, then continue to add dumplings, butter and Parmesan until all ingredients are used up. Keep in a lightly heated oven while you finish the cooking, otherwise the first ones will cool too much. Serve at once.

46. GNOCCHI DI PATATE
(*Potato Dumplings*)

SERVES 4 TO 6

Gnocchi are not Tuscan, they are Northern rather than Central Italian, but are eaten here very often. The word itself seems to indicate the Northern origin, as it apparently comes from the Germanic *knodel*, with numerous intermediate steps such as *knederli, gnocc, gnocarei* and so on. Basically they are dumplings, made with a vegetable or gruel base and held together with egg and flour. They can be seasoned with butter, tomato sauce, meat and tomato sauce or a combination of these. My personal favorite for the recipe below is a piece of fresh butter and a few tablespoons of tomato sauce, a seasoning called *macchiato* in Tuscany, which is very good on *spaghetti*, too.

2 full pounds mealy potatoes	*1¼ cups flour*
Salt	*⅓ cup melted butter*
1 egg	*⅓ cup grated Parmesan cheese*

1. Peel and wash potatoes, cut in half, cook in lightly salted water for 45 minutes and drain. Put back on the stove for a moment or two in order to dry the potatoes completely; do this by moving the pan back and forth on the flame. Mash and allow to cool.

2. Add the egg, 1 cup flour and ½ teaspoon of salt to the cool mashed potatoes, work well together until you have a light, uniform dough.

3. Meanwhile, put 4 or 5 quarts of water in a large, wide pan, add 2 teaspoons salt, bring to the boiling point.

4. Sprinkle some of the remaining flour on a wooden surface. Take a handful of dough and roll on the floured surface until it becomes a long, sausage-like roll the thickness of a finger. Using a sharp knife, cut into 1-inch dumplings.

5. When the water boils add some of the prepared *gnocchi*, no more than 12 or 15 at a time. Allow to cook for a few minutes, and when they come to the surface remove with a slotted spoon. Serve at once, seasoned with melted butter and grated Parmesan or another sauce of your choice.

POLENTA

In ancient Rome the simple citizen's everyday dish was something called *"puls romana,"* a mixture of vegetables and barley or other soft grains cooked in water. During the Middle Ages the European lower classes ate various types of gruel, a form of nourishment based on ground-up cereal cooked in water, milk or broth and seasoned, whenever possible, with more substantial items, such as lard, olive oil, or cheese. Through the centuries that followed, this habit has persisted. In fact, the porridge eaten by the British school boy, the corn pone of the Kentucky farmer, and the Polish peasant's *mamátyga*, are all latter day offspring of the same parent, which in Italy has had, through the ages, a variety of names, such as *farinata, panata, panissa, panicella* and, best known of all, *polenta*.

At first, the cereals used in Italy were rye, spelt, barley and inferior qualities of wheat. They were ground by whatever means were available, and the resulting flour was then cooked in whatever liquid was at hand and enriched with whatever fatty substance was available. It's worth noting that originally olive oil was preferred to animal fats such as lard and butter, but when the olive harvest was bad, the poorer people had to fall back on whatever seasonings they could find.

Coarse flour made of various inferior cereals was also used in the making of bread, and even today the characteristic Tuscan country bread is dark in color and rugged in texture. The big outside baking ovens, heated by means of a wood fire, were lit only once a week, so that bread wasn't always fresh and edible in the form of common slices. Methods were devised for the use of stale bread. One method was simply letting it get hard and then grinding it up again, thus obtaining bread crumbs which were then cooked in milk or broth and seasoned with oil or butter, and so on. Another way of using stale bread was to toast the slices and use them as a base for vegetable soups, *zuppe* and, later, as a base for fish and meat stews—*cacciucco* and *scottiglia*. These last two ways for using stale bread are typical of Tuscany, where bread in general probably finds more applications than anywhere else in Italy. Not only does it serve as a base for the above mentioned recipes, but it's also an important part of the tasty *panzanella* (recipe No. 12), a salad made with raw tomatoes, onions and cucumber or, cooked with hot peppers, garlic and tomatoes, bread is the main ingredient in the spicy Florentine soup called *pappa al pomodoro* (recipe No. 66).

With the discovery of America many new items entered the European diet. Chief among these were: potatoes, which later became a staple in the diet of Germans, Poles, Russians and Great Britons; tomatoes, which rapidly became popular in the south of Italy and were brought north during the Risorgimento, the 19th century movement which culminated in the unification of Italy; and corn, an American cereal that was easy to cultivate and that made a yellow flour the Northern and Central Italians have been eating for about three centuries in the form of *polenta*.

In Tuscany *polenta* is seldom eaten by itself. It is either seasoned with a sauce—meat, fish, mushrooms, tomatoes, or a combination of these—or cooked in a vegetable soup base, thus bringing together the ancient tradition of the cereal mash with that other ancient tradition, the vegetable soup, as they did in ancient Rome with the *"puls romana."*

When Thomas Jefferson came to Florence, he was served *polenta*. He liked it so much that once back in Virginia he had his cook learn how to prepare it the Tuscan way and had it served often, both for himself and for his guests.

Below I have listed several ways of eating *polenta*. To begin with, there are two recipes for cooking the cereal itself, one in a harder version and the other in a softer, more pudding-like version. Then there are three sauces for seasoning it, two combinations of meat and mushrooms and one fish and tomato sauce. Finally, there are three recipes for vegetable soup and *polenta*, all Tuscan, but each from a different area. It should be noted, however, that *polenta* is very good seasoned simply with fresh butter and cheese—any melting cheese, such as Parmesan, Cheddar, Swiss, Gouda, or a combination of these—and many like to eat it straight, with only cold milk poured over it.

47. POLENTA
(*Corn Meal Mush*)

An old recipe says that to make a perfect *polenta* one needs:

— *a round-bottom pot, of the kind that makes mixing possible, without visible joining point between the sides and the bottom,*
— *a good wood fire,*
— *a large, flat wooden spoon for turning,*
— *a large wooden board for pouring it onto when it's ready,*
— *a strong thread to cut it with.*

An up-to-date version of the above would be: a large pot with a long handle, a normal gas fire, a large wooden spoon for stirring, and a large wooden board lined with a large white linen napkin for turning out the *polenta*.

There are two types of yellow corn meal in Tuscany, the local variety, ground fine, and the northern variety, coarser in grain. Strangely enough, the coarser meal makes a softer *polenta* and the finer meal makes a harder *polenta*, though the real determining factor is the proportion of water to meal. Tuscan cooks favor the harder variety, which is probably why the locally milled corn meal is fine. When cooked, it is so firm that it can be cut with a taut thread.

7 cups water
2 teaspoons salt
2 cups polenta, *yellow corn meal, one each of the coarse and fine grained variety*

1. Put the water and salt in a large pot, bring it to the boiling point.
2. Sift the fine *polenta*, eliminating all chaff, and mix it with the coarse polenta.
3. Add the combined corn meal slowly to the water, pouring it with one hand in a continuous thin stream, and stirring with the other hand, always from left to right. It's important that the meal be added

slowly in order not to lower the temperature of the water too much. When all the corn meal has been added, continue to stir for another 5 minutes, scraping the sides of the pot with the wooden spoon, always from left to right, making sure no lumps are formed.

4. Cook on a low fire, uncovered, for another 30 to 45 minutes, or until it starts to stand away from the sides of the pot. Stir often to avoid lumps and sticking. Stirring will get harder as the mixture thickens. *Polenta* should cook for at least 45 minutes, otherwise it tastes slightly bitter.

5. When ready pour out, in one swift motion, onto a damp white linen napkin set on a wooden board. Fold the four corners of the napkin over the *polenta* and serve it on the whole board if your table is big enough. At the table unfold the napkin, cut the round into quarters with a wet knife, and cut the quarters into slices. Put 2 or 3 slices on each dish and season as desired.

48. POLENTA MORBIDA O POLENTINA
(*Soft Corn Meal Mush*)

SERVES 6 OR 7

2½ *quarts water*
1½ *teaspoons salt*
3 *cups* polenta, *half of it coarse and the other half fine-grained*

1. Put water and salt in a large pot and bring to the boiling point. Repeat step 2. of previous recipe.

2. Start pouring in the corn meal slowly and steadily, stirring constantly with your other hand, always from left to right. The corn meal should be added slowly in order to avoid lowering the temperature of the water, and steadily in order to avoid the formation of lumps. The consistency here should be that of a porridge, so stop adding the meal when you feel that the mixture has reached the right consistency. Continue to stir for another 5 minutes, scraping the sides of the pot with the wooden spoon.

3. Cook on a low fire, uncovered, for another 45 minutes. If it starts getting too thick, add a ladle or 2 of hot water. Stir often to avoid lumps and sticking. After about 45 minutes of cooking time the

polenta is ready to be served. Put about 2 ladlefuls on each soup dish and season with one of the sauces described below or any other sauce you like.

49. MATUFFI AL RAGÙ DI FUNGHI
(*Mushroom Sauce for Matuffi*)

SERVES 6 OR 7

Matuffi is another name for *polentina* with a sauce, and its interest lies in the fact that it's made in layers.

1 *large onion*
1 *large carrot*
1 *stalk celery*
A *handful of parsley*
5 *leaves fresh basil or one teaspoon dried*
2 *ounces dried mushrooms*
Two 16-ounce cans peeled *Italian plum tomatoes*
⅓ *cup olive oil*

1 *pound ground beef, chuck or round*
1 *cup Chianti wine*
2 *tablespoons tomato paste dissolved in 1 cup hot water*
Salt and pepper
Nutmeg (*optional*)
1 *bouillon cube*
1½ *cups fresh-grated Parmesan cheese*

1. Clean, wash and chop onion, carrot, celery, parsley and basil. Soak mushrooms in warm water for 30 minutes, remove, wash and clean well, cut into small pieces. Strain the mushroom water through a sieve lined with several layers of cheesecloth, to remove all earth and sand, and reserve. Chop the tomatoes, discarding all hard pieces and seeds, and reserve.

2. In a saucepan, heat the oil, and add chopped vegetables except the tomatoes. Stir while they wilt; do not allow onion to brown. After a few minutes add the ground beef, and stir until it is no longer red. When the meat has released all its fat pour in the wine, stir, turn down the flame and cook, uncovered, for about 15 minutes, until most of the wine has evaporated.

3. Add chopped tomatoes and dissolved tomato paste. Stir, add salt and pepper to taste and a whiff of nutmeg if you like, cover; let

cook on a low flame for at least 1 hour. If the sauce gets too thick add the strained mushroom water, a little at a time.

4. At this point add the mushrooms and the bouillon cube. Stir, cook for another 10 minutes, check the seasoning, correct if necessary, cook on low flame for another 30 minutes, always adding more mushroom water if necessary; remove from fire.

5. Ladle out 2 or 3 spoonfuls of the *polentina* into each soup dish, cover with 1 or 2 spoons of the sauce, sprinkle with Parmesan, then repeat from the beginning. The *matuffi* should have plenty of sauce and cheese, should be served hot, and should be eaten with a spoon, so keep the *polentina* soft.

50. POLENTA CON SPEZZATINO DI AGNELLO
(*Polenta with Lamb Stew*)

SERVES 4

2 ounces dried mushrooms
1 onion
1 pound stewing lamb
4 tablespoons butter
5 tablespoons olive oil

1 teaspoon meat extract
2 tablespoons tomato paste
1 cup warm water
Salt and pepper

1. Soak mushrooms in warm water for 30 minutes, drain, clean well, removing all earth and sand. Clean onion, cut into thin slices. Clean and cut the lamb into cubes.

2. Put butter, oil and onion slices into a saucepan, let the onion wilt. Add the meat, allow to brown on all sides.

3. While the meat is browning dissolve the meat extract and the tomato paste in 1 cup warm water. Add to the saucepan, stir well in order to loosen any pieces that may have stuck to the bottom of the pan; cover, lower the flame, allow to cook for 1 hour. Check the level of the liquid, and if necessary add water. Add salt and fresh-ground pepper to taste.

4. Add the mushrooms and continue to cook for another 30 minutes, remove from fire, serve on top of the *polenta*, or next to *polenta* that has been seasoned with butter and cheese.

Note: For *polenta* with a fish sauce, see recipe No. 97.

51. BORDATINO
(*Vegetable Soup with Polenta*)

SERVES 4 TO 6

This is a specialty of the city of Leghorn and is called *bordatino* because it was made by the sailors on *board* ship.

1½ pounds fresh pinto beans or 6 ounces dried pinto beans	⅓ cup olive oil
1 onion	1 teaspoon tomato paste
1 stalk celery	1 bouillon cube
1 carrot	Salt and pepper
1 clove garlic	1 cup farina gialla (*yellow corn meal*)
1 Tuscan black cabbage (*see note*)	Parmesan cheese, as needed

1. Shell beans if fresh; if dried, soak overnight in warm water, drain, rinse. Cook for about 1 hour in 1 quart water. When cooked, put through a food mill.

2. Clean, wash and chop onion, celery, carrot and garlic. Clean and wash cabbage, cut into strips discarding hard core at center.

3. Measure bean purée and the liquid in which it cooked, put in a large soup pot, add enough water to make 2 quarts. Bring to boiling point, add cabbage, cook on low fire, covered, for about 30 minutes.

4. Put oil in saucepan, add chopped vegetables, allow to wilt but do not brown. Dissolve tomato paste in a little warm water, add to saucepan, cook for a few minutes. Meanwhile, add bouillon cube, a little salt and a few twists of the pepper grinder to the bean and cabbage pot. Add the contents of the saucepan to the soup pot, stir, allow to cook for 5 minutes, taste, correct seasoning if necessary.

5. At this point start pouring in the corn meal with one hand, slowly, while stirring with the other. When it's thoroughly blended (make sure no lumps are formed), let it cook on a very low fire for at least 30 minutes. Serve hot, with fresh-grated Parmesan and/or the sauce of a good pot roast.

Note: If Tuscan black cabbage is not available, use ordinary green cabbage, 1 small head or ½ of a large one.

52. POLENTINA CON FAGIOLI E CAVOLI NERI
(*Polentina with Beans and Black Cabbage*)

Follow the recipe above but do not purée the beans, leave them whole. This variation is typical of Lucca and of the coastal area of the province of Lucca, known as the Versilia. In our house it is the best-liked version of *polenta* and vegetable soup. In order to achieve the right consistency we mix the fine grained *farina gialla* made locally with the coarser grained *farina gialla* made in the north, in the proportion of one-to-one.

53. L'INFARINATA
(*Vegetable Soup with Polenta*)

SERVES 8

This is a specialty of the Garfagnana, the mountainous region of the province of Lucca.

1½ pounds fresh schiaccioni
    white beans or 6 ounces
    dried white lima beans
A few pieces of pork rind, if
    available
Salt
1 onion
1 clove garlic
1 carrot
1 stalk celery
A handful of celery
3 potatoes

1 small black cabbage (see note
    p. 72)
2 ounces lard or bacon (in one
    piece)
2 tablespoons olive oil
1 teaspoon fennel seeds
1 bouillon cube (optional)
1½ cups farina gialla (*yellow*
    corn meal)
Grated Parmesan cheese, as
    needed

1. Shell beans if fresh; soak overnight in warm water if dried. Cook in 2½ quarts of water for about 1 hour, add the pork rind at the beginning and 1 teaspoon of salt toward the end of the cooking time.
2. Clean, wash and chop the onion, garlic, carrot, celery and parsley. Peel and dice the potatoes; clean and wash the cabbage, cut into

strips, removing the hard white core. Chop up lard or bacon. Put oil into a large pot, add the first 5 chopped vegetables and the lard, fry, stirring, for a few minutes.

3. Take the pork rind out of the cooked beans, then add the beans with all of their broth to the frying vegetables. Add the diced potatoes and the strips of cabbage and cook for another 45 minutes. While the vegetables are cooking, crush the fennel seeds and add them to the pot.

4. When all vegetables are cooked, check the water level: there should be at least 2 quarts of liquid, if not, add enough water to bring to that amount. Check the seasoning, and if necessary, add salt or a bouillon cube or both.

5. Start adding the *farina gialla* to the vegetable soup. Pour in slowly with one hand while stirring with the other. Make sure no lumps are formed. Cook on very low fire for 40 minutes. Serve hot, sprinkled with fresh-grated Parmesan and, for those who like it, fresh-ground black pepper. If there is any soup left over, it will harden and can be sliced and fried in oil, or grilled, then served with grated Parmesan.

54. PASTA E CECI
(*Pasta and Chick Peas*)

SERVES 4 TO 5

7 ounces dried chick peas
1½ teaspoons salt
Baking soda
1 sprig fresh rosemary or ½
    teaspoon dried
1 clove garlic
1 small onion
3 slices bacon

Olive oil, as needed
1 teaspoon tomato paste
1 bouillon cube
7 ounces non-egg noodles
Grated Parmesan cheese, as
    needed
Pepper

1. Soak the chick peas in 2 quarts of warm water to cover for at least 24 hours. Add 1 teaspoon of salt and ½ teaspoon of baking soda.

2. Drain chick peas and rinse, add 1½ quarts of water, the rosemary, garlic and ½ teaspoon salt and let cook on low flame for at least 2 hours.

3. Meanwhile, chop onions and cut bacon into small pieces. Put bacon into large saucepan over low flame, let it melt for a minute or two, then raise heat to medium and add 3 tablespoons oil and the onion. Stir. Dissolve tomato paste and bouillon cube in warm water and add as soon as the onion is wilted. Stir and lower the flame.

4. Take the garlic and rosemary out of the cooked chick peas. Put ½ of the peas through the food mill and pour the purée into the simmering bacon-onion-tomato mixture. Add remaining whole chick peas and their broth, bring to a boil. Add the noodles, bring to a boil again, stir with a slotted spoon in order to separate the noodles and to avoid sticking. Let cook until noodles are tender.

5. The resulting mixture should be semi-liquid. Serve hot and pass the olive oil container, fresh-grated Parmesan and black pepper grinder separately.

55. CACCIUCCO DI CECI
(*Chick Pea Cacciucco*)

SERVES 4 TO 5

This vegetable soup, an inexpensive, hearty, winter dish, is worth trying for anyone who likes chick peas.

10 ounces dried chick peas	*1 tablespoon tomato paste*
Salt	*Warm water, as needed*
Baking soda	*8 to 10 slices toasted Tuscan*
7 ounces Swiss chard	*bread (see recipe No. 220)*
1 onion	*Grated Pecorino or Parmesan*
Olive oil, as needed	*cheese, as needed*
1 clove garlic	*Pepper*
2 anchovy fillets	

1. Soak the chick peas for 48 hours in about 2 quarts of warm water to which 1 teaspoon of salt and 1 teaspoon of baking soda have been added.

2. Clean and wash Swiss chard, cook in ½ cup lightly salted water for about 8 minutes. Drain and save.

3. Clean and slice the onion and put in a large pot with 5 tablespoons olive oil, the cleaned garlic clove and the anchovy fillets. Allow

to simmer on medium flame, and as the onion wilts, take a fork and mash the anchovies until they are practically dissolved. Do this on a low flame, for if anchovies burn they become bitter. Remove the garlic clove.

4. Drain and rinse the chick peas. Dissolve the tomato paste in ½ cup warm water, add to the onion and anchovy mixture. Cut the drained Swiss chard into wide strips and add to the pot. Add chick peas, 2 quarts warm water, cover, and cook on slow fire for 2 to 3 hours, taking the lid off as seldom as possible.

5. Put 2 slices of toasted bread in each soup plate, cover with chick pea mixture, let the bread soak in the broth. Serve hot, with fresh-grated *Pecorino* or Parmesan cheese and olive oil, to be added at will, and pass the black pepper grinder.

56. SCOTTIGLIA O CACCIUCCO DI CARNE
(*Meat Cacciucco*)

SERVES 6

1 *large onion*
1 *stalk celery*
1 *small carrot*
A *handful of parsley*
5 *leaves fresh basil or 1 teaspoon*
    dried
3 *cloves garlic*
½ peperoncino (*Italian hot*
    pepper)
2 *to 3 pounds assorted meats:*
    veal, chicken, lamb, pork,

guinea-hen, pigeon, rabbit,
    pheasant, etc.
One 16-ounce can peeled Italian
    plum tomatoes
¾ cup olive oil
Salt
1 cup dry white wine
1 bouillon cube (optional)
6 slices Tuscan bread (see
    recipe No. 220)
Pepper

1. Clean and wash the onion, celery, carrot, parsley, basil and 1 clove of garlic. Rinse the *peperoncino* and chop everything fine. For those who like their food spicy, a whole *peperoncino* can be added—in Tuscany they think nothing of using 2 hot peppers for this amount of meat, but for me that amount is decidedly too much.

2. Clean and wash all the meats and cut into bite-size pieces. Dry with paper towels. Put the tomatoes through a food mill.

3. Put the oil in a large saucepan, add the chopped vegetables and

let simmer over a medium flame for a few minutes. When vegetables are wilted add the various meats, stir, and allow the pieces to brown on all sides. Salt to taste.

4. When meats are browned pour in the wine and stir, loosening any bits that may have stuck to the bottom of the pan. Lower the flame and allow wine to evaporate slowly. When it's almost gone add the tomatoes. Cover and allow to cook for at least 1 hour, checking the liquid level from time to time.

5. Check seasoning. If salt is needed add a bouillon cube, or part of one, instead. If the gravy gets too thick add a little broth or water, no more than one ladle at a time. When *cacciucco* is done there ought to be at least 3 cups of liquid and the meat should be so well cooked that it will be coming away from the bones.

6. Toast the slices of bread, preferably in the oven. When still warm rub with the remaining clove of garlic. Put 1 slice at the bottom of each soup plate, ladle out the stew, trying to give each person at least 1 piece of each kind of meat. Pass the pepper grinder for those who like it.

Note: For a more elegant, but not-so-Tuscan, meal, serve this with boiled rice. Follow with a salad and dessert, and it's a complete meal.

57. MINESTRONE ALLA LIVORNESE
(*Leghorn Minestrone*)

SERVES 4 TO 5

1 pound fresh pinto beans, or 6 ounces dried
A large handful of Swiss chard
A large handful of spinach
¼ of a large cabbage
2 slices prosciutto (*Italian raw ham, fat if possible*)
1 clove garlic
A handful of parsley
1 tablespoon olive oil
2 potatoes
1 carrot

1 zucchini squash
1 medium onion
1 stalk celery
1 tablespoon tomato paste
2 quarts meat broth or 3 bouillon cubes dissolved in 2 quarts warm water
Salt and pepper
1 cup raw short-grain rice
5 tablespoons grated Parmesan cheese

1. Shell beans if fresh; soak in warm water overnight if dried. Wash Swiss chard, spinach and cabbage, cut into strips. Chop *prosciutto*, garlic and parsley, add oil and simmer on low flame. Put cleaned, cut greens, with just the water that clings to the leaves, in another pan on low flame and let cook until most of their water evaporates. When almost dry, add to the simmering *prosciutto*-garlic mixture.

2. Cook beans in 2 quarts of unsalted water for 1 hour. Drain. Meanwhile, peel and dice potatoes and carrot, dice zucchini, slice onion and celery into thin strips. Add them all, plus the beans, to the simmering greens. Dissolve the tomato paste in a little warm water and add. Pour in the broth, stir, add salt and pepper to taste, let all boil slowly for about 1 hour.

3. Add rice, bring to a boil, stir, lower the flame, let cook until rice is ready, about 15 to 20 minutes. Turn off flame, add Parmesan, stir again. It's good served hot, warm or cold.

58. MINESTRONE CON GRANO FARRO
(*Spelt and Vegetable Soup*)

SERVES 6

Grano Farro or spelt is also known as German wheat. The standard hearty vegetable soup, *minestrone*, is reinforced by this excellent wheat which has a slightly nutty flavor. This was once a traditional winter soup in Garfagnana, the mountainous region of the province of Lucca.

See recipe for *Minestrone alla Livornese*, No. 57. Use the same ingredients, substituting whole grain wheat for the rice in the same quantities.

1. and 2. Make the *minestrone* as in recipe No. 57.

3. Cook the whole grain wheat for about 20 minutes in a separate container, using about 1 quart of lightly salted water. Drain, put into the vegetable soup, cook another 15 minutes, and serve hot, with or without Parmesan.

59. RISO E FAGIOLI ALLA FIORENTINA
(*Florentine Rice and Beans*)

SERVES 5 OR 6

1½ pounds fresh cannellini
    beans or 7 ounces dried
    white beans
Salt
1 onion
2 cloves garlic
A handful of parsley
5 leaves fresh basil, or 1 teaspoon
    dried
1 stalk celery

2 ounces prosciutto (*Italian raw
    ham*)
1 peperoncino (*Italian hot
    pepper*)
3 tablespoons olive oil
One 1-pound can peeled Italian
    plum tomatoes
Pepper
7 ounces raw short-grain rice

1. Shell beans if fresh; soak in warm water overnight if dried. Put in soup pot with about 2 quarts of fresh water, cook until tender, add ½ teaspoon of salt when already cooked (beans harden if cooked in salted water).

2. While beans cook, chop the onion, garlic, parsley, basil, celery and ham fine. Chop the *peperoncino* but add with care, keeping in mind that every seed adds a lot of spice to the soup. Put oil, chopped vegetables and *prosciutto* into a saucepan, let simmer slowly, stirring occasionally. After a few minutes add the tomatoes, squashing them in your hands as you add each one and removing the hard pieces. Add black pepper—1 or 2 twists of the pepper grinder—stir, and allow to simmer for at least 15 minutes.

3. Pour the contents of the saucepan into the beans, stir, let cook for another 15 minutes. Add rice, bring to a boil, stir well in order to loosen the grains of rice, cook until rice is tender, and serve hot.

60. RISO CON POLMONE D'AGNELLO
(*Rice with Lamb's Lung*)

SERVES 4

A simple, hearty, rice dish. The meat sauce can be made with lamb, veal or beef lung, but it's best with a coratella* of lamb.

*14 ounces lamb's lung or coratella**	*2 tablespoons chopped parsley*
5 peeled Italian plum tomatoes	*Salt and white pepper*
1 onion	*3 bouillon cubes dissolved in 4 cups hot water*
4 tablespoons butter or margarine	*1½ cups raw long-grain rice*

1. Cut the lung or *coratella* into small cubes. Chop the tomatoes, discarding hard pieces and seeds. Clean, wash and slice the onion.

2. Put 3 tablespoons of butter in a saucepan, add the onion and parsley. When the onion is wilted, add lung and brown on all sides, no more than 5 or 6 minutes. Then add the tomatoes, salt and pepper to taste, lower the flame, and cook, uncovered, for about 30 minutes, checking often and stirring occasionally.

3. Put the bouillon cube broth on a high flame and when it boils add the rice. When the liquid returns to the boil, stir carefully with a slotted spoon, making sure that all grains of rice are separated. Cook for 12 minutes, taste; if starchy taste is gone, remove from fire and drain. Put in a bowl, add the remaining butter, stir to blend well. Serve the rice on a warm platter and pass the lung sauce separately.

---

   * The *coratella* of an animal consists of its lungs, heart, liver and spleen. In small animals these are removed together and are united by the windpipe or trachea. The expression is used mainly for lamb, sometimes for rabbit or hare.

   Lung may not be available in all parts of the United States, but the recipe is included here for all those lucky enough to find it, and because it is authentically Tuscan.

61. RISOTTO CON LE BECCACCE
(*Risotto with Woodcock*)

SERVES 4 OR 5

Many varieties of rice are grown in Italy, but they can be essentially reduced to three types: the *risotto* type, of which Arborio and Vialone are the best known, the cooking or steaming type, known in commerce as Razza 77 or R.B., and the type that is added to soups, called *riso da minestra* or *riso originario*. Since none of these names is known in other countries, it might be helpful if I explain what differentiates one type from another.

Beginning with the last one, the *riso originario* is a soft rice, with an abundant starch coating and very little gluten content. This means that it cooks quickly and becomes sticky when steamed. This starchy quality makes for a thicker soup, and the rice reaches the right consistency faster. This type is similar to what is known in the United States as short-grain rice.

The second quality, Razza 77 or R.B., is advisable for plain cooked rice, steamed rice or rice salads, because it has little starch on the surface and a substantial amount of gluten. It therefore stays firm when cooked through, but because of the lack of starch on the outside, it makes a poor *risotto*.

The best varieties of Italian-grown rice are the ones used for *risotti*, because they combine a hard, gluten heart with a starchy exterior, and that is what a good *risotto* requires. The Arborio or Vialone types cook slowly, remain firm on the inside, and at the same time make a sticky sauce that means a good *risotto*.

Rice of the right quality for a *risotto* can be had from an importer of Italian products, otherwise U.S. long-grain rice is adequate.

1 ounce dried mushrooms
1 small onion
3 slices of bacon, blanched
2 woodcocks or 1 pigeon, cooked
   (*see recipe* No. 174)
2½ cups good quality meat broth
   (*see recipe* No. 21)

3 tablespoons olive oil
3 tablespoons butter
12 ounces long-grain or risotto
   rice
3 peeled Italian plum tomatoes
Salt and pepper

1. Soak mushrooms in lukewarm water for 30 minutes. Clean and wash the onion. Chop the onion and bacon.

2. Bone the cooked birds with a sharp knife, removing every bit of skin and meat. Chop up the larger pieces. Put back into their sauce and reserve. Bring the broth to a boil.

3. Put oil, chopped onion and bacon into a large saucepan, simmer on medium flame for a few minutes. When onion is wilted add the meat of the woodcocks and 2 tablespoons of their cooking juices, stir, and allow to heat through.

4. When meat is warm add 2 tablespoons of butter and the rice. Stir, continue to cook on medium flame, uncovered, until the rice becomes transparent. At this point add 3 ladles of boiling broth, stir, lower the flame and allow the liquid to absorb slowly.

5. Meanwhile, remove the mushrooms from the water, wash well, be sure to remove all sand, and cut into strips. Add to the cooking rice, stir. Chop the tomatoes, discarding seeds and hard parts, add to the rice, stir. Continue adding the hot broth and stirring until the rice is cooked *al dente*, about 20 minutes total cooking time.

6. When rice is cooked, taste for seasoning and, if necessary, add salt and pepper, stir, add the remaining tablespoon of butter, cover, allow to stand for 2 or 3 minutes, serve hot with fresh-grated Parmesan cheese on the side.

Note: The right consistency for a *risotto* is that of a very thick soup. In Italy a good *risotto* is said to be *all'onda*, wavelike, meaning that it should be soupy enough to make a wave. It isn't easy to get the right consistency the first time around, so try, try again.

62. RISOTTO AI CARCIOFI
(*Artichoke Risotto*)

SERVES 4

This is a delicate, pale *risotto* that is especially popular in the city of Siena. To make *risotto* Italians always use good, homemade beef broth, but I've had very good results with Campbell's beef bouillon.

6 medium artichokes, cleaned
    and quartered (*see recipe*
    No. 189, step 1)
Juice of 1 lemon
1 quart hot beef broth
2 ounces prosciutto (*Italian raw*
    ham)
1 small onion

A handful of parsley
6 tablespoons butter
12 ounces risotto *type or long-*
    grain rice
Grated Parmesan cheese, as
    needed
White pepper (*optional*)

1. Put the artichoke quarters in a bowl of cold water and add the lemon juice. Heat the broth. Chop the *prosciutto* into small pieces. Clean, wash and chop the onion. Separately, clean, wash and chop the parsley.

2. Put 4 tablespoons of the butter in a medium saucepan, add the *prosciutto*, onion, and half the parsley, and let them fry for a few minutes; be careful not to brown the onion. Drain the artichokes and, as soon as the onion is straw colored, add the artichokes to the saucepan. Stir and cook on a low flame, adding a ladleful of broth when and if necessary.

3. When the artichokes are almost cooked, stir in the rice and let it absorb the butter. After a few minutes add 2 or 3 ladles of hot broth (it must be hot), stir, let it get absorbed by the rice, add more broth, stir again; continue to cook this way, uncovered, stirring often, until the rice is cooked *al dente*, usually about 20 minutes.

4. The *risotto*, when ready, should be like a very thick soup. If it's too dry add a little more broth—there should be some broth left over if all quantities were respected. Generally 1 quart of broth is enough for 1 pound of rice. Turn off the flame. Add the remaining butter, the remaining parsley, and about ⅓ cup grated Parmesan. Stir, cover, let stand for 2 or 3 minutes, serve at once with additional Parmesan and pass the white pepper grinder for those who want it.

63. RISOTTO ALLA TOSCANA
(*Tuscan Risotto*)

SERVES 4 OR 5

In the classical *risotti* of Northern Italy the hot liquid is added slowly to the simmering rice, but in Tuscany the opposite is sometimes the case. This recipe is the simplest one I've come across of the Tuscan variety, made by putting the rice into the meat sauce base. Serve it with the sliced pot roast and a salad and it turns into a whole meal.

2 ounces dried mushrooms	⅓ cup olive oil
5 slices bacon	One 16-ounce can peeled Italian
1 medium onion	plum tomatoes
1 stalk celery	3½ cups hot water or more, as
1 carrot	needed
1 clove garlic (optional)	1 bouillon cube
2 pounds rump, chuck or bottom	3 tablespoons butter
round pot roast	3 cups long-grain rice
Salt and pepper	Grated Parmesan cheese

1. Soak the mushrooms in warm water. Chop the bacon. Clean and chop the onion, celery, carrot and garlic. Sprinkle the meat with salt and pepper.

2. Put the oil in a large saucepan, add the meat and brown on all sides, then add the chopped bacon and vegetables and continue to simmer for another few minutes, until vegetables soften.

3. Add the peeled tomatoes, mashed slightly with a fork, and the liquid in the can. Wash the mushrooms carefully, removing all sand, cut into small pieces and add to the saucepan. Add the mushroom water, strained through several layers of cheesecloth. Bring to a boil, lower the flame, cover and cook for 1 to 2 hours, until meat is tender, checking the liquid level constantly. If it looks low, add hot water, no more than ½ cup each time.

4. When meat is done take out and keep in warm place. Measure the amount of liquid left. Put 2½ cups back into the saucepan; save the rest to serve over the meat. Add 3½ cups hot water to the saucepan, for a total of 6 cups of liquid. Add bouillon cube and half of the

butter, and bring to a boil. Add the rice, let the liquid boil again, stir well, lower flame, and allow to cook slowly for 15 to 20 minutes, until rice is *al dente*. Stir occasionally to prevent sticking. *Do not cover*. The *risotto* should be soupy and dark. Blend in the rest of the butter and serve hot, sprinkled with the grated Parmesan cheese.

64. RISOTTO ALLA PAESANA
(*Country Style Risotto*)

SERVES 4

This is a springtime *risotto*, made with early peas, carrots and zucchini squash. It can be made with frozen peas and older carrots, but the flavor will be slightly different. In Tuscany this recipe is made with hot, salted water rather than with beef broth, in order to have no interference with the good fresh flavor of the vegetables, but in case the vegetables used are not of the early spring kind, I would recommend good, hot, beef broth instead of the water.

10 ounces fresh peas, or 6 ounces
    canned or frozen peas
1 medium onion
1 stalk celery
1 small, young carrot
A handful of parsley
5 leaves fresh basil or 1 teaspoon
    dried
1 young zucchini
5 or 6 peeled Italian plum
    tomatoes

2 ounces blanched bacon
1 quart water
Salt and white pepper
2 bouillon cubes (optional)
⅓ cup olive oil
12 ounces of risotto type or
    long-grain rice
Parmesan cheese, as needed

1. Shell peas if fresh. Clean, wash and chop coarse the onion, celery, carrot, parsley, basil and zucchini. Chop the tomatoes, discarding seeds and hard parts. Cut bacon into small strips.

2. Put 1 quart water on fire, add a teaspoon of salt or the bouillon cubes and bring to a boil. Put bacon in a saucepan over medium flame, allow it to get crisp, add oil and all chopped vegetables except for the

zucchini and tomatoes, let them simmer for a few minutes. When onion is the color of straw add the tomatoes, the zucchini and the peas. Stir and allow to cook for about 20 minutes on a medium-low flame.

3. When vegetables are almost cooked add the rice, stir, let it absorb the fats for a few minutes, then add 2 or 3 ladles of the boiling water. Stir, let rice absorb the water, add more water, stir again, continue to cook this way, uncovered, until rice is cooked *al dente*, about 20 minutes. For rice, the *al dente* point is reached when it has lost the starchy flavor but is still consistent to the bite; by the time the grain is evenly soft it's overcooked, and the passage from the desired, *al dente*, stage to the overcooked stage can be as little as 2 minutes.

4. Remove from fire, add about ¼ cup fresh-grated Parmesan cheese, stir, serve hot.

65. BOMBA DI RISO ALLA LUNIGIANA
(*Rice Mold from the Lunigiana*)

SERVES 6 TO 8

⅓ cup olive oil
1 small onion, sliced thin
2 squabs or 1 broiling chicken, cleaned
10 peeled Italian plum tomatoes
½ cup dry white wine
Salt and pepper
3 leaves fresh sage or ½ teaspoon dried
3 leaves fresh basil or ½ teaspoon dried

½ cup beef broth, as needed
1½ pounds long-grain Carolina white rice
2 eggs
⅓ cup grated Parmesan cheese
½ cup cubed Swiss cheese
8 tablespoons butter
Dry bread crumbs, as needed
5 chicken livers, plus livers of squab
Flour, as needed
¼ cup Vin Santo or sweet sherry

1. Put olive oil and sliced onion into a large saucepan, allow to simmer for 2 minutes, add squabs or chicken. Chop the tomatoes, discarding seeds and hard parts.

2. When squabs have browned on all sides add white wine, allow to evaporate. Add tomatoes, sprinkle with salt and fresh-ground pepper, add sage and basil, stir, cover, and cook on a low flame for about 30

minutes or until birds are cooked through. Do not allow sauce to get dry. If necessary, add broth.

3. Meanwhile, boil rice for 8 to 9 minutes in a pan of lightly salted water, drain well, reserve.

4. Take birds out of their sauce, reserve. Put rice, the wine-tomato sauce left in the saucepan, eggs, grated Parmesan and cubed Swiss, and 3 tablespoons of the butter into a large bowl, and mix well. Preheat the oven to 350° F.

5. Butter a 2-quart mold, sprinkle well with dry bread crumbs. Put half of the rice mixture into the mold.

6. Cut chicken and squab livers into pieces, and roll in flour. Melt 3 tablespoons butter in a frying pan, add livers, simmer for 2 or 3 minutes. Add *Vin Santo* or sherry, sprinkle with salt, cover, lower the flame, cook for another 2 or 3 minutes, reserve.

7. Bone the squabs or chicken carefully, cutting meat into large pieces. Mix these pieces with the liver sauce made in step 6 and spread this mixture on the rice in the mold. Cover with remaining rice, sprinkle with bread crumbs, dot with about 2 more tablespoons of butter, bake for 20 to 30 minutes, until the surface has browned. Remove from the oven, allow to cool slightly, then unmold onto a warm platter and serve.

66. LA PAPPA AL POMODORO I
(*Bread and Tomato Soup I*)

SERVES 6

One of the famous Florentine soups—ideally it should be made in late summer, when fresh tomatoes and fresh basil are available.

*2 pounds fresh, ripe plum
    tomatoes*
Olive oil, as needed
4 garlic cloves, crushed
*10 leaves fresh basil or 2
    teaspoons dried*
*12 slices stale Tuscan bread,
    sliced (see recipe No. 220)*

Salt and pepper
1 peperoncino (*Italian hot
    pepper*)
*3 bouillon cubes dissolved in 6
    cups hot water*

1. Wash the tomatoes, cut into pieces, put into a saucepan and cook, uncovered, for about 30 minutes. Remove from fire and put through a food mill.

2. Put ½ cup olive oil into a saucepan, add the garlic and basil, simmer for 2 minutes, add the slices of bread, salt and pepper to taste, fry on medium flame for 5 to 10 minutes, add the tomatoes, stir, continue to cook for another few minutes. Cut the *peperoncino* into a few pieces, add.

3. At this point add the bouillon cube broth (or equivalent in homemade or canned broth), stir well, and continue to cook on low flame until the bread is reduced to a complete mush. Serve hot or cold. One or 2 tablespoons of olive oil should be poured on top of each portion and the black pepper grinder can be passed for those who like it.

67. LA PAPPA AL POMODORO II
(*Bread and Tomato Soup II*)

SERVES 6

Besides bread and tomatoes this soup has garlic as a third important ingredient. Use of this Asiatic plant goes so far back in time that we don't know who brought it to Italy. What we do know is that in Roman days it was considered a potent vermifuge and for this reason was given often to children and adults alike, either in raw or cooked form. The Egyptians adored it as a minor god. One old source says that garlic ". . . is potent against poisons, kills worms, clears the voice and induces coitus and urine." The navies made abundant use of it in order to avoid "the bad smells of decay" and because it "gave strength and vigor to those who manned the oars." On the other hand, the Romans said it was food fit only for the plebeians, and Alfonse, King of Castille, hated it so that anyone who smelled of garlic at court was severely punished. Nowadays, the use of garlic is regulated only by personal taste, and the *pappa al pomodoro* is a dish for garlic lovers.

2 *pounds fresh, ripe plum tomatoes*

5 *cloves garlic, cleaned and crushed*

12 *ounces stale Tuscan bread* (*see recipe No.* 220)

10 *leaves fresh basil or* 1 *teaspoon dried*

1 peperoncino (*Italian hot pepper*)

Salt and pepper

Olive oil, as needed

1. Wash the tomatoes, cut into pieces, put into a saucepan and cook, uncovered, for about 20 minutes. Remove from fire and put through a food mill.

2. Put the tomato purée into a clean saucepan, add the crushed garlic cloves, the bread, the basil, the *peperoncino*, torn into several pieces, salt and pepper to taste and ½ cup of olive oil. Cook for another 20 minutes, stirring often and adding a little water if the mixture should become too dry. When ready, the *pappa al pomodoro* should have the consistency of oatmeal. This happens when the bread is completely blended with the other ingredients.

3. Serve in soup bowls, with olive oil and the black pepper grinder on the side. This version is more delicate than the previous one and it's a little quicker to make. But, personally, I like the previous recipe better because frying the bread improves the flavor a bit.

68. BRODO DI FAGIOLI CON PASTA
(*Bean Broth with Pasta*)

SERVES 5 OR 6

Beans and pasta are eaten all over Italy. This is the Tuscan version of this classic dish.

12 ounces dried pinto beans
7 cups water
2 cloves garlic, cleaned
7 tablespoons olive oil
Salt
1 small onion
1 small carrot
1 stalk celery
5 slices bacon
5 peeled Italian plum tomatoes

2 potatoes
1 tablespoon chopped parsley
1 tablespoon chopped fresh basil
   or 1 teaspoon dried
1 bouillon cube
¾ cup broken-up noodles or
   spaghetti, *or the equivalent*
   in homemade pasta
Fresh-grated Parmesan cheese,
   as needed

1. Soak beans overnight, drain, rinse, cover with 7 cups water. Add 1 clove garlic and 2 tablespoons of the oil and cook, covered, for about 1 hour, or until tender. Add ½ teaspoon salt.

2. Clean and wash the onion, carrot, and celery, and chop fine

with the remaining garlic. Dice the bacon. Chop the tomatoes, discarding seeds and hard parts. Peel, wash and dice potatoes.

3. Put remaining oil, bacon, parsley, basil and vegetables, except the tomatoes and potatoes, into a large saucepan, simmer on medium flame for 5 to 10 minutes. Add tomatoes, potatoes and bouillon cube, stir, cover, lower flame and cook for another 15 or 20 minutes.

4. Meanwhile, put half of the beans through a food mill. Then add all beans, puréed and whole, plus their liquid, to the saucepan. Stir and bring to the boiling point. Then add the *pasta*, stir again, and cook on very slow flame for another 10 to 15 minutes, or until the *pasta* is cooked through. Stir frequently in order to avoid sticking.

5. Serve hot, and pass the black pepper grinder and the fresh-grated Parmesan cheese. In Tuscany they also season the broth with a tablespoon of good olive oil.

69. ZUPPA MATTA
(*Crazy Soup*)

SERVES 4 OR 5

This is the simplest of soups, but I'm very fond of it. It's based on those beige and red beans they call *borlotti* here in Tuscany which, when cooked, become light brown. If it's true that beans are "the poor man's meat" this could easily be called the "poor man's soup."

There is much to be said about beans, which are such a substantial part of Tuscan cooking. It seems that while the lentil was known as far back as Biblical days, the bean arrived on the gastronomical scene much later. Only one variety of this leguminous plant, *fagiolo dell'occhio*, the black-eyed pea, was cultivated during the Greco-Roman period. Later, with the discovery of America, other bean varieties arrived in Europe. One of the first to introduce American beans to Italy was the humanist Piero Valeriano. He got his first seeds from Pope Clement VII, one of the Florence Medici, otherwise famous for refusing to annul the marriage of Tudor Henry VIII and Catherine of Aragon, a situation which laid the base for the schism which eventually led to the foundation of the Church of England. But to go back to beans, Valeriano's variety, planted in 1532, became known as *bellunesi*, from the city of Belluno, and are considered excellent.

Nowadays, several varieties are grown in Tuscany, of which the white *cannellini* are the most frequently used. The broad, flat *schiaccioni* (similar to U.S. lima beans) make the best *zuppe*, and the aforementioned *borlotti* are my favorites for this recipe. Closest to them on the U.S. market are the pinto beans, which make a brown broth of very similar flavor.

12 ounces dried borlotti or pinto beans, or 2 pounds fresh	8 cups water
2 cloves garlic	8 slices Tuscan bread (see recipe No. 220)
3 leaves fresh sage or ½ teaspoon dry	Salt
Olive oil, as needed	Grated Parmesan cheese
	Pepper

1. Soak dried beans in lukewarm water overnight, shell if fresh. Rinse, add cleaned garlic, sage, and 2 tablespoons olive oil, and cook in 8 cups of water for at least 1½ hours. If using fresh beans, cook for about 45 minutes. Beans should be very soft.

2. Toast the bread in the oven. Remove garlic and sage leaves from beans. Serve about 2 ladles of hot beans with their liquid and 2 slices of bread to each person. Let everyone add salt, cheese, olive oil and fresh-ground pepper to taste. Pour the *zuppa matta* over the bread or serve the bread on the side.

70. ZUPPA DI FAGIOLINI
(*String Bean Soup*)

SERVES 4 OR 5

This is the lightest, most digestible of Tuscan soups. String beans rather than beans, and no cabbage. And it's delicious—try it!

1 pound string beans, Blue Lake
    type if possible, fresh,
    canned or frozen
7 cups water
8 tablespoons olive oil
1 bouillon cube
5 leaves fresh basil or 1 teaspoon
    dried
A handful of parsley
½ onion

3 cloves garlic
2 tablespoons butter
5 peeled Italian plum tomatoes
½ teaspoon sugar
Salt
8 slices toasted Tuscan bread
    (see recipe No. 220)
½ cup grated Parmesan cheese

1. Clean and wash string beans, cut each in 2 or 3 pieces, put into a pot with 7 cups of water, 5 tablespoons olive oil and the bouillon cube, and boil for 25 minutes. If using canned beans, boil for only 10 minutes.

2. Meanwhile, wash basil and parsley, clean onion and 1 clove garlic, and chop all fine. Put butter and 3 tablespoons olive oil in saucepan; when hot add chopped vegetables and cook for about 5 minutes, until wilted. Stir often to avoid sticking.

3. Put tomatoes through a food mill, add to the vegetables. Add the sugar, salt to taste, stir and cook on low flame for another 10 minutes.

4. Clean remaining garlic and rub on the toasted bread, put 4 slices on the bottom of a large bowl, pour in half of the string beans and their broth, add half of the vegetable-tomato mixture, sprinkle with half of the grated Parmesan, repeat with remaining ingredients. Cover and allow to stand for a few minutes. Serve with a big spoon, giving each person some bread, some vegetables and some broth.

71. ZUPPA ALLA FRANTOIANA, VERSIONE ESTIVA
(*Oil-press Soup, Summer Version*)

SERVES 6 TO 8

The literal translation of this exquisite (and exquisitely Tuscan) dish sounds strange to uninitiated ears, and it's a little misleading, besides. *Zuppa* is a generic term used in Central Italy to designate all vegetable soups, as well as meat and fish stews that are eaten with slices of toasted bread soaking inside. In this case, the *zuppa* is a thick vegetable soup eaten with fresh-pressed olive oil poured over it as dressing. The best versions of this dish are eaten in late fall, at olive harvest time, thus the name *alla frantoiana*, from *frantoio*, olive- or oil-press. This recipe is a lighter version, made off season, but it happens to be my favorite.

1 *pound dried white* cannellini *Tuscan beans or 3 pounds fresh*
4 *garlic cloves*
Water, as needed
1 *sprig fresh sage, or ½ teaspoon dried*
Good quality olive oil, as needed
3 *carrots*
2 *stalks celery, including leaves*
1 *large onion*
A handful each fresh parsley and basil, or 1 tablespoon each if dried

1 *sprig fresh thyme, or ½ teaspoon dried*
5 *medium potatoes*
2 *zucchini squash*
1 *large green cabbage* (cavolo verza)
2 *bouillon cubes*
Salt
15 *slices stale Tuscan bread, toasted* (see recipe No. 220)
Pepper
Grated Parmesan cheese

1. Soak the dried beans in water to cover, overnight, or shell the fresh beans. Rinse and cook in fresh water to cover plus 4 cups, with 1 clove of garlic, 3 leaves of sage, and 2 tablespoons olive oil, until tender, 1 hour if fresh, more if dried.
2. Meanwhile, clean, wash and chop carrots, celery, onion, 1 clove garlic, parsley and basil, and simmer in ⅓ cup olive oil for about 15 minutes. Use a low flame and a large kettle, and stir frequently to

avoid browning onion too much. Add sprig of thyme, or ½ teaspoon if dried.

3. Dice potatoes and zucchini, shred the cabbage. Add the potatoes to the simmering vegetables; after 5 minutes add the zucchini, stir after each addition. Finally, add the cabbage, keeping the flame medium-low and stirring occasionally in order to avoid sticking. Cook for another 10 minutes, adding water if necessary, but no more than one ladle each time.

4. Take the sage and garlic out of the cooked beans and put the beans through a food mill. Include the liquid. Add all to the simmering vegetables, stir well, bring to boiling point, then lower flame, cover and cook for about 1 hour, checking now and then to make sure the bean purée isn't sticking to the bottom of the kettle.

5. Add bouillon cubes, stir, wait about 10 minutes, and taste. If necessary, add salt, but be careful not to oversalt; recipes that contain beans are better undersalted. Cook for another 45 minutes, keeping flame low.

6. Rub the remaining garlic on the toasted bread and put 2 or 2½ slices at the bottom of each soup dish. Then ladle out the *zuppa,* making sure all bread is covered. Allow to stand for a few minutes and serve with pepper grinder, fresh-grated Parmesan cheese and good olive oil (in Tuscany, fresh-pressed olive oil, greenish and with an aftertaste that stings). Each person should add these ingredients according to individual taste.

Note: Another way of serving *zuppa alla frantoiana* is by putting it all in a large soup bowl. In this case take the garlic-flavored bread and line the bottom of the bowl (about 5 slices), cover with soup, add next 5 slices, cover with soup again, then the last 5 slices, and cover with the remaining soup. Let stand for about 20 minutes, covered. The bread will soak up the vegetable mixture. Ladle out with a big serving spoon and serve with pepper, cheese and olive oil, as above.

72. ZUPPA ALLA FRANTOIANA, VERSIONE INVERNALE
(*Oil-press Soup, Winter Version*)

SERVES 6 TO 8

12 ounces dried or 24 ounces
    shelled fresh borlotti, *or*
    pinto beans
2½ quarts water
1 ham bone or the equivalent in
    pork bones
3 pieces ham or bacon rind
4 cloves garlic, cleaned
3 leaves fresh sage or ¼ teaspoon
    dried
Olive oil, as needed
Salt
2 carrots
3 stalks celery

1 large onion
A handful of parsley
½ pound spinach
1 black cabbage (see recipe
    No. 146)
½ green cabbage
3 potatoes
3 peeled Italian plum tomatoes
1 sprig fresh thyme or ½
    teaspoon dried
Pepper
16 slices of stale, toasted,
    Tuscan bread (see recipe
    No. 220)

1. If using dried beans soak overnight in lukewarm water. Rinse the soaked beans and cook in 2½ quarts of water with the ham bone, bacon rind, 1 garlic clove, the sage and 3 tablespoons of olive oil. If the beans are fresh-shelled, cook unrinsed with same amount of water and same ingredients. Allow to cook slowly, covered, on a low flame, for about 1 hour, or until tender. To check if beans are cooked, take one out and blow on it gently. If the skin breaks and rolls back, it's cooked. Add ½ teaspoon of salt toward the end of the cooking period.

2. Clean and wash the carrots, celery, onion, parsley, spinach and cabbages. Peel and dice the potatoes. Chop the tomatoes, discarding seeds and hard parts. Chop the carrots, celery, onion, 1 clove garlic and the parsley. Cut spinach and cabbage into strips. Put 5 tablespoons olive oil into a large soup kettle, add chopped vegetables, except the tomatoes, simmer for a few minutes, add the tomatoes and thyme; after 5 minutes add the potatoes and finally add the spinach and cabbage strips. Add salt and pepper to taste.

3. When the vegetables are wilted, add some of the bean broth, cover and allow to cook for about 30 minutes. Meanwhile, remove the ham bone and rinds and put half of the beans through a food mill.

Add whole beans, puréed beans, all the liquid and bacon rinds to the vegetables, stir, cover, and cook for another 20 to 30 minutes.

4. Rub remaining garlic on the toasted bread, put 2 slices in each soup plate, cover with hot soup, and serve. Make sure each person has a piece of the bacon rind. Pass the black pepper grinder and the olive oil.

73. ZUPPA DI MAGRO
(*Lenten Soup*)

SERVES 6

This is the poor relative of the *zuppa* family. With the exception of the beans, bread, oil and garlic, any one or two of the other ingredients can be omitted with small damage to the final result.

12 ounces dried or 1½ pounds
　shelled fresh pinto beans
2 quarts water
3 cloves garlic, cleaned
Olive oil, as needed
Salt
2 carrots
2 stalks celery
1 large onion
1 tablespoon each parsley and
　fresh basil, chopped
5 peeled Italian plum tomatoes

2 potatoes
¼ large green cabbage
1 small black cabbage (see recipe
　No. 146)
A handful of spinach
A handful of Swiss chard
1 bouillon cube
12 slices stale, Tuscan bread,
　toasted (see recipe No. 220)
Pepper

1. If using dried beans, soak in lukewarm water overnight. Rinse the soaked beans, cook in about 2 quarts of water with 1 clove garlic and 1 tablespoon olive oil. Allow to boil slowly for about 1 hour or until tender. Add 1 teaspoon of salt toward the end of the cooking period—not before, otherwise beans get hard.

2. Clean and wash carrots, celery, onion, and 1 garlic clove. Chop coarse. Put 4 tablespoons of olive oil in a soup kettle and allow the chopped vegetables to simmer in it gently until wilted. Stir frequently to avoid sticking and add some of the bean broth, if necessary. Add parsley and basil.

3. Chop the tomatoes, discarding seeds and hard parts. Peel and dice the potatoes. Clean and wash both cabbages, spinach and Swiss chard, cut into strips. Discard the thick white stalks of the black cabbage.

4. Add the tomatoes to the simmering vegetables, after 5 minutes add the potatoes, allow to cook for another 5 minutes, stir, add the strips of cabbage, spinach and Swiss chard. If liquid is needed add bean broth, but cooking on low flame, covered, should produce enough liquid from the vegetables.

5. Put half of the beans through a food mill, add to the simmering vegetables together with remaining whole beans and the rest of the bean broth; stir. Add bouillon cube, let it dissolve, taste for salt, add a little if necessary. At this point the soup should be medium thick. Cover it, and allow to cook on low flame for another 30 minutes.

6. Rub the toasted bread with garlic. Put 2 slices into each soup plate, cover with hot soup, serve with black pepper grinder and olive oil.

Note: This soup is also good with *pasta* rather than bread. Add broken-up egg noodles or other small *pasta* about 10 or 15 minutes before serving, and serve as above, adding fresh-grated Parmesan cheese.

74. ZUPPA IGNORANTE
(*Ignorant Soup*)

SERVES 4 OR 5

This is a simple bean-zucchini soup which is called *zuppa* because served with bread and *ignorante* because it was once made by the simple, uneducated peasants. Nowadays it's also made by the busy housewife, but the name has stuck.

7 ounces dried borlotti or pinto
    beans
1 small onion
1 small carrot
1 small stalk celery
1 clove garlic
7 cups water
Salt

3 large zucchini
5 tablespoons olive oil
1 tablespoon chopped parsley
1 bouillon cube
Tuscan bread, as needed (see
    recipe No. 220)
Pepper

1. Soak the beans overnight. Clean, wash and chop the onion, carrot, celery and garlic.

2. Rinse the beans and cook, covered, on medium flame, in 6 cups water. After 45 minutes add ½ teaspoon of salt and cook for another 30 minutes.

3. Wash and dice the zucchini. Put oil in large saucepan, add chopped vegetables and parsley, simmer for 5 minutes. Add zucchini and 1 cup water, cover, cook for 15 more minutes. Add bouillon cube, stir.

4. Add beans and their liquid to the vegetables on the stove, cook everything together for 15 minutes, serve hot, pass the bread, salt and pepper. In Tuscany the bread is put into the soup, but it can just as well be eaten on the side.

75. ZUPPA DI LENTICCHIE
(*Lentil Soup*)

SERVES 5 OR 6

Lentils can be bought dried or canned. If dried, they should be soaked ahead of time; if canned, they can be used as they come, including the liquid.

9 ounces dried lentils, about
     twice that amount if canned
Water as needed
2 cloves garlic
1 stalk celery
5 tablespoons olive oil
1 small onion
1 small carrot

3 slices bacon
1 tablespoon chopped parsley
1 tablespoon chopped fresh basil
5 peeled Italian plum tomatoes
1 bouillon cube
Salt and pepper
Grated Parmesan cheese, as
     needed

1. If using dried lentils soak for 3 hours. Drain, rinse, cover with water, add 1 clove garlic, ½ stalk celery and 1 tablespoon olive oil, and cook for 1½ hours, or until tender.

2. Clean, wash and chop the onion, carrot and remaining garlic and celery. Chop bacon. Put remaining oil, bacon, chopped vegetables, parsley and basil into a large saucepan and simmer lightly for 5 minutes.

3. Chop tomatoes, discarding seeds and hard parts. Add to simmering vegetables and cook, uncovered, on medium flame, for 15 minutes. Add bouillon cube, stir.

4. Remove garlic and celery from lentils, then add them and about 7 cups of their liquid to the saucepan. If there isn't enough liquid in the lentils, add water. Stir, cook for another 20 or 30 minutes. Taste for seasoning and add salt if necessary. Serve hot, pass the pepper grinder and the fresh-grated Parmesan.

SALSE

(Sauces)

76. BESCIAMELLA
(*Béchamel or White Sauce*)
ABOUT 1½ CUPS, SERVES 5 OR 6

Besciamella, béchamel or white sauce, this is one of the standard sauces of any cuisine. Remember that it can be made thicker by lowering the milk content and thinner either by raising the milk content or by cutting down on the flour. The recipe below is for a medium-thick béchamel, as used in the Tuscan *sformati*.

> *3 tablespoons butter*
> *3 tablespoons flour*
> *1½ cups milk*
> *Salt*

1. Melt the butter in a saucepan without letting it brown. Stir in flour, keeping on a medium flame. Be sure that the mixture, at this point, is completely smooth and cream colored, not dark.

2. Meanwhile, bring milk almost to the boiling point. When the *roux* made in step 1 is well blended but still light, add the hot milk, stirring constantly.

3. Continue to stir until the sauce boils, at which point it will thicken and become a smooth cream. Add a pinch of salt, and the white sauce is ready.

77. SALSA DI CAPPERI
(*Caper Sauce*)

ABOUT ONE CUP, SERVES 4

This sauce is used mainly for boiled meat or fish, but it's also good on meat loaf and meat balls.

A *small handful of parsley*	3 *tablespoons flour*
2 *tablespoons capers*	1 *bouillon cube, dissolved in* ⅔
1 *egg yolk*	*cup warm water*
3 *tablespoons milk*	⅓ *cup dry white wine*
3 *tablespoons butter*	

1. Wash, clean and chop parsley. Chop capers. Beat together the egg yolk and milk.

2. Melt butter on medium flame, add flour, stir well and allow to simmer until mixture turns golden. Add the bouillon and the wine, stir and allow sauce to thicken. Remove from stove and allow to cool slightly.

3. Add egg yolk and milk mixture, the chopped parsley and capers and stir well. Put back on low flame, heat through, while stirring constantly, serve at once.

78. SALSA DI CAPPERI ED ACCIUGHE
(*Caper and Anchovy Sauce*)

SERVES 3 OR 4

This sauce is very good on fried fish, lamb or veal, but it can also be put on sliced tomatoes and, diluted with half a cup of olive oil, makes a spicy salad dressing.

3 anchovies
2 tablespoons capers
2 tablespoons chopped parsley
2 tablespoons wine vinegar
Salt and pepper

1. Clean anchovies and chop. Chop capers.
2. Put chopped anchovies, capers and parsley in a small bowl. Add vinegar, very little salt and fresh-ground pepper to taste. Mix well.

79. SALSA DOLCE E FORTE
(*Sweet and Pungent Sauce*)

ABOUT ½ CUP, SERVES 3 TO 4

I've come across several recipes for sweet and pungent sauces that accompany non-feathered game such as venison, boar or hare. The one given here is the one I find easiest to make. Guests seem to find it delicious—there's never enough. The ingredients used in this sauce all date back to antiquity—except for the sugar, which is our modern-day substitute for honey—and it seems that a sauce similar to this was used by the Romans to accompany all meats. In those days the lack of refrigeration caused meat to deteriorate quickly, so strong sauces were appreciated not only because they increased thirst and therefore made for greater wine consumption and a merrier party, but also because they covered a multitude of sins. For a latter day version of this sauce, add 1 ounce of melted baking chocolate.

1 ounce dried raisins
3 dried prunes
2 cloves garlic, cleaned and
    crushed
1 bay leaf, broken into small
    pieces
6 tablespoons sugar, or more if
    necessary
6 tablespoons wine vinegar, or
    more if necessary

6 brandied cherries (optional,
    but do not use Maraschino
    cherries)
3 tablespoons cleaned pinoli
    nuts
2 ounces candied lemon and
    orange peel, mixed

1. Soak raisins and prunes in warm water.

2. Put garlic, bay leaf, 6 tablespoons of sugar and 6 tablespoons of vinegar in a saucepan on medium flame. Stir until sugar is liquefied.

3. Drain raisins and prunes, cut up the prunes into raisin-size pieces, eliminate pits. Cut up the cherries, eliminating pits. Cut up the *pinoli* nuts and candied fruit, add all these ingredients to boiling sugar mixture.

4. When mixture has returned to the boiling point stir well and taste to see if the sweet and pungent taste is balanced. Correct with additional vinegar or sugar until ideal point is reached. It tastes good hot, warm or cold, but I prefer it warm.

80. SALSA DI DRAGONCELLO
(*Tarragon Sauce*)

SERVES 3 OR 4

3 slices soft white bread (crusts
    removed)
Wine vinegar, as needed
2 cloves garlic

2 sprigs fresh tarragon
Salt
½ cup olive oil, or more if
    necessary

1. Break the bread into pieces, cover with vinegar. Clean and wash garlic and tarragon, dry, then chop fine.

2. Squeeze out the bread, chop, put into a bowl, add the chopped garlic and tarragon and a pinch of salt and blend well.

3. Take about ½ cup of oil and add slowly with one hand while stirring with the other. Taste for seasoning and, if necessary, add more vinegar, salt or oil. Serve with boiled meat or fish; also good with roast chicken.

81. SALSA ALL'ESTRATTO DI CARNE
(*Meat Extract Sauce*)

SERVES 4

This is a sauce that goes well with *pasta*, eggs or fish. It's quick and easy to make and it's a good way to use up pregrated Parmesan cheese.

> *4 tablespoons butter*
> *1 teaspoon meat extract*
> *⅔ cup heavy cream*
> *½ cup grated Parmesan cheese*
> *Salt*

1. Put the butter and meat extract into a small saucepan, allow both to melt slowly.

2. Keep the saucepan on a low flame and add the cream, stir, allow to heat through, then add the grated Parmesan. Stir, bring to the boiling point, taste for seasoning and add a little salt if necessary.

3. Serve on *spaghettini* cooked *al dente*, on boiled rice, potatoes, poached or hard-boiled eggs or boiled trout.

Note: For a richer version, remove saucepan from heat, add an egg yolk and stir briskly.

82. SUGO CHIARO
(*Light Sauce*)

SERVES 4 TO 6

This is a modified version of the previous recipe. It uses no cheese and adds flour, milk and the spicy perfume of nutmeg.

4 tablespoons butter	*½ cup heavy cream*
2 tablespoons flour	*⅓ cup milk*
1 teaspoon meat extract	*Nutmeg (optional)*
Salt and pepper	

1. Melt butter on slow flame, add flour, stir.
2. Just as the mixture starts to brown add meat extract, a little salt and fresh-ground pepper, stir well to incorporate.
3. Add the cream and stir constantly until the sauce has no lumps. Add milk and nutmeg, stir and allow to thicken. This sauce is very good on *tortelli, spaghetti* or egg noodles. Good on boiled eggs or rice as well.

83. SALSINA PICCANTE
(*Hot and Spicy Sauce*)

SERVES 3 OR 4

1 onion	*5 peeled Italian plum tomatoes,*
1 clove garlic	*mashed; or 10 tablespoons*
A handful of parsley	*pomarola (see recipe No.*
1 carrot	*86)*
3 slices bacon	*1 peperoncino (Italian hot*
¼ cup olive oil	*pepper)*
Salt and pepper	

1. Wash and clean onion, garlic, parsley and carrot. Chop onion and garlic fine, chop the parsley, dice the carrot. Cut the bacon into squares.
2. Allow bacon to crisp in a small saucepan. Add oil, onion and garlic, cook 2 minutes and add parsley and carrot. Add salt and pepper

to taste. When vegetables are wilted add the mashed tomatoes or the tomato sauce, stir, lower flame, let cook uncovered for 15 to 20 minutes, until sauce thickens.

3. At this point add the *peperoncino*, cut into several pieces. Stir, let boil for another 1 to 2 minutes, serve on anything from meat or fish to *spaghetti* or scrambled eggs.

84. SALSINA PICCANTE CRUDA
(*Spicy Raw Sauce*)

SERVES 3 OR 4

5 cloves garlic
1 small onion
5 leaves fresh basil or ½ teaspoon
    dried
2 very ripe tomatoes

½ teaspoon paprika
½ teaspoon salt
1 tablespoon wine vinegar
¼ to ½ cup olive oil

1. Clean and wash garlic and onion, cut into large pieces; wipe basil leaves with a damp cloth, then chop; wash and dry the tomatoes, dip in boiling water, peel, cut into quarters and remove the seeds and liquid.

2. Put the garlic and onion into a mortar and work into a paste— this is a delicate operation because it will make you cry, but otherwise the sauce won't be the same—add the paprika, the salt, the vinegar, the basil and the tomatoes, continue to mash until it all becomes a homogeneous pulp.

3. When everything is reduced to a paste, pour in the oil, slowly, as if making a mayonnaise. It should absorb anywhere from ¼ to ½ cup of oil. When ready, this sauce can be kept in the refrigerator for a few days. Serve on boiled meats, fish or as a relish.

85. CIBREO DI FEGATINI
(*Chicken Liver Sauce*)

SERVES 3 OR 4

½ onion
A *small handful of parsley*
5 *chicken livers*
2 *tablespoons butter*
1 *tablespoon flour*

1 *shotglass of* Vin Santo *or sweet*
    sherry
Salt
1 *egg yolk*
½ *cup broth*

1. Clean, wash and chop onion and parsley. Wash and cut chicken livers into small pieces.

2. Melt butter in saucepan, add vegetables and livers, simmer on medium flame for a few minutes. Sprinkle with flour and continue to simmer for another 2 or 3 minutes.

3. Pour the Vin Santo or sherry over the chicken livers, reduce the flame and carefully scrape up the flour attached to the bottom of the saucepan. Add salt to taste and cook for another 8 to 10 minutes. Remove from stove and allow to cool slightly.

4. Stir the egg yolk into the cold broth, add to saucepan. Mix briskly because egg yolk has a tendency to solidify quickly when combined with warm liquids. Put back on a low flame, allow to heat through while stirring constantly. Serve at once.

86. POMAROLA
(*Tomato Sauce*)

SERVES 8 OR 10

The recipe below is for a large quantity of sauce because it's so basic in Italian and Tuscan cooking that making it once a week and keeping it in the refrigerator for constant use is normal procedure. Use it with eggs, as in recipe No. 20. Use it to season *pasta*, adding only a piece of fresh butter and grated Parmesan. Use it to liven up a vegetable *sformato*, add it to the *umidi* instead of using peeled and chopped tomatoes. With the addition of fresh basil, this sauce becomes the excellent *Penne alla Giovanni,* recipe No. 30, one of the most refreshing summer *pastas* I know.

1 carrot	tomatoes or equivalent
1 onion	canned
5 tablespoons olive oil	2 bouillon cubes
2 pounds ripe Italian plum	Salt and sugar (optional)

1. Clean and wash carrot and onion and chop coarse. Put oil in a saucepan, add chopped vegetables, simmer 3 to 5 minutes on medium flame.

2. Meanwhile, wash tomatoes, dry them, cut in half and add to the saucepan. Add the bouillon cubes, stir, cook on medium-low flame, uncovered, for about 20 minutes.

3. Remove from fire and pass the mixture through a food mill. Put the purée back on a low flame, allow to cook for another 30 minutes. At this point taste for seasoning and, if necessary, add a little salt or ½ teaspoon of sugar. The need for this last ingredient depends on the ripeness of the tomatoes: if they are very ripe, they are sweet enough, but if any of the tomatoes are less than perfectly mature the sauce may taste slightly acid. A touch of sugar neutralizes this excess sourness.

87. SALSA DI POMODORI E PISELLI
(*Pea and Tomato Sauce*)

SERVES 4 OR 5

This is a tasty, light sauce that can be served over a plain omelet, over meat loaf and meat balls, or on *spaghetti.* By doubling the amount of peas and leaving the other ingredients in the quantities listed below it becomes a new way of cooking peas and can be served as a vegetable.

1 small onion	3 tablespoons olive oil
1 clove garlic	1 bouillon cube
5 slices bacon	10 ounces tender, small peas
3 leaves fresh basil or ½ teaspoon dried	(shelled fresh, canned or frozen)
One 16-ounce can peeled Italian plum tomatoes	

1. Clean and wash onion and garlic and chop fine. Dice bacon and cut basil leaves into strips. Chop the tomatoes, removing hard parts and seeds.

2. Put oil, bacon and chopped onion and garlic in a saucepan and simmer for a few minutes. Add the tomatoes and basil, stir, allow to cook for another few minutes.

3. Add the bouillon cubes and the peas, stir again, lower the flame, cook until peas are ready—this will depend on whether they were fresh, canned or frozen. Fresh take from 15 to 25 minutes, should be cooked covered and with a little additional water; frozen will take 8 to 10 minutes, and should be cooked covered with only the liquid in the tomatoes; canned just need heating through, about 3 to 5 minutes, and should be cooked uncovered, otherwise the sauce may become too liquid. Serve this sauce hot.

88. RAGÙ
(*Meat and Tomato Sauce*)

SERVES 6 PLUS

Ragù or meat and tomatoes cooked into a thick sauce, is eaten all over Italy as seasoning for egg noodles, *polenta* or other *minestre*. While the city of Bologna can claim its paternity with unquestioned authority— on most restaurant menus it's listed as *ragù bolognese*—this sauce is at home in all of Central Italy and finds its regional counterparts in almost every corner of the peninsula. The recipe below is the one I found most commonly used in Tuscany, even if tradition demands it be made with nothing but ground beef and called *la ghiaiosa*, meaning "pebbly." For the "pebbly" version use 1 pound ground beef and eliminate the pork and chicken liver.

1 *small carrot*
1 *medium onion*
1 *stalk celery*
5 *leaves fresh basil or ½*
   teaspoon dried
2 *tablespoons chopped parsley*
⅓ *cup olive oil*
8 *ounces ground chuck or round*
8 *ounces pork, in one piece*

1 *whole chicken liver*
   (*optional*)
½ *cup dry red wine*
2 *tablespoons tomato paste*
1 *bouillon cube*
1 *cup hot water*
8 *peeled Italian plum tomatoes*
Salt and pepper

1. Clean and wash carrot, onion, celery and basil and chop fine. Put in saucepan with parsley and oil; simmer on medium flame for a few minutes.

2. Add all meats, continue to cook, stirring occasionally, for another 10 to 15 minutes, until all meats are browned.

3. Pour in the wine, stir, cover and cook on low flame until the wine has evaporated. Meanwhile, dissolve the tomato paste and bouillon cube in 1 cup of hot water and add to the saucepan.

4. Stir well and cover again. Allow to cook on low flame for about 60 minutes, being sure the liquid level doesn't drop too much.

5. Chop the tomatoes, discarding seeds and hard parts. Add to the saucepan, stir and cover again. Cook for another 30 minutes, then remove the pork and chicken liver, if used. Chop them as fine as possible or put through the meat grinder and put back into saucepan, stir.

6. The *ragù* is almost ready. This is a sauce that improves with cooking, so at this point taste for seasoning, add salt and pepper if necessary, and continue to cook for at least another 30 minutes. Use for seasoning egg noodles, *polenta* or *tortelli*. Some add a tablespoon of fresh butter at the end, which makes the sauce smoother and more delicate.

89. SUGO ANTICO
(*Old-fashioned Sauce*)

SERVES 6 TO 8

2 ounces *good quality dried mushrooms*
1½ cups *dry white wine*
1 *cleaned onion*
4 ounces prosciutto (*Italian raw ham*)
4 ounces *sliced bacon*
⅓ cup *olive oil*
8 ounces *ground beef, preferably round*

1 *breast of chicken, cut into a few large pieces*
1 *bouillon cube*
One 16-ounce *can peeled Italian plum tomatoes, drained*
Pepper
Salt

1. Put the mushrooms into 1 cup of the white wine, add warm water to cover. Let soak for an hour. Clean mushrooms carefully, remov-

ing all earth and sand. Chop coarse. Filter the wine-water mixture through several layers of cheesecloth and reserve.

2. Chop the onion, *prosciutto* and bacon. Put bacon in medium saucepan, allow to crisp, then add oil, onion and *prosciutto*. As soon as the onion becomes straw colored, add the mushrooms, ground beef, chicken breast pieces and bouillon cube. Let cook on medium flame for about 15 minutes, stirring now and then to avoid sticking.

3. Add the remaining ½ cup of wine and the drained tomatoes, squashing them with your hands as you drop them in and discarding the hard pieces. Add some fresh-ground pepper. Lower the flame, cover and allow to simmer for 30 to 45 minutes.

4. Remove the pieces of chicken breast from the sauce and chop fine. Put back in. Check the taste. If needed, add salt. If sauce thickens too much add some of the strained wine-water mixture saved in step 1. Continue to cook for another 30 minutes on very low flame. When ready this sauce should be thick and brown. It's excellent with *spaghetti* or as a filling for *cannelloni* (see recipe No. 43).

90. PESTO

SERVES 4 OR 5

This sauce is famous in its Genoese version, but since Northern Tuscany borders on Liguria, it's eaten in Tuscany as well. Ideally, it should be made with both Parmesan and *Pecorino* cheese, but since good *Pecorino* is hard to find even in Italy, I've written the recipe with Parmesan as an alternative. The amount below is about enough for one pound of *spaghetti*, but this sauce is also used with boiled beef or boiled tongue.

30 to 40 fresh basil leaves
1 clove garlic
30 pinoli *nuts, about 2*
    tablespoons

10 tablespoons grated Parmesan
    or Pecorino *cheese*
Salt
⅔ cup olive oil

1. Clean the basil by wiping each leaf with a damp cloth. Clean the garlic.
2. Chop the basil, *pinoli* and garlic, put in a bowl, add the cheese

and a pinch of salt, mix well. Add oil slowly with one hand while stirring with the other. When all oil has been added and well blended
the sauce is ready.

Note: Step 2 can be modified by putting all ingredients into a
blender. In old days it was done by using a mortar and pestle, and I
heartily recommend the method to all those who possess these lovely
utensils.

91. SALSA DI NOCI
(*Walnut Sauce*)

SERVES 4 OR 5

This is a Tuscan version of *pesto*, and I find it more delicate. The
quantities given here will season about one pound of *spaghetti*.

> *30 to 40 leaves fresh basil*
> *About 15 walnuts, shelled*
> *⅓ cup grated Parmesan cheese*
> *Salt*
> *½ cup olive oil*

1. Clean basil as in previous recipe.
2. Chop basil and walnuts fine, put in a bowl, add cheese, salt and
oil, and stir briskly. Otherwise, put everything in a blender and mix for
2 or 3 minutes.

PESCE

(*Fish*)

92. ANGUILLE O SOGLIOLE MARINATE O IN CARPIONE
(*Marinated Eels or Sole*) .

SERVES 4 OR 5

Marinating fish is an old Mediterranean custom. The method was used in ancient Egypt, Greece and Rome and is still used today. People who live near the sea find it useful to preserve the fresh-caught fish this way, because it can then be eaten later. With the advent of modern refrigeration this method of preserving has become reduced to the level of a curiosity, but in Tuscany it is still in use because it renders fish both palatable and digestible.

The expression *in carpione* is probably derived from the carp, a fish that is exquisite when cooked with white wine, as in *Carpe à la Chambord,* one of the great dishes of French *haute cuisine.* Later, the *carpione* was modified and is now made with vinegar instead of white wine, but the method is similar.

1 teaspoon salt

4 tablespoons flour

8 cleaned fillets of sole or 1 large eel, washed and cleaned

1 cup peanut or other frying oil

1½ cups wine vinegar

1 tablespoon maple syrup

5 leaves fresh sage or 1 teaspoon dried

3 cloves garlic, cleaned and cut in half

1 tablespoon pinoli nuts

2 tablespoons raisins

1 tablespoon candied fruit, cubed

2 bay leaves, broken into small pieces

1. Add 1 teaspoon of salt to about 4 tablespoons of flour. Mix well. For sole: dredge with the seasoned flour, then fry in 1 cup hot oil, about 3 minutes on each side. Remove and drain on absorbent paper. For eel: cut into pieces about 1½ inches long, dredge with the seasoned flour and put under the grill. Turn after 10 minutes, and grill for 10 minutes longer. Remove when the eel has rendered its fat.

2. Put all the remaining ingredients in an enameled or earthenware cooking vessel, stir and bring to a boil. Put the fish in a container where it will lie flat. Pour the hot vinegar mixture over the fish, cover and let stand for at least ½ hour, or as much as necessary for vinegar to penetrate. Serve warm or cold.

93. ARAGOSTA CON SALSETTA DI VIN SANTO
(*Lobster with Wine Sauce*)

SERVES 4

The lobsters available in Tuscany—and in the whole Mediterranean area—are not like Maine lobsters. They are smaller and don't have the heavy front claws. Nonetheless, their meat is juicy and sweet. This recipe is good whether made with Maine lobster, European lobster or even large shrimp.

4 *lobsters*
½ *cup butter*
Nutmeg
Salt and white pepper
1 *shotglass of* Vin Santo *or sweet sherry*

1. Prepare the lobsters your favorite way, boiled or broiled.

2. Meanwhile, melt the butter on a slow flame, add just a touch of nutmeg, very little salt and as much fresh-ground pepper as you like. When all this is foaming, pour in the V*in Santo* or sherry, stir and allow the liquid to evaporate for 2 or 3 minutes. It should be reduced by half.

3. Put the hot lobsters on the table, pass the hot sauce, stand back for the applause.

Note: For a change, try the above sauce with brandy rather than V*in Santo* or sherry. Some like it even better.

94. BACCALÀ MARINATO
(*Marinated Salt Cod*)

SERVES 4

10 *ounces salted, dried cod*
Flour, as needed
¾ *cup peanut or other frying oil*
3 *sprigs fresh rosemary or* 1½
    teaspoons dried

3 *cloves garlic*
1 peperoncino (*Italian hot*
    pepper)
¾ *cup wine vinegar*

1. Cover dried cod with warm water, allow to stand from 12 to 24 hours. Clean, wash well, and cut into 1½ to 2 inch pieces. Put in a saucepan, cover with cold water, bring to boiling point, allow to cook for 10 to 15 minutes; drain.

2. Dredge pieces of boiled cod with flour. Put oil in frying pan, let it get very hot, fry the cod, a few pieces at a time. Remove with slotted spoon and drain well on several layers of paper towels.

3. Meanwhile, chop the rosemary leaves, the garlic and the *peper-*

oncino. Pour half of the oil out of the frying pan, reheat the remaining oil, add the chopped rosemary, garlic and *peperoncino* and heat through. Add vinegar, let it come to a boil, turn flame low. Put fried cod back into the frying pan, heat through, turn, keep on fire for another minute, cover and remove from heat. Allow to stand for a few minutes. Serve warm, as a second course, with boiled beans or tomato salad.

95. BACCALÀ ALLA LIVORNESE
(*Codfish, Leghorn Style*)

SERVES 6 TO 8

Whenever a recipe is identified as *alla Livornese* it usually means that it's made with garlic, parsley and tomato, plus fish. The following is a recipe used during the Lenten period, but for those who like codfish it's good all the year round.

2 cloves garlic
2 pounds dried codfish, soaked in water to cover and 1 teaspoon baking soda for at least 12 hours
Flour, as needed

⅔ cup olive oil
1 cup pomarola (see recipe No. 86)
1 tablespoon chopped parsley
Salt

1. Clean and wash garlic, chop. Take the skin off the soaked codfish, clean the fish well and cut it into 1½ to 2 inch squares. Dry the pieces and coat with flour.

2. Put oil and garlic into large frying pan, heat the oil, add the pieces of codfish and allow them to brown well on both sides.

3. When all codfish is browned add the *pomarola*, lower the flame and simmer for about 1 hour, stirring occasionally.

4. When the pieces of codfish are cooked add the chopped parsley, salt if needed (keep in mind that the dried codfish is salty), and serve hot with *polenta* or boiled potatoes.

96. BACCALÀ PARADISO
(*Paradise Codfish*)

SERVES 4 OR 5

This is a specialty of the city of Grosseto, where they serve it with slices of the ubiquitous Tuscan bread. I like it with boiled beans.

> *12 ounces dried codfish*
> *4 cloves garlic*
> *7 whole black peppercorns*
> *Olive oil, as needed*

1. Soak the codfish overnight, then clean and wash well. Clean garlic.
2. Put a large pan of water on the fire, bring to the boiling point, add the garlic, the peppercorns and the fish. Boil for at least 45 minutes, or until tender. Drain.
3. Serve at once, as is, passing the olive oil and the pepper grinder.

97. BACCALÀ CON CAPPERI E POMODORO
(*Codfish with Capers and Tomato Sauce*)

SERVES 6 TO 8

1½ pounds dried codfish, soaked in water and baking soda for at least 12 hours
1 small onion
1 clove garlic
A handful of parsley

5 or 6 peeled Italian plum tomatoes
½ cup olive oil
3 tablespoons drained capers
Salt and pepper

1. Wash the codfish, put in a saucepan, cover with cold water, cook for about 20 minutes and drain. Clean, wash and chop the onion, garlic and parsley. Chop the tomatoes, discarding the seeds and hard parts.
2. Take the skin off the codfish, remove bones and break the fish into small pieces, following its natural grain. Heat the oil in a saucepan,

add the chopped onion, garlic and parsley, allow to simmer for a moment, add the capers and chopped tomatoes, very little salt and a few twists of the pepper grinder; stir, and cook for about 10 minutes.

3. At this point add the codfish flakes, stir, and cook on low flame for another 15 to 20 minutes. If the sauce gets too dry add a ladleful of hot water. Serve over *polenta* made with about 3 cups of corn meal.

98. CALAMARI IN ZIMINO
(*Squids with Spinach or Swiss Chard*)

SERVES 4 TO 5

1 small carrot
1 stalk celery
1 clove garlic
1 small onion
12 ounces small, fresh squid

¼ cup olive oil
1 tablespoon chopped parsley
Salt and pepper
12 ounces cleaned spinach or
    Swiss chard

1. Clean and wash the carrot, celery, garlic and onion, chop fine. Clean and wash squid, cut into pieces.

2. Put oil, chopped vegetables, squid and parsley into a frying pan, cook on medium flame for about 10 to 15 minutes, until the fish is tender. Add salt and fresh-ground pepper to taste.

3. Meanwhile, cook the spinach in 1 or 2 cups of lightly salted water. After 8 or 10 minutes, drain and save.

4. When the squid is ready add the cooked spinach to the frying pan, stir, heat through and serve at once.

99. CEFALO IN GRATICOLA
(*Grilled Grey Mullet*)

SERVES 4

Grey mullet is one of the most interesting fish in the Mediterranean. It's a vegetarian, and eats only algae and other sea greens. A poet of ancient Greece said it was one of the most romantic animals in creation, because the males are caught when they go to the rescue of a trapped female, but modern research shows that they do so only when the female specimen is in good health and has a well formed body. Incidentally, this method of catching mullet is still in use today.

4 slices of grey mullet, about 6
   to 7 ounces each
½ cup olive oil
Salt and pepper

1 teaspoon oregano
Juice of 1 lemon
1 tablespoon chopped parsley

1. Put the cleaned fish slices on a large plate, pour ¼ cup of the olive oil over them, sprinkle with salt, fresh-ground pepper and oregano, and allow to stand for about 1 hour, turning once.

2. Light the broiler or, if using a wood fire, put the griddle on the embers, and when hot put the slices of fish on it. Allow to cook about 5 minutes on each side or until cooked through.

3. Meanwhile, mix the remaining oil with the lemon juice, add salt and pepper and beat well with a fork or wire whisk. As soon as the fish slices are ready put on a warm platter, pour the oil-lemon juice sauce over them, sprinkle with chopped parsley and serve at once.

100. CEE ALLA PISANA
(*Baby Eels Pisan Style*)

SERVES 5 OR 6

Baby eels are available only in November, December and January. The sexually mature eel, when ready for parenthood, goes to sea and multiplies. The tiny baby eels, little wormlike fish no more than 3 inches in length and about as thick as a strand of *spaghetti*, come back to the river in late fall and are caught on most of the Tyrrhenian coast as they try to go upstream. The word "cee" is Tuscan for "cieche" which means "blind"—at this stage, in fact, the little eel is blind and transparent.

2 pounds of fresh baby eels, cee
1 cup coarse corn meal
3 cloves garlic
½ cup olive oil
6 leaves fresh sage or 1 teaspoon
   dried

½ cup good quality meat broth
   (see recipe No. 21)
Salt and pepper

1. Wash the baby eels well with cold water and then add the raw corn meal and mix with both hands. This helps to remove the slimy material that may cling to the outside of the little fish. Rinse again, putting everything into a sieve so that the corn meal will go down the drain while the fish remain.

2. Clean the garlic, bruise slightly. Heat the olive oil and garlic in a large frying pan that has a tight fitting lid. Remove the garlic when it gets dark and add the sage.

3. Turn the *cee* into the hot oil with one swift motion, cover at once. This is a delicate operation because the little fish tend to jump out as soon as they hit the hot oil. Once the pan is covered, lower the flame and allow to cook for 5 minutes.

4. Uncover, add the broth, stir, cook covered for another 10 minutes. At this point the fish should be totally white, and the sauce should be just enough to coat them. Add salt and fresh-ground pepper to taste, and serve at once. Pass fresh-grated Parmesan cheese for those who like it; personally, I like these little fish straight off the kitchen range with only a touch of salt.

101. CEE ALLA VIAREGGINA
(*Baby Eels Viareggio Style*)

SERVES 2 OR 3

Another way of cooking this delicious little fish, a bit more spicy than the previous one.

1 *pound baby eels*, cee
½ *cup coarse corn meal*
2 *cloves garlic*
½ *onion*
3 *leaves fresh sage or* ½ *teaspoon dried*

¼ *cup olive oil*
⅓ *cup dry white wine*
5 *peeled Italian plum tomatoes*
1 *peperoncino* (*Italian hot pepper*)
Salt and pepper

1. Follow instructions for cleaning eels as in previous recipe.

2. Clean and wash garlic, onion and sage, chop fine. Heat the oil in a frying pan, add chopped vegetables, fry until wilted, add the baby eels, cover at once.

3. Lower the flame, cook for 5 minutes, uncover. Add the wine, stir, cover.

4. Meanwhile, chop the tomatoes and discard seeds and hard parts. Add to the eels, chop the *peperoncino* into several pieces and add, stir again and cook for another 10 minutes, or until the sauce is thick and coats the fish. Add salt and pepper to taste and serve at once.

102. FRITTATA DI COZZE
(*Mussel Omelet*)

SERVES 3 TO 4

2 *pounds fresh mussels*	⅔ *cup dry white wine*
2 *cloves garlic*	8 *eggs*
6 *tablespoons olive oil*	*Salt and pepper*
2 *tablespoons chopped parsley*	1 *tablespoon ketchup*

1. Soak mussels in water for 30 minutes, then scrub each one well in order to remove all sand.

2. Clean garlic and chop fine. Put 2 tablespoons of the olive oil, the garlic and parsley in a large frying pan, add mussels; put on medium heat, cover, and allow to cook, shaking pan occasionally. When all mussels have opened, remove from fire. Discard any that did not open.

3. When mussels have cooled, remove them from their shells and save their liquid together with the pan juices, but be sure to filter through several layers of cheesecloth in order to remove all sand particles. Put 3 tablespoons of the liquid in a bowl, add the wine and the mussels, allow to marinate for 30 minutes.

4. Meanwhile, break the eggs into a bowl, add ½ teaspoon of salt and some fresh-ground black pepper and whip with a fork. Remove the mussels from the marinade, drain well and stir them into the eggs. Save the marinade.

5. Heat the remaining oil in a clean frying pan, pour in the eggs and mussel mixture and lower the flame. Allow the bottom of the omelet to set, slip onto a plate, turn and fry on the other side.

6. Add the marinade to the liquid from the other frying pan and, while the omelet is cooking, allow ⅔ of this to evaporate. Add ketchup, stir, cook for another few minutes. Serve the omelet hot, folded in half and covered with the sauce.

103. GAMBERONI ALLO CHAMPAGNE
(*Giant Shrimp in Champagne Sauce*)

SERVES 4

This is a very special dish, cooked by our friend Sergio who owns the "Risacca," an elegant restaurant overlooking the sea. It's a recipe that can be served at an elegant meal, but it's very easy to make. Omit the *peperoncino* if you don't want it spicy.

20 *large shrimp, peeled, washed and deveined*	½ *teaspoon salt*
About ¼ *cup flour*	1 *small* peperoncino (*Italian hot pepper*)
2 *tablespoons butter*	⅔ *cup dry champagne*
2 *tablespoons olive oil*	

1. Roll the shrimp in the flour.
2. Heat the butter and oil in a large frying pan, add all shrimp and fry on both sides, about 2 minutes on each side. Sprinkle with ½ teaspoon of salt and add the *peperoncino*, broken into several pieces.
3. Pour in the champagne, lower the flame and, with a spatula or wooden spoon, scrape the pan in order to incorporate all flour that may have got stuck to the bottom.
4. Cook for another 5 minutes uncovered. When the sauce has acquired a sticky consistency, serve. There should not be much sauce in this dish, just enough barely to cover each shrimp.

104. SOFFIATO DI GAMBERI
(*Shrimp Soufflé*)

SERVES 4

1 *pound raw shrimp*	5 *eggs*
Butter, as needed	3 *tablespoons fresh-grated Parmesan cheese*
4 *tablespoons flour*	
1 *cup milk, or more, as needed*	1 *tablespoon ketchup*
Salt and white pepper	½ *teaspoon lemon juice*

1. Wash shrimp, put in a saucepan, cover with cold water, bring to a boil, allow to boil for 10 minutes, drain. When shrimp are cool, peel and devein them.

2. Meanwhile, make a béchamel with 3 tablespoons butter, the flour and 1 cup of milk (see recipe No. 76). If too solid add a little more milk. Add salt and fresh-ground white pepper, stir, and allow to cool.

3. Chop all shrimp fine and add to the béchamel. Separate 4 eggs. Reserve the whites and add the yolks, one at a time, to the béchamel-shrimp mixture. Make sure each one is fully incorporated before adding the next one. Add grated Parmesan, and the ketchup.

4. Preheat oven to 325° F. Separate the last egg, add the white to the other 4 and save the yolk for another use. Add the lemon juice to the 5 egg whites, whip until stiff.

5. Fold the whipped egg whites into the other ingredients, mix slowly and with even strokes until well blended.

6. Butter well a medium-size soufflé dish. Fold in the shrimp soufflé, put in the preheated oven and bake for about 30 minutes. It should puff up and increase by at least half its original volume. Take out of the oven carefully and serve immediately.

105. SPAGHETTI CON SUGO DI VONGOLE
(*Spaghetti with Clam Sauce*)

SERVES 4 TO 5

3 pounds clams
2 cloves garlic
Salt
⅔ cup olive oil
1 small onion, sliced
½ cup dry white wine
One 16-ounce can peeled Italian
    plum tomatoes

White pepper
1 peperoncino (*Italian hot
    pepper*)
1 pound spaghetti
2 tablespoons chopped parsley

1. Put clams in salted water to cover for at least 1 hour. Clean garlic. Put about 4 quarts of water on fire, add 2 teaspoons salt, bring to a boil. Rinse the clams thoroughly, be sure to remove all sand.

2. Put a few tablespoons olive oil in a frying pan, add garlic and clams, cover and cook on a high flame for a few minutes, shaking the pan a few times. When you uncover the pan most of the clams should be open. Discard any that are not.

3. Remove the clams from their shells and reserve about ⅔ cup of the liquid that has formed in the frying pan, straining it through a few layers of cheesecloth in order to remove all sand. Put the remaining oil in a saucepan, add the onion, let it wilt, add the wine, allow it to evaporate. Chop the tomatoes, discarding seeds and hard pieces, add to the saucepan. Season with salt and fresh-ground white pepper, stir, cover, allow to cook on a medium flame for about 20 minutes.

4. Add the *peperoncino* and the ⅔ cup of reserved clam liquid, stir and cook for another 10 to 15 minutes.

5. Meanwhile, cook the *spaghetti al dente* in the boiling salted water (see recipe No. 27). While the *pasta* is cooking add the clams to the sauce and heat through. Drain the *spaghetti*, put in a large preheated bowl, season with the clam-tomato sauce, toss, sprinkle with the chopped parsley and serve at once.

106. RISOTTO AI GAMBERI E CURRY
(*Shrimp and Curry Risotto*)

SERVES 5 OR 6

This *risotto* is for shrimp lovers. Rice, unlike *pasta*, is not just seasoned with fish but is actually cooked in the shrimp broth and thus absorbs the flavor completely. The curry adds color and complements the shrimp.

1 clove garlic
1 onion
1 carrot
1 stalk celery
A few sprigs of parsley
1 tablespoon vinegar
Salt
6 cups water
1 pound medium-size shrimp, fresh or frozen

2 tablespoons olive oil
¼ cup butter
Pepper
1 pound long-grain rice
¼ cup dry white wine
5 tablespoons pomarola (see recipe No. 86)
1 teaspoon curry powder

1. Clean and wash the garlic, onion, carrot, celery and parsley; make a *bouquet garni* with half the onion, the celery and the parsley, put into an enameled saucepan with the carrot, the vinegar and ½ teaspoon salt, add 6 cups of water and bring to the boiling point.

2. Wash the shrimp well, clean but do not peel, add to the boiling water. Allow to cook for a few minutes, then remove with a slotted spoon, reserving the broth.

3. Meanwhile, chop the rest of the onion and the garlic. Put oil and ½ of the butter into a saucepan, add chopped onion and garlic, simmer for a few minutes, until the vegetables are wilted.

4. Peel and devein the shrimp, save the largest 12 or 15, chop the rest. Add the chopped shrimp to the simmering fats, add salt to taste and a little fresh-ground pepper, allow to cook for a few minutes then add the rice, stir.

5. Let the rice cook for a few minutes on a low-to-medium flame, stirring often to help it absorb fats. Add the wine and a few ladles of the shrimp broth, which should be kept simmering on the side. Continue to stir and to add shrimp broth until the rice is ⅔ cooked, about 10 to 12 minutes.

6. At this point add the *pomarola* and curry powder, stir to blend evenly, add a little more broth if necessary, remove from fire as soon as the rice is cooked *al dente*; add the remaining butter, cover, let stand for 2 or 3 minutes, stir again and serve at once, decorating each dish with 2 or 3 whole shrimp.

107. OSTRICHE ALLA LIVORNESE
(*Oysters Leghorn Style*)

SERVES 3 TO 4

The recipe calls for oysters but it can be made with clams or mussels as well.

1 scallion	4 tablespoons chopped parsley
1 clove garlic	4 tablespoons bread crumbs
2 anchovy fillets, cleaned	1 teaspoon fennel seeds
¼ cup olive oil	16 oysters

1. Clean and wash onion and garlic, chop fine. Clean and chop the anchovies. Put all in a bowl and add all other ingredients except oysters and mix well. Preheat the oven to 350° F.

2. Wash the oysters well, scrub with a hard brush, then, with a short, sharp knife remove their upper shell. Put 1 teaspoon of the filling mixture into each lower shell.

3. Line up the filled shells on a baking dish and put in the oven for about 15 minutes or until the oysters curl around the edges. Serve hot, about 4 to each person, more if there are oyster lovers at the table.

108. PESCE PICCOLO MARINATO
(*Small Marinated Fish*)

SERVES 4 OR 5

1 pound fresh small fish, such as
    sardines or anchovies
Approximately ¼ cup flour
1 cup peanut oil or other light
    oil for frying
½ onion, chopped

2 cloves garlic, chopped
2 tablespoons chopped parsley
2 tablespoons chopped fresh basil
    or 1½ teaspoons dried
1 bay leaf, broken into pieces
¾ cup wine vinegar

1. Clean fish by cutting off heads and removing intestines. Wash, roll in flour.

2. Put oil in frying pan, let it get very hot. Fry the fish, a few at a time, turning with a slotted spoon. Remove after 2 to 3 minutes, or when fish flesh turns white. Drain on paper towels.

3. When all fish are fried pour out about half the oil from the pan. Put the frying pan with remaining oil on medium flame, add chopped onions, garlic, parsley, basil and bay leaf. Let simmer for a few minutes, stirring constantly. When onion is golden, lower the flame and add vinegar. Do it carefully, because when the cold vinegar hits the hot oil it makes a lot of steam.

4. Let the vinegar heat through, keep the flame low, put the fried fish back into the pan, let them soak in the sauce. Cover, turn off flame, let stand for 10 to 15 minutes. Serve warm as an appetizer or cold for a summer lunch.

109. SOGLIOLA CON FUNGHI
(*Sole with Mushrooms*)

SERVES 4

1 ounce dried mushrooms	3 tablespoons olive oil
1 onion	Salt and white pepper
8 fillets of sole	⅔ cup dry white wine
3 tablespoons butter	½ lemon

1. Soak mushrooms in warm water for ½ hour. Clean well, chop. Slice the onion into thin rounds. Clean and trim the fillets of sole. Preheat the oven to 350° F.

2. Heat ½ the butter and ½ the oil in a frying pan, add ½ of the onion rounds, all the mushrooms, salt and pepper, and cook on medium-low flame for about 15 minutes, stirring now and then.

3. Meanwhile, butter a pyrex dish, put the fish in it, add the remaining butter, oil and onions, add salt and pepper to taste. Bake for about 10 minutes, then cover with the mushroom-onion mixture, pour in the wine, bake for another 15 minutes.

4. When ready, squeeze the lemon over the sole and serve at once.

110. ROTELLE DI PALOMBO IN SALSA
(*Swordfish Slices in Tomato Sauce*)

SERVES 4

Palombo does not translate exactly into swordfish, but this recipe can be made with any large fish that slices evenly and has no bones.

4 *slices swordfish*, palombo or *other fish of the shark family*	1 teaspoon flour
	2 tablespoons butter
1 egg	¼ cup pomarola (*see recipe* No.
Salt	86)
5 tablespoons bread crumbs	Pepper
3 tablespoons olive oil	1 tablespoon chopped parsley

1. Rinse fish in cold water, dry well. Put the egg and ½ teaspoon salt in a bowl, beat well, put the fish into the egg and allow to marinate for about 1 hour. Turn the slices at least once during that time.

2. Take fish slices out of egg and roll in the bread crumbs. Then put back into the egg and back into the bread crumbs.

3. Put the oil in a large frying pan and allow to get hot. Fry the fish slices for about 3 minutes on each side, remove, drain on paper towels, and reserve.

4. Blend flour into butter with a wooden spoon, add to the frying pan, put on low flame, stir while butter melts. As soon as the resulting *roux* begins to darken, add tomato sauce and salt and pepper to taste. Stir to blend well and allow to boil for a few minutes. Put the fish back into the pan, cover, let it cook in the sauce for 5 or 10 minutes and sprinkle it with chopped parsley. Serve at once with plain boiled rice or potatoes. Most of the sauce will be absorbed by the breading on the fish; whatever is left should be spooned onto the fish slices before serving.

111. TOTANI AL PREZZEMOLO
(*Squid with Parsley*)

SERVES 4 AS MAIN DISH,
6 IF USED AS APPETIZER

3 pounds very small fresh squid, octopus or cuttlefish
½ cup olive oil
2 cloves garlic, crushed
Salt and pepper

6 slices white bread
3 tablespoons butter
Juice of 1 lemon
2 tablespoons chopped parsley

1. Clean and wash the squid (or other fish), drain well, dry on paper towels. Cut the top part of each squid into 2 or 3 pieces. Put oil and garlic into a frying pan; when garlic turns brown take it out and put in the fish. Add salt and pepper to taste, stir, allow to cook on a medium-high flame for about 10 minutes.

2. Meanwhile, fry the bread in the butter (see recipe No. 179—step 4). Dry on absorbent paper, cut each slice diagonally into 2, making 12 triangles.

3. When the fish is cooked, add the lemon juice and the chopped parsley, stir, cook for another 1 or 2 minutes, then serve very hot, on top of the bread triangles.

Note: The squid, octopus or cuttlefish get reduced by 50% when cleaned. If using frozen or already cleaned fish, half of the above amount is sufficient.

112. TRIGLIE ALLA LIVORNESE
(*Red Mullet, Leghorn Style*)

SERVES 4

12 small red mullets, cleaned
Flour, as needed
A handful of parsley
1 small onion
1 clove garlic
⅓ cup olive oil

1 sprig fresh thyme or ½
  teaspoon dried
1 bay leaf, broken into pieces
Salt and pepper
4 tablespoons pomarola (*see
  recipe No. 86*)

1. Wash the red mullets well, dry with paper towels, dredge with flour. Clean, wash and chop parsley, onion and garlic.
2. Put oil in frying pan; when hot add the mullets, fry about 3 minutes on each side.
3. Add the chopped onion and garlic, the thyme and bay leaf, salt and fresh-ground black pepper and allow to cook for 2 more minutes.
4. Add tomato sauce, stir carefully, moving the fish as little as possible. Lower the flame, allow to cook for a few minutes, and when the sauce is thick, sprinkle with the chopped parsley and serve at once.

113. TRIGLIA IN FORNO AL POMODORO
(*Baked Red Mullets in Tomato Sauce*)

SERVES 6

12 *red mullets, about 4 ounces*
    each
2 *eggs*
Salt
Flour, as needed
½ *cup olive oil mixed with*
½ *cup peanut oil*
One 16-ounce can peeled Italian
    plum tomatoes

3 *cloves garlic*
A large handful of parsley
5 *leaves fresh basil or* ½ *teaspoon*
    dried
A few leaves of fresh mint, if
    available
Pepper

1. Clean and wash red mullets, dry well. Break the eggs into a bowl, add a little salt, beat with a fork. Dip the fish in the egg, one by one, then roll in the flour.

2. Put ½ of the mixed oils in a frying pan, heat until they start to smoke, then fry the fish, 2 at a time, for about 5 minutes or until the flesh comes away easily from the backbone. Drain on paper towels. Preheat oven to 350° F.

3. Wipe the basil and mint leaves with a damp cloth to clean. Chop the tomatoes, discarding seeds and hard parts. Clean and wash garlic and parsley, chop fine. In another frying pan put 3 tablespoons of the oil you've used for frying the fish. Heat through, then add the tomatoes, basil, mint, and salt and pepper to taste. Stir, allow to cook, uncovered, for about 20 minutes, or until the sauce gets fairly thick.

4. Line up the fish in a baking dish, cover them with the tomato sauce, bake for about 15 to 20 minutes. Remove from oven, sprinkle with the chopped garlic and parsley, serve at once, with plain boiled potatoes and a green salad.

114. TRIGLIE GRAVIDE
(*Pregnant Red Mullet*)

For this dish the red mullets should be fairly big, at least 6 ounces each. After cleaning carefully, remove as much of the spine as possible—this should be done with a small, sharp knife, in order to leave the fish as whole as possible. If you don't think you can do it, better leave the fish as is—the stuffing won't have as close a contact with the meat of the fish, but the overall taste will be about the same.

Juice of 2 lemons
¼ cup dry white wine
½ cup olive oil
Salt and white pepper
4 red mullets weighing at least 6 ounces each, cleaned, washed, and prepared for stuffing (see above)

4 ounces prosciutto (*Italian raw ham*)
4 tablespoons chopped parsley
2 tablespoons butter
⅓ cup bread crumbs

1. Put the lemon juice, wine, oil, salt and fresh-ground white pepper to taste in a bowl and beat briskly with a fork until the mixture is well blended. Add the cleaned red mullets and allow to steep in the liquid for about 30 minutes. Preheat the oven to 350° F.

2. Meanwhile, chop the *prosciutto* (fat included) and mix with 2 tablespoons of chopped parsley, the butter, and a generous amount of fresh-ground white pepper. Blend well.

3. Remove the red mullets from the marinade, fill the opening of each fish with ¼ of the mixture made in step 2, place the 4 fish in a baking dish, side by side, sprinkle with the bread crumbs and pour the marinade over all.

4. Bake for 20 to 25 minutes. Serve hot, sprinkled with the remaining parsley.

115. TROTE AL VINO BIANCO
(Trout with a White Wine Sauce)

SERVES 4

Of all fish that swin in sea, river or lake, trout is probably the most universally known, appreciated and available. In Tuscany, trout is either served very plain, roasted or broiled and seasoned with rosemary and garlic, or else it's drowned in sauces of white wine, tomato or a combination of both. The three recipes that follow are my favorites.

*4 medium-size trout, fresh or
    frozen
2 tablespoons flour
Salt and white pepper*

*2 cloves garlic
¼ cup olive oil
2 tablespoons chopped parsley
⅔ cup dry white wine*

1. Clean and wash trout, drain. Mix 2 tablespoons of flour with 1 teaspoon salt and abundant fresh-ground white pepper. Roll the trout in this mixture.

2. Clean garlic and chop fine. Heat the oil in a frying pan large enough to hold all 4 fish, add the parsley and garlic, simmer for 1 or 2 minutes, add the floured trout, simmer on medium flame for 3 minutes on each side. Be sure to turn only once, carefully, because fish are delicate and break easily.

3. When both sides are browned pour in the wine and continue to cook, uncovered, until ¾ of the wine has evaporated. Carefully remove the fish to a warm platter. Keeping the frying pan on a low flame stir with a wooden spoon, scraping the bottom in order to incorporate the flour that is attached there. This should make the sauce rather creamy. If necessary, add a little more flour or wine, put the sauce through a sieve and blanket the fish with it. Serve at once, with plain boiled potatoes that have been sprinkled with chopped parsley.

116. TROTE AL POMODORO
(*Spicy Trout with Tomato Sauce*)

SERVES 4

4 medium-sized trout, fresh or
    frozen
3 cloves garlic
1 small peperoncino (*Italian
    hot pepper*)
2 peeled Italian plum tomatoes
3 tablespoons chopped parsley

1 teaspoon oregano, fresh or
    dried
Salt
¼ cup olive oil
½ cup dry white wine
Juice of 1 lemon

1. Clean and wash fish, allow to drain well. Clean garlic, chop 2 cloves, leave 1 whole. Chop up the *peperoncino*. Chop the tomatoes, discarding seeds and hard parts.

2. Make a mixture of the chopped garlic, 2 tablespoons of the parsley, the oregano and *peperoncino* and put some of it into the stomach cavity of each fish. Close with a skewer. Sprinkle with salt on both sides.

3. Heat oil in a frying pan over medium flame; add 1 tablespoon parsley and the whole garlic clove, simmer for a few minutes, remove garlic as soon as it gets brown. Ease fish into the pan, allow to brown on both sides, pour in the wine.

4. Cook, uncovered, on medium flame, until the wine has almost completely evaporated. Add lemon juice, turn the fish carefully, and after 1 or 2 minutes add the tomatoes. Allow to cook for another 3 minutes, serve at once.

117. TROTE IN SALSA DIVINA
(*Trout in Wine Sauce*)

SERVES 4

1 small carrot
1 small onion
4 slices of blanched bacon
2 slices white bread
¾ cup white wine
Salt and white pepper

4 medium-size trout, fresh or
    frozen
3 tablespoons olive oil
3 tablespoons butter
1 tablespoon flour

1. Clean and wash the carrot and onion; chop fine. Chop the bacon. Remove crusts from bread slices and soak the soft white part in ¼ cup of the wine. Squeeze out excess wine and chop the bread. Put all in a bowl, add ½ teaspoon salt and some fresh-ground white pepper and mix well.

2. Clean and wash the trout, allow to drain well. Fill the stomach cavity of each fish with some of the stuffing made in step 1, close with a skewer. Sprinkle salt on both sides of the trout.

3. Put oil and 2 tablespoons of butter in a frying pan large enough to hold all 4 fish, allow to get hot, ease in the fish. Fry on medium flame for about 5 minutes, turn carefully, fry for 3 to 4 minutes on second side, cover and remove from fire.

4. In a small frying pan make a sauce by combining the remaining butter, the flour, the rest of the wine and some fresh-ground white pepper. Carefully remove the fish from the frying pan to a hot platter, cover with the sauce and serve at once.

CACCIUCCO

Cacciucco means fish soup in Tuscany. Every port has its own version, but essentially it's a lot of fish in a spicy wine and tomato sauce, served on toasted, garlic-flavored bread. In fact, the *cacciucco* is also called *zuppa di pesce*, since anything with bread in it is a *zuppa*.

There's an interesting legend about the origins of this famous dish. It seems that *cacciucco* was invented by a *livornese* lighthouse keeper who, living out at sea, had all the fish he wanted but wasn't allowed to fry it because the oil was needed to keep the light going. So, with a little ingenuity, a little wine and a little hot pepper he invented this excellent specialty, which tastes better than fried fish ever did. Incidentally, *cacciucco* should be made with at least five varieties of fish, one for each "c" in its name. The origins of the name are not clear, some say it means "mixture" or "confusion"; others say it comes from the Turkish word "*kacùkli*" which means "minute stuff" or "tid-bits."

Don't be surprised at the large quantity of fish necessary for each person, because so much of it gets discarded: heads, tails, bones, shells and insides. What remains is just enough; when you make it you'll see why!

The fish should be bought in these proportions: half of it should be regular scaled fish such as small soles, bass, tub fish, hake, swordfish, or any other salt-water fish available; of the remaining half two-thirds should be squid, shrimp, cuttlefish, crawfish and so on, and the remainder should be shellfish such as clams, mussels, dateshells or whatever other mollusks are available. The scaled fish should be cleaned as usual, removing scales and insides, and the larger specimens cut into pieces. The meatier varieties should be eaten whole, the smaller ones cooked first so that they can lend their flavor to the sauce. The squids are cleaned by removing the mouth and insides, and in the case of the cuttlefish remember to remove the little bladder that contains the black liquid. Shrimp are rinsed well but left in their shells, and the mollusks are soaked well and scraped carefully in order to get rid of all sand.

118. CACCIUCCO ALLA LIVORNESE I
(*Fish Soup Leghorn Style I*)

SERVES 5 OR 6

5 *pounds fish* (*see above*)
One 16-*ounce can peeled Italian*
   plum tomatoes
1 *onion*
3 *cloves garlic*
1 *carrot*
1 *stalk celery*
1 *peperoncino* (*Italian hot*
   pepper)

¾ *cup olive oil*
2 *tablespoons chopped parsley*
¾ *cup dry white wine*
About 10 *slices of Tuscan bread*
   (*see recipe No. 220*),
   toasted and rubbed with
   garlic
Salt *and* pepper

1. Clean all fish (see above), cut up the bigger fish, leave the small ones whole. Chop the tomatoes, removing seeds and hard parts. Clean, wash and chop the onion, garlic, carrot and celery. Wash and chop the *peperoncino*.

2. Heat the oil in a large saucepan, add chopped onion, garlic, *peperoncino*, carrot, celery and parsley. Simmer for a few minutes on medium flame, stir to avoid sticking, then add the pieces of squid and cuttlefish. The fish will release a little water which should be allowed to evaporate. Add the wine, stir, allow to evaporate.

3. When wine has almost evaporated add the tomatoes, stir, cook

for another 5 to 10 minutes, then remove the pieces of squid and cuttlefish and reserve.

4. Add the small fish and the heads and tails of the big ones, lower the flame, cover and cook for about 20 minutes, adding a little hot water if necessary. Remove all fish from the sauce and put through a sieve. Throw out the bones and hard parts and put the fish purée back into the saucepan.

5. Stir the sauce, which should be the consistency of a light vegetable soup. If too thick add a little hot water. At this point add the remaining pieces of fish, cover and allow to cook slowly for about 15 minutes, always checking to be sure the sauce is not getting too dry.

6. Finally, put the previously cooked squid and cuttlefish back into the saucepan, add the shrimp and the shellfish and a little hot water, cover and allow to cook for another 5 to 8 minutes, until the shrimp are cooked through and the mollusks have opened up.

7. Put 2 slices of bread into each soup bowl. Then put the steaming saucepan on the table and ladle out some of the sauce, then a few pieces of fish and squid, 1 or 2 shrimp and several shellfish into each bowl. Discard any shellfish that haven't opened. Be sure that each portion has a sample of every, or almost every, type of fish used. Let each person add salt and fresh-ground pepper.

119. CACCIUCCO ALLA LIVORNESE II
(*Fish Soup Leghorn Style II*)

SERVES 5 OR 6

5 pounds mixed fish (see p. 134, but do not use too many of the smaller variety of scaled fish)
2 onions
2 carrots
2 stalks celery
2 cloves garlic
3 peeled Italian plum tomatoes
1 small peperoncino (Italian hot pepper)
5 cups water
Salt

½ cup olive oil
½ cup dry white wine
1 tablespoon tomato paste
1 cup hot water
3 tablespoons chopped parsley
1 tablespoon chopped fresh basil or 1 teaspoon dried
About 10 slices of Tuscan bread (see recipe No. 220), toasted and rubbed with garlic on both sides
Pepper

1. Clean all fish (see p. 135). Clean and wash onions, carrots, celery and garlic. Chop 1 onion, 1 carrot, 1 stalk celery and all the garlic. Chop tomatoes, discarding seeds and hard parts. Wash and chop *peperoncino*.

2. Make a broth with 5 cups of water, the heads of the larger fish and the few smaller fish, the whole onion, carrot and celery and the 3 chopped tomatoes. Add a little salt and cook for about 30 minutes. The broth should be thick and in small quantity. Strain it and reserve.

3. Put oil, chopped vegetables and *peperoncino* in a saucepan, simmer on medium flame for a few minutes, then add the pieces of squid and cuttlefish. When they have rendered their liquid allow it to evaporate, then add the wine, stir and cook until ⅔ of it has also evaporated.

4. Dissolve the tomato paste in 1 cup of hot water, add to the saucepan. Stir, cook on low flame for another 10 or 15 minutes, then add the pieces of larger fish and cover.

5. Cook for another 10 minutes, then add shrimp and shellfish, cover again, cook for another 5 to 8 minutes or until mollusks have opened. Sprinkle with fresh chopped parsley and basil, cover again.

6. Take the hot broth, the saucepan with the fish and sauce and the garlic-flavored bread to table. Each person should take as much bread as he or she likes, cover it with as much broth as desired, then take his or her favorite fish and some sauce. Pass the black pepper grinder for those who like their food very, very spicy.

120. CACCIUCCO ALLA VIAREGGINA
(*Fish Soup Viareggio Style*)

This version is almost identical to *Cacciucco alla Livornese I*. The one notable difference is that it eliminates the *peperoncino*, making it digestible for those with delicate stomachs. But most Tuscans add plenty of fresh-ground pepper, making things about even. Another difference is that the fish is added gradually, according to the length of cooking time required, and is left in. Evidently, the small fish are not reduced to purée and the sauce isn't as thick as in the *Livornese* version, but personally I like this one beter; it's easier and faster to make and the sauce is lighter.

121. CACCIUCCO VELOCE
(*Quick Fish Soup*)

SERVES 3 TO 4

⅓ cup olive oil
2 cloves garlic, cleaned and
    chopped
2 tablespoons chopped parsley
Salt and pepper
3 pounds fish, at least 5 different
    varieties (see p. 134),
    cleaned and washed
⅔ cup dry wine, red or white

3 peeled Italian plum tomatoes,
    3 tablespoons tomato sauce
    or 1 teaspoon tomato paste
    diluted in ⅓ cup water
Small piece of peperoncino
    (Italian hot pepper)
A few slices of dark bread,
    toasted and rubbed with
    garlic on both sides

1. Put oil, garlic and parsley into a saucepan, simmer on medium flame for 2 or 3 minutes. Add salt and pepper to taste.

2. Add the fish, beginning with the tougher varieties and larger pieces. After 5 minutes add wine, the tomatoes and the *peperoncino*. Allow to simmer, covered, until all fish is cooked through.

3. Put some bread into each soup bowl and ladle the hot soup over it. Be sure to give each person a sample of each kind of fish.

122. TEGAMACCIO ETRUSCO
(*Etruscan Fish Stew*)

SERVES 5

This recipe is to sweet water fish what the *cacciucco* is to salt water fish. There are fewer versions of this than of its sea-flavored brother; it's easier to get several varieties of salt water fish. But the fact that it's called Etruscan may be an indication that this wasn't so in ancient times. Not that there were fewer fish in the sea, but it was easier to fish in rivers and lakes than to venture into the not always friendly Mediterranean.

The main idea here, just as in the *cacciucco*, is to use as many kinds of fish as possible. An eel adds a delicate touch; sweet water crabs and a few frogs, if they can be had, are excellent additions. The varieties should be no less than five,. at any rate. Personally, I prefer this dish to the *cacciucco*, because it's lighter and more digestible, and because I like the fish included in it.

About 3 pounds sweet water fish	*A handful of fresh basil leaves*
(pike, tench, eel, trout, carp,	*A few leaves of* nepitella*
perch, crabs, frogs, etc.)	*Salt and pepper*
1 large onion	*1 peperoncino (Italian hot*
3 cloves garlic	*pepper, optional)*
One 16-ounce can peeled Italian	*10 slices stale Tuscan bread (see*
plum tomatoes	*recipe No. 220), toasted and*
5 tablespoons olive oil	*rubbed with garlic*
1 cup good, dry red wine	

1. Clean and wash the fish well, cut into large pieces, heads included. Clean and wash the onion and 1 clove garlic, chop. Chop the tomatoes, discarding seeds and hard parts.

2. In an earthenware casserole, if possible (otherwise in an enameled or stainless steel saucepan), put oil, onion and chopped garlic. Simmer on a medium flame and when the vegetables are wilted start adding the fish, beginning with the larger, meatier pieces. This is a delicate operation because the fish should be moved about as little as possible in the pan, and touched only with a wooden spoon. Metal forks or spatulas can break the flesh of the fish, which tends to become flaky as it cooks. When all fish has been added, pour in the cup of wine, cover, lower the flame and simmer for about 15 minutes.

3. Wash, dry and chop the basil and the *nepitella*. Uncover the casserole, sprinkle with 1 teaspoon of salt, a little fresh-ground pepper, the whole *peperoncino*, the chopped herbs and the tomatoes. Allow to cook, uncovered, on a very low flame, or until the sauce is the right consistency, which should be like that of a thick vegetable soup. At this point clean the remaining cloves of garlic, chop fine, and sprinkle on the soup.

4. Turn off the flame and gently remove all fish heads and large bones that may have become loose during the cooking. Take the bread slices and ease them into the casserole, one by one, covering them with

* *Nepitella* is an herb of the mint family which grows wild in Tuscany and can be found from May to November in the fields. When not available use mint, fresh or dried.

as much sauce as possible. The bread should soak in most of the sauce, so that when the *tegamaccio* is ladled into the individual bowls it's mostly fish, soggy bread and tomatoes. Serve with a crisp salad or with thin, crackly, fried potatoes.

123. ZUPPA DI FRUTTI DI MARE
(Seafood Soup)

SERVES 5 TO 6

This is a *cacciucco* made with mussels, clams, shrimp, lobster and any other mollusk or crustacean, but no scaled fish. It is therefore more expensive but also more delicate and a dish I heartily recommend to all seafood lovers.

½ small onion
3 cloves garlic
½ cup olive oil
5 tablespoons chopped parsley
1 small peperoncino (*Italian hot pepper, optional*)
5 pounds mixed seafood, see pp. 134–5, well cleaned but with all shells left on

6 peeled Italian plum tomatoes
⅔ cup dry white wine
10 to 12 slices of Tuscan bread (*see recipe No. 220*), toasted and rubbed with garlic

1. Clean and chop the onion and 2 cloves garlic. Put oil in a large frying pan, add 2 tablespoons of the chopped parsley and the chopped onion and garlic. Allow to heat through, add the whole *peperoncino* if desired, then add all seafood, mollusks and crustaceans and continue to cook on medium flame, shaking the frying pan slightly in order to avoid sticking.
2. Chop the tomatoes, discarding seeds and hard parts. Add them to the frying pan, then add the wine and stir carefully. Allow to cook for about 15 minutes, or until all fish are cooked through.
3. Clean and chop the remaining garlic, mix with the remaining parsley, reserve.
4. Put the prepared bread into the soup bowls, spoon the soup and

seafood over it, sprinkle with the garlic-parsley mixture, serve at once. This soup should have abundant liquid; if necessary, add a few ladles of hot water.

124. ZUPPA DI GRANCHI
(*Crab Soup*)

SERVES 4

This soup is made with the small Mediterranean soft-shell crabs which have plenty of flavor but not much substance. If the larger, ocean crab is used, it is well to leave some of the pulp in pieces, adding to the consistency of the dish.

2 pounds whole soft-shell Mediterranean crabs	⅓ cup olive oil
	1 tablespoon chopped parsley
1 small onion	½ cup dry white wine
3 cloves garlic	Salt and pepper
2 slices bacon	8 slices Tuscan bread (see recipe
4 peeled Italian plum tomatoes	No. 220)

1. If crabs are bought fresh let them sit in salt water for at least 2 hours, then clean well. Chop onion and 1 clove garlic. Cut up bacon into small strips. Chop tomatoes, removing seeds and hard parts.

2. Let the bacon crisp in large frying pan, then add the oil, onion, chopped garlic and parsley and simmer for a few minutes. When onion has wilted add the crabs and cook for 3 more minutes. Add the wine, lower the flame, cover and cook for about 10 minutes, or until about half of the wine has evaporated.

3. At this point add the chopped tomatoes, a generous amount of fresh-ground black pepper, a touch of salt and 1 or 2 ladles of warm water. Stir, cover and continue to cook for another 20 minutes.

4. Remove the crabs from the soup, reserve the best looking 4, put the rest of the crabs through a food mill and strain the resulting purée in order to eliminate pieces of shell or bone. Toast the bread, rub with the remaining garlic. Put the crab purée back into the frying pan, stir, check the seasoning and correct if necessary; allow to heat through.

5. Place garlic-flavored bread in an earthenware casserole or other covered container, pour crab soup over it, cover, allow bread to soak up the liquid. Serve at once, giving each person 2 large spoonfuls of bread and soup and adding one of the reserved whole crabs on top.

CARNE
(*Meat*)

125. BISTECCA
(*Steak*)

SERVES 4

Here, to go into a restaurant and ask for a *fiorentina* is to ask for a steak. Tuscany has always had the best beef in Italy, and Florence had first choice of Tuscan beef. Cows here are butchered at an early age—in fact, the best Italian beef is called *vitellone*, which means "large veal." As a result the cross-section of the rib is not large, and one very thick steak is just about enough for two people.

Ideally, the *bistecca fiorentina* should be cooked on a wood fire and shouldn't be salted before cooking. It should be rare; a well-done steak is not a *fiorentina*.

> *2 steaks, cut 1-inch thick*
> *Salt and pepper*
> *1 lemon*

1. Light a fire in your barbecue or fireplace, using fragrant, dry wood, if possible. About 2 hours later, when the wood is reduced to glowing embers, put an iron grill over these embers and let it get very hot. Otherwise, preheat the broiler in your oven.

2. Meanwhile, take the steaks out of the refrigerator and let them reach room temperature. This is very important, as there is nothing worse than a well-grilled steak that remains cold on the inside. Put 1 steak on the hot grill, allow it to set—about 2 to 3 minutes—turn. Sprinkle the cooked side with salt and fresh-ground pepper, turn after 3 to 5 minutes (this is a matter of taste, whether you want the steak very rare, rare or medium-rare). Allow to cook for 3 more minutes, sprinkle other side with salt and pepper, remove to a warm platter.

3. Carve first steak, separating the sirloin and the tenderloin from the bone and cutting each into 3 or 4 pieces. Meanwhile, grill the second steak. When ready carve like the first and serve with lemon wedges.

Note: For the thickness indicated, grill 3 minutes per side for rare, 5 minutes for medium-rare, provided the embers are 6 inches away from the grill.

126. IL LESSO
(*Boiled Meat*)

SERVES 6 TO 8

Recipe No. 21 describes how to make good broth and how to make good boiled meat. There is only one thing to add here. Remember that boiled beef, unlike chicken, is not easily digestible. This does not mean it's a heavy dish, it only means that to digest it the stomach works from 5 to 6 hours.

Lesso should be served with at least two sauces (choose from recipes No. 77, 83, 84 or 90), plus mustard, plus Tuscan mustard (see recipe No. 249). For those who like boiled meat, a mixed *lesso* is a feast.

1 *small veal tongue*
4 *quarts water*
1 *pound muscle of beef*
1 *pound short ribs of beef, cut*
    into pieces
1 *pound beef breast*
1 *piece calf's foot*
Several beef bones, including 1
    marrow bone and 1 *knee*
    bone

Chicken bones or ¼ *stewing hen*
    (*optional*)
1 *onion*
2 *carrots*
1 *stalk celery*
A few leaves of fresh basil, if
    available
A few sprigs parsley
Salt
2 *bouillon cubes*

1. Boil the tongue in water to cover for about 30 minutes, drain, remove white outer skin.

2. Put a large pot with 4 quarts of water on the stove, bring to the boiling point. Add all the meats, the bones and the chicken.

3. Clean and wash the vegetables, basil and parsley, add to the pot. Add ¾ teaspoon salt, allow to return to the boiling point, then skim off the grey foam that forms. Turn the flame down to the minimum, cook covered for about 2 hours, or until all meats are tender.

4. Add the bouillon cubes, stir until they are dissolved, taste broth for seasoning. If necessary, add a little salt. Remove meats to a warm platter, cut the muscle, tongue and breast into pieces, serve at once. Each person should get one piece of each type of meat.

Note: The resulting broth is usable as a base for sauces or *risotti*, but will not be as good as the broth in recipe No. 21.

127. LESSO RIFATTO
(*Boiled Beef Made Over*)

SERVES 3 OR 4

We often find ourselves with a leftover piece of boiled or even pot-roasted beef that served by itself would be a little flat. For those who like onions the recipe below is a good solution.

3 *onions*
About 1 *pound leftover boiled*
    or pot-roasted beef
4 *or* 5 *peeled Italian plum*
    tomatoes

⅓ *cup olive oil*
Salt and pepper
5 *leaves fresh basil or* 1 *teaspoon*
    dried

1. Slice onions into thin rounds. Cut meat into slices. Chop up tomatoes, discard seeds, hard parts and excess liquid.

2. Put oil in frying pan, add onions, let them fry slowly until they turn the color of straw. Add slices of meat, salt and pepper to taste and tomatoes. Cut fresh basil leaves into strips and add. Stir and allow to cook for 5 to 10 minutes.

3. Serve slices of meat on a warm platter, covered with the onion and tomato sauce.

128. BRACIOLINE ALLA FIORENTINA
(*Florentine Meat Slices*)

SERVES 4

1 *small carrot*
1 *stalk celery*
½ *onion*
¼ *cup olive oil*
8 *slices round or flank steak,*
    cleaned and pounded

Flour, as needed
Salt and pepper
5 *peeled Italian plum tomatoes*
½ *cup dry red wine*

1. Clean and wash carrot, celery and onion, chop. Put the oil in a deep frying pan or shallow casserole, add chopped vegetables, allow to fry on medium flame for 2 or 3 minutes.

2. Roll the meat slices in the flour, shake off excess, sprinkle with salt and pepper. Add to the simmering vegetables, raise the flame, allow all slices to brown on both sides.

3. Chop the tomatoes and discard seeds and hard parts. Add wine and tomatoes to the cooking meat, cover, lower the flame and cook for at least 30 minutes, or until the meat is tender.

4. Remove the meat to a warm platter and save. With a spatula, scrape the bottom of the frying pan in order to incorporate everything into the sauce. Allow the sauce to thicken for a few minutes, then put it through a sieve. Cover the meat slices with the resulting smooth sauce and serve at once with boiled rice or potatoes.

129. STRACOTTO ALLA TOSCANA
(*Tuscan Pot Roast*)

SERVES 4 TO 6

Stracotto means overcooked and that's what you do to this piece of meat —you overcook it. There are many versions of *stracotti* in Tuscany. The following is the most delicate, the one after is slightly different but also good. Make the recipe below with veal instead of beef and white wine instead of red and it becomes a party dish.

2 cloves garlic	3 carrots
Salt and pepper	1 whole celery stalk
About 2 pounds of round, chuck or rump	⅔ cup dry red wine
½ cup olive oil	1 tablespoon tomato paste dissolved in 1 cup of hot water
2 onions	
5 leaves fresh basil or ½ teaspoon dried	Hot meat broth (see recipe No. 21), as needed

1. Clean garlic and cut into sticks. Mix 1 teaspoon salt with an equal amount of fresh-ground pepper and roll the garlic in this mixture. Make small, deep cuts in the meat (be sure to follow the grain), insert the garlic sticks. Sprinkle remaining salt and pepper mixture on the meat.

2. Heat ¼ cup oil in a casserole or Dutch oven, add meat and brown on all sides.

3. Meanwhile, clean, wash and slice onions, basil, carrots and celery. Put remaining oil in a saucepan, add vegetables and ½ teaspoon salt, cook covered on low flame for 10 to 15 minutes. Stir often to avoid sticking.

4. Add wine to cooking vegetables, stir, cover, cook for another 15 minutes. Add the dissolved tomato paste, stir again, cook for another 10 minutes, always on a low flame.

5. When vegetables are very soft, remove from fire and allow to cool slightly. Put through a food mill or into a blender and pour the resulting purée over the meat. Cover and cook on very low flame for at least 2 hours, possibly more. Check the liquid level often, add a little hot broth whenever necessary. Serve the meat on a hot platter, sliced and covered with its thick vegetable gravy.

130. STRACOTTO ALLA FIORENTINA
(*Florentine Pot Roast*)

SERVES 4 TO 6

3 tablespoons olive oil
3 tablespoons butter
2 to 3 pounds beef pot roast
    (*rump, chuck, round*)
¼ pound salt pork or bacon, in
    one piece
1 onion
1 carrot

1 stalk celery
¾ cup Chianti wine
2 tablespoons tomato paste
1 bouillon cube
1½ cups hot water or more, as
    needed
Pepper

1. Heat oil and butter in a Dutch oven, add the meat and brown well on all sides.

2. Meanwhile, dice salt pork or bacon, clean, wash and dice onion, carrot and celery. When meat is browned, add diced pork and vegetables and let them wilt. Keep flame high, add wine, then lower flame and let wine evaporate for about 10 minutes.

3. Dissolve tomato paste and bouillon cube in 1½ cups hot water. Pour over cooking meat and vegetables, stir, add fresh-ground pepper; cover and allow to cook on low flame for at least 2 hours, or until meat is tender. If sauce thickens too much add hot water, no more than ½ cup each time.

4. Serve sliced meat with half of the sauce. Save the other half for seasoning *pasta* or rice.

131. PEPOSO
(*Peppery Stew*)

SERVES 4 OR 5

This is a goulash made in Versilia, a name that defines the seacoast area of the Lucca province. It's called *peposo* because it's a very spicy meat stew, and it could have been called *aglioso* because it's also very garlicky. I don't recommend it to people with delicate palates. When you serve it, make sure there is plenty of light, dry red wine on hand.

1 calf's or pig's foot (*optional*)
Salt
12 cloves garlic
1 stalk celery
1 carrot
½ onion
¼ cup olive oil
20 to 30 whole peppercorns,
    broken into pieces
1 pound veal or beef stewing
    meat, cleaned and cubed

Flour, as needed
One 16-ounce can peeled Italian
    plum tomatoes
1 cup dry red wine
1 cup beef broth, canned or
    homemade
8 or 10 slices Tuscan bread (*see
    recipe No. 220*)

1. Put the calf's or pig's foot in water to cover, add salt, cook until tender, about 1 hour. Drain, cut into small pieces, reserve.

2. Clean the vegetables. Chop coarse 5 cloves garlic, the carrot, celery and onion. Put oil in large saucepan, add chopped vegetables and 3 additional whole cloves garlic. Simmer for 3 to 4 minutes on medium flame, stirring occasionally. Add salt to taste and about half of the pepper.

3. Roll meat in the flour, shake off excess. Add pieces of foot and floured meat to the saucepan, brown.

4. Drain and chop tomatoes, discard seeds and hard parts. Add to the casserole, stir, cook for about 10 minutes on medium flame, then add the wine.

5. Stir well, cover, allow to cook for 90 minutes, or until meat is very tender and sauce is thick. If it gets too thick during cooking time, add a little hot broth.

6. Taste for seasoning, add the remaining pepper. Chop 2 of the remaining garlic cloves, sprinkle over stew before serving.

7. Rub the bread with the last garlic cloves, put 2 slices of bread at the bottom of each plate, pour some sauce and some meat over them and serve.

132. INVOLTINI TOSCANI
(*Tuscan Beef Rolls*)

SERVES 4 TO 5

1 pound round or flank steak, cut
    into even, thin slices
4 ounces prosciutto (*Italian
    raw ham*)
½ cup grated Parmesan cheese
Capers, as needed
Flour, as needed
Salt and pepper

3 tablespoons olive oil
2 tablespoons butter
1 onion, chopped
⅔ cup dry red wine
5 or 6 peeled Italian plum
    tomatoes
1 bouillon cube

1. The secret of this recipe is to have the meat as clean, thin and square as possible. Pound the slices to get them even thinner, but be careful not to cause breaks. Lay out flat, cover each slice with a piece of the *prosciutto*, sprinkle with Parmesan, add a few capers, then close up the roll by tucking in one corner, then the opposite corner, then rolling up diagonally and securing with a toothpick or skewer.

2. Dredge the rolls with flour, then sprinkle lightly with salt and pepper. Put oil and butter in a frying pan, heat, add the meat rolls and fry on all sides.

3. Add the chopped onion, let it wilt, then pour in the wine and cook on medium flame until it evaporates. Chop the tomatoes, discard seeds and hard parts, add. Break up the bouillon cube into small pieces, add. Stir, cover, lower the flame, and cook for 30 to 40 minutes.

4. At this point, check the sauce for seasoning. If necessary, add salt and pepper. Check several times during cooking time. The sauce should be velvety but not too thick. If necessary, add hot water, one ladle at a time. When the meat is fork tender remove the toothpicks or skewers and serve the meat hot, covered with its own sauce.

Note: This recipe can also be made without tomatoes, and with white wine rather than red. In that case, add a slice of *fontina* cheese to the meat rolls (on top of the *prosciutto*) and substitute ¼ of a hard-boiled egg for the capers.

133. POLPETTE I
(*Fried Meat Balls I*)

SERVES 4 OR 5

The Tuscan meatball is light and soft. Unlike its southern sister, it is seldom cooked in a tomato sauce and served over *spaghetti*. Following are two recipes for meatballs as made in Tuscany, the third is a sauce originally meant for leftover meatballs, but it can be made purposely and, for those who are fond of it, used as a sauce for *spaghetti*. In our home we eat it with boiled potatoes or *polenta*.

2 *large potatoes*	2 *eggs*
2 *slices slightly stale white bread*	3 *tablespoons grated Parmesan*
¼ *cup milk*	*cheese*
1 *clove garlic*	*Salt and pepper*
A *handful of parsley*	*Bread crumbs*
12 *ounces leftover cooked beef*	*Oil for frying, as needed*
or veal	

1. Wash the potatoes, boil until soft, peel. Break up the bread into small pieces and soak in the milk. Clean and wash garlic and parsley, chop fine.
2. Squeeze the excess milk out of the bread. Cut the meat into cubes. Put the meat, bread and potatoes through the meat grinder twice. Add the chopped garlic and parsley, the eggs, the grated Parmesan and salt and fresh-ground pepper to taste. Blend everything well.
3. Form small meatballs by rolling a small amount of the mixture in your hands. Flatten slightly and roll in the bread crumbs.
4. Put a large frying pan on a high flame, add ½ inch oil, allow to reach frying temperature. Fry the meatballs, a few at a time, and when ready transfer to a platter lined with paper towels. When all fat has been absorbed by paper, transfer to a clean, warm platter and serve at once.

134. POLPETTE II
(*Fried Meatballs II*)

SERVES 4 OR 5

This recipe uses Tuscan sausage, if available. If not, diced bacon is equally good, but it should be blanched first—simmered for a few minutes in boiling water then rinsed with cold water. Blanching bacon removes the smoky flavor.

2 *slices white bread*	*Salt and pepper*
Milk, as needed	2 *eggs*
1 *small onion*	12 *ounces ground beef, chuck*
4 *ounces Tuscan sausage or*	*or round*
blanched bacon (see above)	*Oil for frying, as needed*
1 *tablespoon chopped parsley*	*Flour, as needed*
Nutmeg	*Bread crumbs, as needed*

1. Break up the bread into pieces and cover with milk. Remove and squeeze out excess milk. Chop the onion and the sausage or bacon. Put in a bowl and add the parsley, a touch of nutmeg, salt, fresh-ground black pepper, the eggs, the soaked bread and the ground meat. Mix well in order to blend thoroughly. If too soft, add a little flour; if too dry, add a little milk.

2. Start heating the oil for frying. Meanwhile, form small meatballs by rolling a small amount of the mixture in your hands. The meatballs should be approximately 1-inch in diameter. Roll lightly in the flour, then in the bread crumbs. When the oil is ready for frying put in the meatballs, a few at a time (see recipe No. 162). When done, transfer to a platter lined with paper towels. When excess fat has been absorbed by paper, transfer to a clean platter, and serve at once.

135. POLPETTE RIFATTE
(*Leftover Meatballs in Tomato Sauce*)

SERVES 4 OR 5

If you have made one of the two preceding recipes and there are any leftovers, they can be livened up with this simple sauce. The amount below is for 8 to 10 meatballs; if there are fewer they will swim in the sauce which, by the way, is no crime.

One 16-ounce can peeled Italian plum tomatoes
1 onion
1 stalk celery
1 carrot
3 slices bacon

3 tablespoons olive oil
1 bouillon cube
8 to 10 leftover meatballs
3 tablespoons chopped parsley
Salt

1. Drain and chop the tomatoes, discarding seeds and hard parts. Clean, wash and chop the onion, celery and carrot. Chop the bacon.

2. Put the oil, bacon and chopped vegetables, except the tomatoes, into a saucepan, allow to simmer for a few minutes. When the onion is wilted, add the bouillon cube and the tomatoes, stir, lower the flame and cook, uncovered, for 15 to 20 minutes.

3. When the sauce is thick, add the leftover meatballs, 1 tablespoon of the chopped parsley, and stir gently. Cover and cook for another 3 to 5 minutes, enough to heat the meatballs through. Check the sauce for seasoning and add salt if necessary. Serve at once, over *spaghetti*, noodles, boiled potatoes, rice or *polenta*, sprinkled with the remaining chopped parsley.

136. POLPETTONE ALLA FIORENTINA
(Florentine Meat Loaf)

SERVES 4 TO 6

1 *ounce dried mushrooms*
8 *peeled Italian plum tomatoes*
3 *cups stale white bread, broken
    into small pieces*
1½ *cups milk*
A handful of parsley
2 *sprigs fresh thyme, or 1
    teaspoon dried*
4 *ounces cooked ham or Bologna*
1 *pound ground beef, round or
    chuck*

2 *eggs*
7 *tablespoons grated Parmesan
    cheese*
Salt and pepper
*Flour or dry bread crumbs, as
    needed*
⅓ *cup olive oil*
¾ *cup Chianti wine*

1. Soak mushrooms in warm water for 30 minutes, wash well, chop fine. Chop tomatoes, discarding seeds and hard parts. Soften the pieces of bread in milk, squeeze out excess liquid. The result will be a ball of bread; chop it and reserve. Wash and chop parsley. Remove little thyme leaves from the stalk, add to chopped parsley. Chop ham.

2. Put ground beef into large mixing bowl, add eggs, chopped bread, ham, parsley, thyme, grated Parmesan, salt and pepper. Mix well, preferably with your hands, until mixture is uniform. Shape into large sausage, a bit shorter than your largest frying pan, flatten it. Roll in flour or dry bread crumbs.

3. Put oil in frying plan, let it get hot, then fry the loaf on all sides. When it's well browned add wine, lower flame, cook, uncovered, until wine evaporates.

4. When wine has almost evaporated add chopped mushrooms and tomatoes, cover, cook on low flame for about 45 minutes. Check liquid level occasionally. If necessary, add a little warm water or broth. Serve on a warm platter, with sauce poured over loaf.

137. ARROSTO DI VITELLA AL LATTE
(*Veal Pot Roast in Milk*)

SERVES 5 TO 6

3 *cloves garlic*
Salt
2 *pounds roasting veal*
½ *cup butter*

¼ *cup wine vinegar mixed with*
½ *cup water*
3 *cups milk*

1. Clean garlic and chop fine. Make a mixture of the chopped garlic and 1 teaspoon of salt and rub into the veal.
2. Melt the butter in a casserole or Dutch oven on a medium flame; put the meat in and let it brown on all sides.
3. Pour the vinegar and water mixture over the meat. Continue to cook, uncovered, until all liquid has evaporated.
4. At this point start adding the milk, keeping the flame low. Stir well, and scrape the bottom of the pan in order to incorporate the juices that have coagulated there. Cover and cook for at least 1 more hour, or until the meat is tender. Check often and, if necessary, add a little hot water and stir, always remembering to scrape the bottom of the pan.
5. When it is tender remove the veal and put the sauce through a sieve. Slice the meat, arrange on a warm platter, cover with the sauce and serve surrounded with small, boiled potatoes and creamed spinach.

138. SPEZZATINO DI VITELLA
(*Veal Stew*)

SERVES 5 OR 6

This is a veal stew that can be used as a base for many things. It can be served with boiled or mashed potatoes, boiled rice, *polenta*, or egg noodles. It can be enlarged by the addition of potatoes, carrots, peas, string beans, celery, mushrooms, or combinations of these. I am particularly fond of it with carrots, potatoes and string beans (added during the last 40 minutes) and served with white rice on the side; my husband likes it plain, served over *polenta*. In either of these combinations, plus a green salad and dessert, it's a quick, tasty meal.

1 onion
1 clove garlic
¼ cup olive oil
3 tablespoons butter
1¼ pounds stewing veal, cleaned
  and cut into cubes

½ cup dry white wine
1 teaspoon tomato paste
  dissolved in ½ cup warm
  water
1 bouillon cube

1. Clean and chop the onion. Without removing the outer skin of the garlic clove, bruise it with a meat pounder. Put oil and butter in saucepan, add onion and garlic. Add the meat and allow to brown well on all sides.

2. Pour in wine, stir, cover, cook for about 10 minutes. Add the dissolved tomato paste and the bouillon cube. Stir again, bring to boiling point, lower flame, cover, cook until meat is tender. Remove garlic before serving. With these proportions, salt should not be necessary; the bouillon cube is enough. If not, add another bouillon cube.

139. STUFATINO DI VITELLA COI FINOCCHI
(*Veal Stew with Fennel*)

SERVES 4 TO 6

This is especially good if made with breast of veal. If not available, use any piece of good stewing veal.

1 clove garlic
1 small carrot
1 stalk celery
2 slices blanched bacon
1¼ pounds veal breast or veal
  stew
3 tablespoons olive oil

Salt and pepper
1 tablespoon tomato paste
  dissolved in 1 cup hot water
1 bouillon cube
3 fennel bulbs
4 tablespoons butter
1 tablespoon chopped parsley

1. Clean, wash and chop garlic, carrot and celery. Dice the bacon. Cut veal into cubes, if using the breast leave the bones in; they add flavor.

2. Put chopped vegetables and bacon, oil and veal into a casserole or Dutch oven. Simmer on medium-high flame until the meat is

browned, then sprinkle with salt and pepper and lower the flame.

3. Pour the dissolved tomato paste over the meat, add the bouillon cube, stir, cover, and cook for at least 40 minutes or until the meat is tender.

4. Meanwhile, clean the fennel bulbs, wash well and cut into quarters, and then cut the quarters into slices. Boil in lightly salted water for 8 minutes and drain well.

5. Melt half the butter in a frying pan and sauté the fennel in it for another 5 minutes.

6. When the veal is almost done add the fennel, the butter in the frying pan and the remaining 2 tablespoons of butter. Stir, cover, and cook for another 10 minutes or until everything is cooked through. Sprinkle with parsley and serve hot, possibly with plain boiled rice.

140. COTOLETTE DI VITELLA SAPORITE
(*Savory Veal Chops*)

SERVES 4

2 tablespoons capers	3 tablespoons olive oil
A handful of parsley	2 tablespoons butter
A few leaves of fresh basil or 1 teaspoon dried	4 large veal chops, about 6 ounces each
Flour	½ cup dry white wine
Salt	

1. Drain the capers and squeeze out excess vinegar. Wash parsley and basil, add to the capers and chop fine with a sharp knife or *mezzaluna*—the Italian chopper shaped like a half-moon.

2. Mix the flour with ½ teaspoon of salt and dredge the chops well. Put the oil and butter in a frying pan large enough to hold all four chops, heat well, then add chops and fry on both sides. Add the wine, lower the flame to medium, and cook uncovered until most of the wine has evaporated. At this point the chops should be cooked through. Remove to a hot plate.

3. Scrape the bottom of the pan carefully and stir. The sauce should be creamy. If not, correct with additional wine or flour or both. Add chopped capers and herbs. Heat through. Put chops back into

sauce, cover, let stand for 2 minutes. Most of the sauce should be absorbed by the chops. Serve on a hot plate with remaining sauce poured over the meat.

141. BISTECCHE DI VITELLA CACCIATORA
(*Veal Chops Cacciatora*)

SERVES 4

1 *medium onion*
1 *ounce dried mushrooms*
5 *peeled Italian plum tomatoes*
Flour
4 *veal chops*
3 *tablespoons olive oil*

2 *tablespoons butter*
Salt and pepper
½ *cup Chianti wine*
*One 2- to 3-inch slice of lemon
rind*

1. Slice onion into thin rounds. Soak mushrooms in warm water for ½ hour, clean well, removing all sand and earth. Cut the tomatoes into small pieces, discarding seeds and hard parts.

2. Flour the chops on both sides. Put oil and butter into large frying pan over medium flame, heat through, add onion rounds. When onions are wilted, add the chops and brown well on both sides. Add salt and pepper to taste.

3. Add Chianti and lemon rind, lower the flame to medium, allow wine to evaporate. Remove chops to a platter; keep warm. Add tomatoes and mushrooms to the sauce, stir, cook on moderate flame for about 15 minutes, until mushrooms are cooked and sauce is thick.

4. Put chops back into frying pan, cover, heat through, turn off flame. Allow to stand for 2 minutes, then serve.

142. INVOLTINI DI VITELLA
(*Veal Rolls*)

SERVES 3 TO 4

8 *thin slices of veal, as for*
    scaloppine
8 *small slices cooked ham*
8 *slices* fontina *or other melting*
    cheese
White pepper
Nutmeg
Flour, as needed

Salt
5 *tablespoons butter*
¼ *cup milk*
½ *cup white wine*
3 *tablespoons* Vin Santo *or*
    sweet sherry
1 *bouillon cube, if needed*

1. Pound the *scaloppine* as thin as possible without breaking, lay out flat, cover with a slice of ham and a slice of cheese. Grind some pepper and grate a touch of nutmeg over the cheese, then fold meat into rolls (see recipe No. 132) and secure with a toothpick. Dredge these rolls with flour, sprinkle with salt, and fry in 2 tablespoons of simmering butter.

2. Make a liquid béchamel with 3 tablespoons butter, 3 tablespoons flour, the milk and the white wine (see recipe No. 76). Add *Vin Santo* or sherry and, if the sauce is too thick, dissolve the bouillon cube in 1 cup of hot water and use it to dilute the sauce. It should be the consistency of a cream soup.

3. When the veal rolls are browned on all sides, pour the béchamel over them, lower the flame, cover and cook for about 35 minutes. When meat is tender, remove the toothpicks and serve the rolls on a warm platter, covered with the sauce. These delicate veal rolls are very good with mashed potatoes.

143. ARISTA DI MAIALE ARROSTO
(*Roast Loin of Pork*)

SERVES 6 TO 8

Loin of pork is called *àrista* in Tuscany. Some philologists and social historians connect this name with an episode that apparently took place in Florence during the Ecumenical Council of 1430. The Byzantine bishops, upon tasting the Tuscan roast, broke out with "Aristos, àristos" which means "excellent" or "best" in Greek, and from then on the name has stuck. However, this explanation for the origin of the name of this excellent roast is denied by other scholars who claim that the word was in use before 1430 and derives from mediaeval Latin, meaning the higher or upper part.

> *1 sprig fresh rosemary or 1 teaspoon dried*
> *2 cloves garlic*
> *Salt and pepper*
> *1 loin of pork, weighing about 4 pounds*

1. Remove the leaves from the sprig of rosemary. Clean the garlic. Chop leaves and garlic fine, combine with 1 teaspoon of salt and plenty of fresh-ground pepper.

2. With a small, sharp knife make holes in the meat, staying as close as possible to the bone. Insert some of the rosemary-garlic mixture into these holes, then sprinkle the outside of the roast with additional salt and pepper.

3. If you have a rotisserie, skewer the meat on the spit and cook, turning, for about two hours. If a turning spit is not available, put the roast on a rack inside a baking dish and roast in a 425° F. oven for 30 minutes. Then reduce the heat to 350° F. and roast for another 60 minutes, basting occasionally with the juices formed at the bottom of the pan. Serve hot, carving carefully around the bones, or cold, which is the way I prefer it. Roast pork keeps in the refrigerator for 3 or 4 days.

144. ARROSTO DI MAIALE AL LATTE
(*Pork Cooked in Milk*)

SERVES 4

Another delicious way of cooking pork.

> *1 boned loin of pork weighing about 1½ pounds*
> *Salt*
> *Milk, as needed*

1. Tie the loin of pork into a sausage–like shape, salt it and put it into a casserole or Dutch oven.

2. Pour 2 cups of milk over the meat, cover and allow to cook slowly on low flame until most of the milk has evaporated. It should cook for at least 1 hour—if milk evaporates earlier add more milk.

3. When pork is ready, take it out and raise the flame to medium. The curdled milk at the bottom of the pot will become dense and the fat will sizzle. Remove fat and add a few tablespoons of fresh milk to the curdled milk, stirring to blend well. Slice the pork and pour the lumpy sauce over the slices. Serve hot, with mashed potatoes and a crisp, cool salad. Correct salt, if necessary.

145. IL GIRATO MISTO
(*Mixed Roast-on-a-Spit*)

SERVES 4 TO 6

The recipe below is not a definitive one. Many different meats can be used, and there are countless variations. The important thing to remember is that the spit should be just far enough from the fire to allow the meat time to cook through without burning the outside. Keep in mind that meats cooked on the same spit should have approximately the same cooking time.

1 guinea fowl	*Salt and pepper*
1 pound pork	*Fresh sage leaves, as needed*
4 Tuscan sausages	*Olive oil, as needed*
4 thick slices Tuscan bread (see	
recipe No. 220)	

1. Clean and wash the guinea hen, cut into 8 or more pieces. Clean pork, cut into large cubes. Cut sausages in half. Cut each slice of bread into quarters. Sprinkle everything generously with a mixture of salt and fresh-ground black pepper. About 1 hour before cooking time, build a strong fire with large pieces of fragrant wood. Otherwise, preheat the broiler. When most of the wood has burned to embers start putting the meat on the spits.

2. Alternate pieces of guinea fowl with a leaf of sage, a piece of bread, a piece of pork, a piece of sausage, and so on until everything is used up. The quantities listed above should be enough for 3 spits. Brush

everything generously with olive oil, put the spits into their slots, near the fire, and start turning slowly.

3. After about 40 minutes—during which time you've repeatedly basted the turning meats and bread with olive oil—stop the spits and check if the guinea hen is cooked. If so, remove everything from the spits and serve at once, with a *contorno* of crisp, fresh salad and plenty of good Chianti wine. A Tuscan meal at its simplest and at its best!

146. BISTECCHE DI MAIALE CON CAVOLO NERO
(*Pork Chops and Cabbage*)

SERVES 4

There are two versions of this recipe. The Tuscan uses *cavolo nero*, black cabbage (actually it's dark green), the other uses regular cabbage. The Tuscan way is slightly bitter, a hearty winter dish. The other version (see Note p. 163) is a little sweeter, reminiscent of the Austrian-Polish method of cooking cabbage, but I must say it was greeted with great enthusiasm by Tuscans.

2 pounds black cabbage (use green cabbage if black is not available)	*Salt and pepper*
	1 teaspoon fennel seed
	1 tablespoon tomato paste
2 cloves garlic	*dissolved in ½ cup warm*
¼ cup olive oil	*water*
4 pork chops	

1. Wash and clean black cabbage. In order to clean it, hold each leaf in your left hand and run the right hand over the leaf, from bottom to top, tearing the outer part of the leaf as you go along, and removing the hard stalk that forms the center. At the very top you can leave the stalk, which will have thinned down considerably. Cut the dark green part into strips.

2. Without removing outer skin, crush the garlic. Put the oil in a large frying pan, and when it's simmering, add garlic. When garlic is golden, add the chops, sprinkle them generously with salt, pepper and fennel seed. Brown well on both sides, add the dissolved tomato paste. Cover, lower the flame, cook for about 30 minutes.

3. Meanwhile, put the strips of cabbage in boiling water for about 5 minutes, drain and squeeze out the remaining water. Remove the pork chops to a preheated platter and keep warm. Add the cabbage to the frying pan, stir, allow to cook for 10 to 15 minutes, adding a little warm water if the mixture looks too dry. Arrange the cabbage around the chops and serve while very hot.

Note: The second version of this dish uses the same ingredients as above plus: 1 tablespoon sugar, 1 teaspoon wine vinegar, and 1 head of ordinary cabbage instead of the black cabbage.

1. Clean and shred cabbage, discarding hard core.
2. As above.
3. As above, up to the removal of the chops. Then add the shredded cabbage, sugar and vinegar. Stir, cook as above, check the taste, correct seasoning if necessary, and serve as above.

147. AGNELLO IN FRICASSEA
(*Lamb Fricassée*)

SERVES 5 OR 6

Lamb *fricassée* or in egg sauce is a delicious spring dish that can be made in several ways. The following is my own favorite, the one after that is a little faster to make and almost as good. In Tuscany these recipes are made with lamb, but both of them are equally good with chicken or veal.

About 1½ pounds lamb, leg or shoulder	⅔ cup hot water
	1 teaspoon flour
2 cups dry white wine	White pepper
1 onion	3 tablespoons lemon juice
6 tablespoons butter	1 egg yolk
Salt	2 tablespoons chopped parsley
1 bouillon cube	

1. Clean lamb, remove as much fat as possible, cut into 1-inch cubes. Cover with wine, allow to stand at least 3 or 4 hours.
2. Clean onion, cut in half, slice.

3. Take the pieces of lamb out of the wine and put into a clean, hot frying pan. Put the pan on a medium-low flame and let the meat secrete its liquid. Move pan back and forth to avoid sticking.

4. When all liquid secreted by meat has evaporated add ¾ of the butter, the sliced onion and a little salt. Simmer on medium flame until meat and onion are browned.

5. Dissolve the bouillon cube in ⅔ cup hot water. Add half of this broth and 3 tablespoons of the marinade wine to the simmering lamb, cover, cook on low flame for about 30 minutes or until the meat is tender. If necessary, add remaining broth.

6. Cream the rest of the butter with the flour, add to the lamb. Sprinkle with a little fresh-ground pepper. Stir, cover, continue to cook on low flame for another 3 minutes.

7. Put lemon juice and egg yolk into a small bowl, mix well. Pour over the lamb, stir, let the egg set (about 2 minutes), sprinkle with chopped parsley, serve at once, with boiled rice and tender peas on the side.

148. AGNELLO TRIPPATO O IN FRICASSEA
(*Lamb in Egg Sauce*)

SERVES 4

1 *clove garlic*
1 *pound stewing lamb*
Salt and white pepper
2 *tablespoons butter*
1 *tablespoon chopped parsley*

2 *egg yolks*
5 *tablespoons grated Parmesan*
    cheese
Juice of ½ lemon

1. Clean garlic and chop fine. Cut lamb into cubes and sprinkle with salt and fresh-ground white pepper.

2. Melt the butter in a large frying pan, add the lamb, brown on all sides, remove the lamb and reserve.

3. Put chopped garlic and parsley into the same frying pan, allow to warm through for 1 minute, put the lamb back in, stir, cook for another few minutes, adding a little warm water if necessary and scraping the bottom of the pan.

4. Meanwhile, put the egg yolks, Parmesan and lemon juice into a

bowl and mix well. Pour this over the lamb, reduce the flame, stir and cook for another few minutes, until the eggs have set. Serve at once, with plain boiled rice or a simple *risotto*.

149. AGNELLO E FAGIOLI ALLA TOSCANA
(*Tuscan Lamb and Beans*)

SERVES 5 OR 6

9 ounces dried white beans
Salt and pepper
About 2 pounds leg of lamb, cleaned
2 cloves garlic, cleaned and cut into sticks

1 sprig fresh rosemary or 1 teaspoon dried
One 16-ounce can peeled Italian plum tomatoes
Warm water, as needed
¼ cup olive oil

1. Soak beans in warm water overnight. Drain, rinse, cover with fresh water, cook for at least 1 hour or until tender. Towards end of cooking time add ½ teaspoon salt. When ready, drain and save.

2. Sprinkle lamb with salt and pepper. Make a few deep holes with a small, sharp knife and insert garlic sticks and rosemary leaves in these holes. Chop tomatoes, discarding seeds and hard parts.

3. Heat oil in a large casserole, add the lamb and brown on all sides. Add tomatoes and 2 ladlefuls of warm water, cover, allow to cook on low flame for about 90 minutes or until meat is tender.

4. Uncover casserole, check sauce level (it should just cover the meat), then add the cooked beans. Stir, cover, allow to cook for another 10 or 15 minutes, taste, correct seasoning if necessary. Serve hot, with plain boiled rice on the side.

Note: For a spring-like version of the above recipe, use peas instead of beans. Remember that peas take less time to cook.

150. BISTECCHINE FRITTE DI AGNELLO
(Fried Lamb Chops)

SERVES 4

> 2 *eggs*
> *Salt*
> 4 *large lamb chops or 8 small*
> *Bread crumbs, as needed*
> *Peanut oil, as needed*

1. Put eggs and ½ teaspoon of salt into a soup dish, whip together.

2. Clean the lamb chops, pound well. Put chops into the egg, allow to steep for at least 1 hour, turning them once or twice.

3. Put 4 or 5 tablespoons of bread crumbs on a flat surface, roll lamb chops in them on both sides.

4. Take a large frying pan and pour in enough oil to cover the bottom. Allow to get hot, then fry the lamb chops until they are golden brown.

5. Remove chops from frying pan and drain on paper towels. Serve at once. For extra spiciness pass the sauce in recipe No. 78.

151. FEGATELLI DI MAIALE ALLA TOSCANA
(Tuscan Pork Liver)

SERVES 4 TO 6

One of the most typical Tuscan dishes, this recipe for pork liver can be made as described below or roasted on a spit. When the bay leaves used come on a twig of good size, the twig is cleaned of all excess leaves and bark and used as a spit. This produces a very special scent which adds to the flavor of the dish. Nonetheless, the fried version is just as good, and personally I find it almost better because the meat becomes more tender. *Rete di maiale*, pork net or caul fat, is a membrane that lines the stomach of the animal and adds juices and fat to this succulent dish. If no caul fat is available, wrap the liver in bacon. The result is less traditionally Tuscan but the smoky taste of the bacon adds sophistication.

About 1⅓ pounds pork liver
About 1 pound of caul fat (see above) or sliced bacon
3 tablespoons bread crumbs
3 tablespoons grated Parmesan cheese

1 tablespoon fennel seed
3 bay leaves, crushed
Salt and fresh-ground pepper to taste
5 tablespoons olive oil
⅓ cup dry red wine

1. Cut the liver into fairly large cubes. Dip the *rete* quickly in hot water, spread out and cut into large squares.

2. Put all other ingredients except oil and wine in a bowl and mix well. Roll the cubes of liver in this mixture, then place on a square of *rete* or on 2 slices of bacon and wrap it around the liver. Secure with a toothpick or small skewer.

3. Put oil in a frying pan, allow to get hot, then fry the *fegatelli* on all sides. This should take 10 to 15 minutes. Add wine, lower flame, cover, cook for another 10 minutes. Remove toothpicks or skewers and serve at once. The sauce that will have formed in the pan is a little greasy but very tasty.

152. FEGATO DI VITELLO ALLA TOSCANA
(*Tuscan Veal Liver*)

SERVES 4

2 tablespoons butter
2 tablespoons olive oil
2 cloves garlic, cleaned
5 leaves fresh sage or 1 teaspoon dried

1 pound veal liver, sliced
Flour, as needed
Salt and pepper

1. Put butter, oil, garlic and sage in a large frying pan; remove garlic as soon as it gets dark.

2. Meanwhile, roll liver in flour, shake off excess. Put liver into hot fats, fry rapidly on both sides, just long enough for it to cook through. Sprinkle with salt and pepper to taste, serve at once.

153. FRITTO MISTO
(*Mixed Fried Meats and Vegetables*)

SERVES 4 TO 6

This recipe is a great Tuscan favorite. Its one disadvantage is that it has to be cooked at the last minute, but for those who like fried food, its advantages are many.

2 brains of veal
1 veal sweetbread
2 medium zucchini
4 small artichokes
Some lemon juice plus 1 whole
    lemon cut into wedges

2 eggs
Flour, as needed
Salt and pepper
Peanut oil or vegetable
    shortening for frying

1. Clean the brains and sweetbread carefully, divide each into several pieces. Clean and wash zucchini, cut into rounds. Clean artichokes, cut into halves and each half into 2 to 4 pieces; put in acidulated water.

2. Mix the 2 eggs with about 4 tablespoons of flour, add 1 teaspoon of salt and some fresh-ground pepper. This mixture, called *pastella*, should be on the liquid side. Put pieces of meat and vegetables into the *pastella* and make sure each piece is entirely covered.

3. Fill a frying pan with oil or shortening, allow to get very hot. Fry a few pieces at a time, for about 5 minutes, turning so that all sides become equally golden. Remove onto paper towels.

4. Continue to fry until all pieces are done. The *fritto* should be served at once, surrounded by lemon wedges.

154. TRIPPA ALLA FIORENTINA
(*Tripe Florentine Style*)

SERVES 5 OR 6

If steak is a Florentine's favorite meat, tripe is every Florentine's favorite meal, snack or sandwich. In Florence, tripe is sold on little hand-pushed carts at all hours of the day. It is served plain, boiled, on fresh, fragrant bread, seasoned with nothing but good olive oil. The following are three recipes for tripe, the first presumably more Florentine, the others simply Tuscan.

It's important to remember that there are several varieties of tripe, coming from different parts of the intestine, and for the best results possible at least two varieties should be used. Tripe is usually precooked by the butcher, and the recipes below presume that it has gone through this first stage.

About 2 pounds precooked tripe
Salt
1 medium onion
1 small carrot
1 stalk celery
5 leaves fresh basil or ½
    teaspoon dried
½ cup olive oil
4 tablespoons butter
1 clove garlic, cleaned

⅔ cup dry white wine
Grated Parmesan cheese, as
    needed
2 tablespoons tomato paste
    dissolved in 1 cup of hot
    water
Pepper
About 1 cup beef broth, canned
    or homemade

1. Wash tripe very well, cut into little strips, put into a pot of lightly salted boiling water, cook for about 15 minutes, drain.

2. Clean and wash onion, carrot, celery and basil, chop fine. Put oil and ⅓ of the butter in a saucepan, add chopped vegetables and the garlic, simmer on medium flame for a few minutes, add wine, allow half of it to evaporate.

3. Add the drained tripe to the simmering vegetables, sprinkle with 5 tablespoons of grated Parmesan, stir, cook for a few minutes. Pour in the dissolved tomato paste, sprinkle with salt and pepper to taste, cover and cook on low flame for about 1 hour.

4. Taste a strip of tripe; if still chewy add some of the broth and continue to cook until tender.

5. When meat is ready, separate into individual portions, put in small buttered pyrex dishes, sprinkle with additional grated Parmesan, dot with the remaining butter and put in a slow oven for about 10 minutes. Serve hot with boiled rice, noodles or potatoes.

155. TRIPPA ALLA TOSCANA
(*Tripe Tuscan Style*)

SERVES 6

About 2 pounds precooked tripe,
    at least two varieties (see
    recipe No. 154)
Salt
6 or 7 peeled Italian plum
    tomatoes
A large handful of parsley
1 large onion
3 cloves garlic

10 leaves fresh basil or 1
    teaspoon dried
1 sprig fresh rosemary or 1
    teaspoon dried
3 carrots
2 stalks celery
⅔ cup olive oil
Pepper
5 tablespoons Parmesan cheese

1. Wash tripe very carefully, cut into strips, cook in lightly salted boiling water for about 20 minutes, drain, put into a bowl of cold water for about 30 minutes. Chop the tomatoes, discarding seeds and hard parts.

Meanwhile, clean and wash all vegetables and herbs. Chop parsley and onion. Separately, chop garlic, basil and rosemary. Cut carrots and celery into rounds.

3. Put ½ of the oil into a large saucepan, add the chopped onion and parsley, simmer for a few minutes. Then add the carrot and celery rounds, stir, cook for another 10 minutes.

4. Finally, add the chopped garlic, basil and rosemary, the tripe, the tomatoes, salt and fresh-ground pepper to taste. Stir, cover, and cook on low flame for 1 to 2 hours, until the meat is very tender. Add a little warm broth or water if sauce gets too thick.

5. When ready, add the remaining oil and the Parmesan, stir and serve at once. In Tuscany this dish is often served with plain, boiled white beans. Good also with boiled rice or potatoes.

156. TRIPPA E ZAMPA ALLA TOSCANA
(*Tuscan Tripe and Calf's Foot*)

SERVES 6 OR 7

3 *small onions*
3 *small carrots*
3 *stalks celery*
5 *leaves fresh basil or ½
    teaspoon dried*
2 *cloves garlic*
Several sprigs of parsley
*About 2 pounds precooked
    tripe, at least two varieties
    (see recipe No. 154)*

Salt
1 *calf's foot*
6 *or 7 peeled Italian plum
    tomatoes*
½ *cup olive oil*
Pepper
*Grated Parmesan cheese, as
    needed*

1. Clean and wash all vegetables. Take 1 onion, 1 carrot, 1 piece of celery, the basil, garlic and half the parsley and chop coarse.

2. Wash the tripe well. Put in a pot with an onion, a carrot, a stalk of celery and half the remaining parsley. Add water to cover and a little salt and allow to cook for 60 minutes. In a second pot, do the same with the calf's foot and remaining vegetables. Meats are ready when the tripe is soft and the meat comes away from the bones of the calf's foot.

3. Chop the tomatoes, discarding seeds and hard parts. Remove meats from water, drain, and cut into strips.

4. Put oil and chopped vegetables, except the tomatoes, into a large saucepan, allow to simmer for a few minutes, add the strips of tripe and calf's foot, the tomatoes, and salt and pepper to taste; stir, cover, and cook on low flame for another hour. If necessary, add a ladle or two of broth while cooking; the end result should be quite saucy. Serve hot with boiled rice or potatoes. Pass the grated Parmesan cheese separately. Excellent with bread rubbed with garlic.

157. POLMONE IN UMIDO
(*Stewed Veal or Beef Lung*)

SERVES 4 TO 6

(See note, recipe No. 60.)

2 pounds veal or beef lung
⅓ cup olive oil
2 cloves garlic, cleaned and
    crushed
5 leaves fresh sage or 1
    teaspoon dried

½ cup dry red wine
About 6 or 7 peeled Italian
    plum tomatoes
1 bouillon cube
Pepper

1. Boil the lung in water to cover, if veal, 20 minutes, if beef, 40 minutes. Drain, cut into cubes.

2. Put oil into frying pan, add garlic and sage and, when hot, the lung cubes. When the lung is slightly browned add wine and lower the flame.

3. Meanwhile, chop the tomatoes, discarding seeds and hard pieces. When wine is almost evaporated, add the bouillon cube, pepper to taste, and the chopped tomatoes. Cook for another 20 minutes on a low flame, serve when the sauce has thickened. Very good with *polenta*.

POLLAME, CONIGLIO E CACCIAGIONE

(Birds, Rabbit and Game)

158. CONIGLIO AL FORNO
(*Roast Rabbit*)

SERVES 5 TO 6

Rabbit is eaten everywhere in Europe, but in Tuscany it's eaten as often as chicken. The Tuscan peasant keeps his own rabbits, raises them on good grass and good *crusca*, bran, and eats one every ten days or so. The Tuscan city dweller buys his rabbit at the butcher, or directly from the farmer, if he can, or even frozen (a novelty that has been available only since the sixties), but he eats rabbit as often as the farmer. All Tuscan restaurants feature rabbit in various forms, and this book wouldn't be complete without a few recipes for this tasty little beast.

1 rabbit
⅓ cup olive oil
1 sprig fresh rosemary or ½
    teaspoon dried

1 clove garlic, cleaned
Salt and white pepper
⅓ cup dry white wine

1. Preheat the oven to 350° F. Clean rabbit, wash in water acidulated with vinegar, drain, cut into pieces. Put in a frying pan, heat well. The meat will release a liquid, let it dry, moving the pan so that the pieces of rabbit don't stick. This procedure eliminates the slightly gamey taste that is otherwise characteristic of rabbit.

2. Pour about ½ the oil into a baking dish, add rosemary, garlic, and the semi-cooked pieces of rabbit. Sprinkle with salt, fresh-ground white pepper and the remaining olive oil. Bake for about 30 minutes, add the wine, bake for another 30 minutes; check to be sure the meat is tender, if not, allow another 10 or 15 minutes (much depends on the age of the animal). Serve hot, with the sauce poured over the meat.

159. CONIGLIO ALLA TOSCANA
(Rabbit Tuscan Style)

SERVES 5 TO 6

1 rabbit
⅓ cup wine vinegar
⅔ cup Chianti wine
⅓ cup dry white wine
2 garlic cloves, cleaned and
    sliced
2 onions, cleaned and sliced
3 leaves fresh sage or ⅓
    teaspoon dried
1 sprig fresh rosemary or ½
    teaspoon dried

3 pieces lemon peel, about 1
    inch each
One 16-ounce can of peeled
    Italian plum tomatoes
⅓ cup olive oil
1 tablespoon flour
5 leaves fresh basil or one
    teaspoon dried
Salt and pepper

1. The evening before cooking, clean and wash the rabbit, cut into 10 to 12 pieces. Make a marinade with the vinegar, Chianti and white wine, garlic, onion, sage, rosemary, and the lemon peel. Put the pieces of rabbit (including the head, if you have it—it gives added flavor) into the marinade and refrigerate overnight.

2. When ready to start cooking take the pieces of rabbit out of the marinade, then strain the marinade and reserve the other solids. Put the liquid and the rabbit in a large saucepan, allow to cook, uncovered, for as long as it takes to evaporate the marinade.

3. Meanwhile, chop the reserved garlic, onion, sage, rosemary and lemon rind from the marinade. Separately, chop the tomatoes, discarding seeds and hard parts.

4. When the rabbit is almost dry add the olive oil, allow to simmer for a few minutes. Sprinkle with flour, add the basil and the chopped marinade vegetables, sprinkle with salt and pepper to taste. Allow to simmer for 10 to 15 minutes, stirring once or twice and making sure that the onions don't burn.

5. Add the chopped tomatoes, stir well, scraping the pan in order to incorporate any bits stuck to the bottom into the sauce, lower the flame, cover, and cook for at least 1 hour, if possible 90 minutes, until the meat is very tender. Take out the head (it doesn't look too appealing on the table) and serve the rabbit pieces at once on a warm platter. Very good with *polenta*.

160. CONIGLIO IN UMIDO CON OLIVE
(*Rabbit Stew with Olives*)

SERVES 5 OR 6

The *umido* is a Tuscan standby. Like all stews, it requires slow cooking in a covered utensil and a liquid such as wine or broth to enhance the flavor of the base, which can be meat, fish or vegetable. The other ingredients of the Tuscan *umido* are tomatoes, olive oil and, almost invariably, garlic. Occasionally, sage or basil add their perfume to an *umido*.

Umido means "damp," and the word itself tells the whole story. In fact, the main characteristic of the *umido* is that it comes enveloped in a tasty sauce, a sauce that is used either as seasoning for *polenta* or soaked up by pieces of substantial, unsalted Tucan bread, which the men here use, with rugged informality, to "clean the plate." Better to forget your manners than leave some of that good sauce. My advice: to get around the problem, when you make an *umido* for guests, serve it with *polenta*, boiled rice or mashed potatoes, all intended as cushions for the sauce.

1 rabbit

Vinegar, as needed

2 cloves garlic

Salt and pepper

1 sprig fresh rosemary or ½
    teaspoon dried

⅓ cup olive oil

½ cup dry white wine

1 tablespoon tomato paste

1 bouillon cube

1 cup hot water

3 ounces Tuscan salted black
    olives, or small green olives

1. Wash the rabbit well in water acidulated with vinegar, drain. Put in a clean frying pan, then on a high flame. The meat will release a liquid which should be allowed to evaporate. Move the pan back and forth in order to avoid sticking. Clean the garlic.

2. Sprinkle the pieces of rabbit with very little salt, fresh-ground pepper, and the rosemary leaves. Transfer to another frying pan together with the oil and garlic. Simmer for a few minutes, and, when the garlic becomes dark, remove it. Continue to brown the rabbit on all sides.

3. Add the wine, lower the flame, allow wine to evaporate. Dissolve the tomato paste and bouillon cube in the cup of hot water. When wine has almost evaporated add this to the rabbit, stir, cover and continue to cook on a low flame for about 15 minutes.

4. With a small, sharp knife make a small cut in each one of the olives (in order to get some of their bitter flavor into the sauce). Add olives to the pan, stir, cover again, and cook slowly until the meat is tender and the sauce is thick and oily. Serve hot.

161. CONIGLIO PASQUALINO
(Easter Rabbit)

SERVES 5 OR 6

This is a recipe from Siena, which is the only city in Tuscany (and, according to some sources, in Italy) that makes ample use of tarragon. This excellent herb blends extremely well with artichokes and, in this recipe, makes for an unusual rabbit roast.

1 rabbit
3 cloves garlic
1 sprig fresh rosemary or ½
    teaspoon dried
6 large artichokes
Juice of 1 lemon

2 tablespoons fresh, chopped
    tarragon or 1 teaspoon dried
Salt and white pepper
Olive oil, as needed
5 slices bacon
1 cup dry white wine

1. The day before cooking, clean and wash the rabbit in water acidulated with vinegar, drain and dry with paper towels. Clean 2 cloves of garlic and put them, whole, into the stomach opening of the rabbit. Add the rosemary and refrigerate the rabbit overnight.

2. The next day clean the artichokes (see recipe No. 189), cut into quarters, remove the choke, and put the artichokes into a bowl of water and juice of 1 lemon to cover. Clean the remaining clove of garlic, chop fine, mix with the tarragon, 1 teaspoon of salt, ½ teaspoon fresh-ground white pepper and 2 tablespoons of olive oil. Preheat the oven to 350° F.

3. Remove the rabbit from the refrigerator and remove and discard the rosemary and garlic. Remove the artichokes from the water and put in a frying pan together with 2 tablespoons of olive oil. Cook on medium heat for about 10 minutes, until the artichokes are about half done. Stir in the tarragon mixture, then fill the stomach opening of the rabbit with the artichoke stuffing. Sew up well with strong white thread.

4. Wrap the bacon around the rabbit and put in a baking dish. Carefully pour the wine over the rabbit and put the dish into the oven. Allow to bake until most of the wine has evaporated, then sprinkle with salt and pepper and finish baking. Depending on the age and size of the rabbit, it should take from 60 to 90 minutes in total.

5. Before serving remove all thread, take out the stuffing, cut the rabbit into pieces, put on a warm platter with the stuffing in the center and the pieces of rabbit around it. Serve with additional artichokes and baked potatoes.

162. POLLO FRITTO
(Tuscan Fried Chicken)

SERVES 4 OR 5

1 frying chicken
¼ cup olive oil
Juice of 1 lemon
1 tablespoon chopped parsley
Salt and pepper

Flour, as needed
2 eggs
Peanut or corn oil for frying, as
    needed
Lemon wedges

1. Clean the chicken, wash, cut into at least 12 small pieces. Make a marinade with the olive oil, lemon juice, chopped parsley, salt and fresh-ground black pepper to taste, and put the pieces of chicken into it for a couple of hours, stirring occasionally.

2. Take the pieces of chicken out of the marinade, drain, dredge with flour. Add 1 teaspoon of salt to the eggs, beat slightly. Put peanut or corn oil into a large frying pan, start heating it.

3. When oil is very hot, put 4 pieces of chicken into the beaten eggs, take out and let drip for a moment, then transfer quickly to the frying pan. Fry on all sides, for a total of 15 to 20 minutes—the meatier pieces take longer—then remove onto a paper towel and repeat with the next 4 pieces, and the next. While the last pieces are frying, put the others on a warm platter. Remove the last pieces onto the paper towels, and, when excess oil is absorbed, add to the platter and serve at once, surrounded with lemon wedges.

Note: Whenever meat or vegetables are fried remember these three rules:

1. the oil should be very hot;
2. fry only a few pieces at a time, otherwise the temperature of the oil drops and the food boils rather than fries;
3. to insure crispness, let the excess oil be absorbed by paper towels or other absorbent paper.

163. POLLO IN UMIDO CON CIPOLLA
(*Chicken and Onion Stew*)

SERVES 4 OR 5

2 onions
¼ cup olive oil
2 tablespoons butter
1 frying chicken, washed and
    cleaned, cut into 8 or 10
    pieces
Salt and pepper

1 peperoncino (*Italian hot
    pepper, optional*)
1 cup dry white wine
1 tablespoon tomato paste
    dissolved in ½ cup hot
    water

1. Clean and wash the onions, cut into even, thin slices.
2. Put oil and butter into a large frying pan, add onion slices, simmer for a few minutes, remove the onions to a dish.
3. Put the pieces of chicken into the frying pan, add salt and pepper, allow to brown on all sides. Put onions back into the pan and add the hot pepper, if desired. Pour in the wine, lower the flame, allow to cook for about 10 minutes, then cover, and continue to cook.
4. After 15 minutes uncover and add the dissolved tomato paste. Cover again, cook for another 15 minutes or until tender. Check the sauce: if too liquid allow to cook uncovered for a few minutes in order to attain a jam-like consistency. Serve at once, with *polenta*, boiled rice or boiled potatoes.

164. POLLO ALLA DIAVOLA
(*Deviled Grilled Chicken*)

SERVES 2 TO 4

This is a simple and delicious grilled chicken and, depending on the appetites, it can serve 2 or more.

1 broiling chicken
3 tablespoons olive oil
Juice of 1 lemon
1 clove garlic, crushed
1 bay leaf, crushed

The leaves of 1 sprig fresh
    rosemary, or 1 teaspoon
    dried
Salt and pepper

1. Clean the chicken, cut in half and pound each piece flat. If using outdoor grill, start the fire.

2. Make a marinade with all other ingredients, whip well in order to incorporate the oil. Put the chicken into the marinade for 2 hours, turn over after 1 hour.

3. Take chicken out of marinade and put on the grill or preheated broiler. Allow to cook for about 20 minutes on each side, basting with the marinade. Serve hot, with a salad and baked or fried potatoes.

165. POLLO ALL'ARRABIATA
(*Angry Chicken*)

SERVES 4 OR 5

This is an excellent chicken *cacciatora*, with or without the hot pepper Tuscans will always have it with, which explains the name and justifies the good wine that should be served with it. For delicate palates, it's equally good without the hot pepper. For those who like sweet (green) peppers, it can be made into a *pollo con peperonata*, chicken with peppers, by adding one green pepper, cleaned, seeded and cut into strips, at the end of step 2.

1 onion	1 frying chicken, cut into 8 or
1 carrot	10 pieces
½ stalk celery	Salt and pepper
2 cloves garlic	1 cup Chianti wine
½ peperoncino (*Italian hot*	4 peeled Italian plum tomatoes
pepper, optional)	1 bouillon cube
⅓ cup olive oil	2 tablespoons chopped parsley

1. Clean and wash onion, carrot, celery and garlic; chop. Separately, chop the *peperoncino*, and reserve. Put oil into a casserole, add vegetables and pieces of chicken, allow to brown on all sides. Stir occasionally in order to avoid sticking.

2. When chicken is browned, sprinkle generously with fresh-ground pepper and ½ teaspoon salt. Add hot pepper if desired. Add the wine, lower the flame, stir well, scraping the bottom of the casserole with a wooden spoon in order to remove all bits and pieces that may have got

stuck there. This is important in all stews and dishes of this type, because the taste of the sauce depends on how well you scrape the bottom of the pan. Cook for about 15 minutes, uncovered, until at least half the wine has evaporated.

3. Meanwhile, put the tomatoes through a food mill and, when the wine is reduced to half, pour them over the chicken; stir, cover, and continue cooking on low flame for another 20 minutes. If sauce thickens too much, dissolve the bouillon cube in a cup of warm water and add some of this to the cooking chicken.

4. When the meat is tender, remove it, and continue to cook the sauce until it reaches the consistency of thick marinade. Return the pieces of chicken to the casserole, sprinkle with parsley, heat through, serve at once, with boiled rice, potatoes, or *polenta*.

166. POLLO CON OLIVE
(*Chicken and Olives*)

SERVES 4 OR 5

1 frying chicken, washed and
    cleaned, cut into 8 or 10
    pieces
Salt
1 large white onion
3 carrots
1 stalk celery

⅓ cup olive oil
1 cup Chianti wine
1 bouillon cube
10 to 12 small flat yellow onions
8 ounces Brussels sprouts
3 tablespoons butter
4 ounces Spanish olives

1. Season the chicken with 1 teaspoon salt. Clean, wash and chop coarse the white onion, 1 carrot and the celery. Heat oil in a large casserole, add chopped vegetables and chicken, allow to simmer on medium flame until the chicken is browned on all sides.

2. At this point add the wine and bouillon cube, lower the flame, cover and cook slowly. Meanwhile, clean and wash the small onions, the remaining carrots and the Brussels sprouts. Slice the carrots. Put the butter in a frying pan, add carrot slices, yellow onions and sprouts, cook on low flame for about 10 minutes, cover and reserve.

3. Check the sauce of the chicken for seasoning. If necessary, add salt. When meat is tender remove all pieces of chicken from the cas-

serole. Put the sauce through a food mill, return this purée to the cas-serole, return the pieces of chicken, add the yellow onions, carrots and Brussels sprouts with their butter, 1 ladle of hot water and the olives. Cook for another 20 to 25 minutes; about half way, check the liquid level (there should be about a cup of sauce) and add more water if necessary. Serve hot, with boiled rice, noodles, potatoes or *polenta*.

167. POLLO DISOSSATO IN GALANTINA
(*Boned Chicken with Meat Stuffing*)

SERVES 5 OR 6

The chicken *galantina* is an excellent cold dish, usually served in hotels or restaurants that cater to an international clientele. I was pleased to come across this Tuscan version of the *galantine* because it is quicker to make, more rustic in appearance and at least as appetizing as its more sophisticated French sister.

4 ounces cooked ham, in one piece	2 eggs
8 ounces smoked tongue, in one piece	Salt and pepper
6 ounces veal, preferably leg or shoulder	Nutmeg
	20 pistachio nuts
4 ounces pork, leg or shoulder	2 carrots
2 large Tuscan sausages or 10 slices blanched bacon	1 stalk celery
1 large onion	A few sprigs of parsley
1 large roasting chicken, boned, plus its removed bones and its liver	5 cloves
	1 bay leaf
	1 bouillon cube
1 tablespoon butter	2 pounds veal or beef bones, cracked
1 shotglass of Vin Santo or sweet sherry	1 calf's foot

1. Cut ham and tongue into strips. Put veal, pork and sausage or bacon through the meat grinder. Clean the onion, cut in half, chop one half, reserve the other.

2. Simmer the chicken liver and the chopped onion in the butter

for a few minutes, add a little of the *Vin Santo* or sherry, allow to cook for 5 minutes, remove from fire.

3. Put ground meats in a bowl, add the remaining *Vin Santo*, ½ teaspoon of salt, and 1 egg and mix. Chop the cooked chicken liver and onion and add. Grind a little pepper and grate some of the nutmeg and add. Check consistency of filling. If hard, add the other egg, or as much of it as necessary to give stuffing the consistency of a thick porridge.

4. Lay chicken on a clean linen napkin with the opening on top. Put ⅓ of the stuffing mixture into the opening, then add ½ of the pistachio nuts and ½ of the ham and tongue strips, then another ⅓ of the stuffing, then the rest of the nuts and meat strips, then the rest of the stuffing. Sew up the chicken and wrap a napkin around it. Tie napkin with white string.

5. Clean the carrots, celery and parsley. Put about 5 quarts of water into a large pot, add the remaining onion half and the other vegetables, the cloves and bay leaf, the bouillon cube, the chicken bones and the veal or beef bones, the calf's foot and the napkin with the chicken in it. Allow to cook for 1½ to 2 hours; remove from heat and allow to cool.

6. Remove the napkin with the chicken, put on a wood surface with the sewn side down, cover with a plate, put a weight on the plate, and let stand for 1 or 2 hours.

7. Remove the plate, unwrap the chicken, remove thread, slice and serve. If you want to make a gelatin with the broth, proceed as below.

> Broth from recipe above, strained, cooled and degreased
> 4 ounces ground beef
> 2 or 3 egg whites, slightly beaten
> 1 envelope unflavored gelatin

1. Pour the cold broth into an enameled or glass container, add the ground beef and egg whites, put on medium flame, bring to the boiling point. Stir constantly while the broth is heating, so that the ground meat and egg whites can capture all impurities as they solidify.

2. When all egg white has set, remove from fire and strain the broth through several layers of cheesecloth.

3. Put strained broth into a clean container, heat again and add the gelatin. When it has dissolved, pour into a pyrex dish, allow to cool, and refrigerate. When gelatin is ready, cut into cubes and serve with the *galantina*.

168. GALLINA RIPIENA ALL'ANTICA
(Old-fashioned Stuffed Hen)

SERVES 5 TO 8

This dish is a meal in itself. The meats and stuffing are delicious and the resulting broth very tasty and susbtantial. With *pastina* added to the soup and a vegetable as *contorno*, this recipe satisfies the most so-phisticated guests and isn't as much work as it seems.

FOR THE STUFFING

2 *slices* mortadella *or cooked ham*

1 *sprig fresh thyme or ½ teaspoon dried*

3 *slices white bread, soaked in milk*

1 *knee bone and 1 marrow bone*

8 *ounces ground veal*

1 *egg*

5 *tablespoons grated Parmesan cheese*

2 *tablespoons chopped parsley*

Salt and pepper

2 *carrots*

2 *onions*

About 1 *pound muscle of beef*

About 1 *pound beef short ribs*

Bouquet garni

1 *large stewing hen*

2 *bouillon cubes*

Salt

1. To make stuffing: chop the *mortadella* or ham fine; if using fresh thyme tear off the little leaves and discard the stalk; remove bread from milk, squeeze well, break into small pieces. Mix all ingredients in a bowl, and reserve.

2. Clean and wash carrots and onions. Rinse all meats and put them in a pot large enough to hold the hen. Add the cleaned vegetables and the *bouquet garni*, put the pot on the fire, bring to the boiling point, remove the grey foam that forms at the top; lower the flame, cover and continue to cook for 1 hour.

3. Meanwhile, prepare the hen for stuffing. Dry the inside well, stuff with the prepared mixture. Fill loosely, since stuffing tends to swell while cooking. If there is any left over, make small meatballs, roll in flour and fry, serve with other meats.

4. Sew the hen carefully in order to avoid getting the stuffing into the broth.

5. When the beef has cooked for 1 hour, add the hen and bouillon

cubes to the pot. Again, the grey foam will form—though less this time —again, remove it with a slotted spoon. Keeping the flame low and the pot covered, cook for another 2 hours or until the hen is tender. Check for seasoning, add salt if necessary.

6. Remove the hen from the broth. Discard all pieces of string used for sewing, take out the stuffing, and cut it into slices. Carve the hen, put on a warm platter with the boiled beef, the fried meatballs (if there are any) and the slices of stuffing. Serve with the boiled carrots and onions, with boiled beans or potatoes, and pass the mustard or the Tuscan *mostarda* (recipe No. 249).

169. ANITRA ALL'ARANCIA
(*Duck with Orange*)

SERVES 4 OR 5

Duck is always good when prepared with fruit. It seems that this version of it was brought to France by the Tuscan cooks of Catherine de' Medici. While it cannot be considered an everyday staple on Tuscan tables, the better restaurants serve it and, in our house, it's made as often as I can get a good duckling.

1 duckling, about 4 to 5 pounds	2 cups chicken or beef broth,
Salt	homemade, canned or made
1 small white onion	with cubes
2 tablespoons olive oil	2 oranges
1 shotglass of brandy	2 tablespoons butter
Pepper	1 tablespoon flour

1. Clean and wash the duck, dry inside and out, sprinkle with salt. Clean and slice the onion.

2. Put oil, onion and duck into a large oval casserole or Dutch oven. Simmer slowly until the duck is browned; be careful not to burn the onion. Pour in the brandy, cover, and cook on low flame for a few minutes. Uncover, sprinkle with fresh-ground pepper, add the broth, and cover again. Continue to cook on medium-low flame for at least an hour, at which point the duck should be ⅔ cooked.

3. Meanwhile, wash the oranges, peel one of them and squeeze

both. Add the orange juice to the cooking duck and cover. Cut the orange peel into thin strips, be sure to remove the white part. Put the strips into boiling water for a minute, drain.

4. When the duck is ready, remove from the pot and keep warm. Put the sauce through a sieve.

5. In the empty casserole make a *roux* with the butter and flour. Add the strained sauce and the orange peel strips, and combine well. Carve the duck into 7 or 8 pieces and serve at once; pass the sauce separately.

170. ANITRA AL MODO DI AREZZO
(*Duck, Arezzo Style*)

SERVES 4

2 carrots
2 stalks celery
1 large onion
A handful of parsley
4 ounces prosciutto (*Italian raw ham*)
1 young duck, no more than 3 pounds

One 16-ounce can peeled Italian plum tomatoes
1 duck liver or 2 chicken livers
3 tablespoons olive oil
Salt, white pepper and nutmeg
1 bouillon cube

1. Clean, wash and chop the carrots, celery, onion and parsley. Chop the *prosciutto*. Clean the duck carefully, wash and dry. Put the tomatoes through a food mill. Cut the liver into small pieces.

2. Put chopped ham and vegetables, except the tomatoes, the oil and the duck in a casserole or Dutch oven and brown on medium flame. Brown the duck on all sides, and stir the vegetables often in order to avoid burning the onion. If you don't have a Dutch oven with an even, heavy bottom (which helps prevent burning), then add the onion later, otherwise it will burn.

3. When duck is browned, sprinkle it with ½ teaspoon of salt, a few twists of the white pepper grinder and a few gratings of nutmeg. Then add the bouillon cube and the tomatoes, stir in order to loosen any bits that may have stuck to the bottom of the Dutch oven, lower the flame and cover. Allow to cook for about 15 minutes, add the pieces of liver, cook for another hour, or until the duck is tender.

3. If, while the duck is cooking, the sauce gets too thick, add small amounts of hot water. Take the duck out of the sauce, carve it into 6 or 8 pieces, put back into the sauce to heat through, and serve hot, with only part of the sauce over it. Save the remaining sauce, which should be abundant, for a *pappardelle all'aretina*, egg noodles with duck and tomato sauce (recipe No. 39).

Note: The liver is part of the original recipe, but I've made it without liver, and the sauce is equally good though a little lighter in flavor and consistency.

171. FARAONA AL CARTOCCIO
(*Guinea Hen Baked in a Bag*)

SERVES 4 TO 6

The guinea hen is an excellent bird, tender and tasty. Its meat is somewhat drier than chicken, more intensely flavored than turkey. It is not considered game, but raising it is not as simple as raising domestic fowl. It likes to perch in trees, and its voice sounds like the scream of a wounded child. In Tuscany, a platter of mixed roasts, *arrosti misti*, invariably includes this bird. This recipe is simple, but the results are very satisfactory. It doesn't matter whether the outer wrapping is a brown paper bag, aluminum foil or oiled wax paper, the important thing is to keep the juices from drying up.

> *1 guinea hen*
> *2 sprigs fresh sage or 1 teaspoon dried*
> *Olive oil, as needed*
> *Salt*
> *10 to 12 slices of bacon*

1. Preheat the oven to 350° F. Wash the cleaned guinea hen well, dry. Dip 1 sprig of sage into olive oil and put inside fowl. If using dried sage, use 1 tablespoon of olive oil and the teaspoon of sage. Salt to taste, inside and out. Wrap slices of bacon around the bird, tucking them in under the wings and thighs. Tie the bird well, wrapping string over the bacon slices.

2. Put the tied bird in a brown paper bag and bake for about 1 hour. If using aluminum foil or wax paper instead of a brown bag, put a generous amount of olive oil on the surface that will be in contact with the bird and wrap carefully in order to keep the juices in. The brown bag method will give you a drier roast, the other two materials will seal in a little more of the gravy.

3. When the guinea hen is tender, unwrap it carefully and collect the juices. Untie the string, making sure you throw out every bit of it, then remove what's left of the bacon and add to the gravy. Cut the bird into several pieces, and serve on a warm platter covered with its natural drippings.

172. FARAONA IN SALMI
(*Guinea Fowl in Salmi*)

SERVES 4

The *salmi* is a common European way of preparing game or fowl; in France a similar recipe is called a *civet* and the Piedmont, an Italian region that borders on France, has its own *civè*, similar to the French one and to the Tuscan *salmi*. Basically, the recipe consists in pot roasting the animal and including its liver in the sauce. Sometimes (as in the case of *tordi in salmi*, thrushes in *salmi*) rather than using the liver for thickening the sauce, the meat of the bird itself is chopped fine, and added. The effect is similar and, in my opinion, a little tastier, but the *salmi* lover prefers his sauce thick and liver-flavored and the recipe below is the classic Tuscan one which can be made with guinea hen, pheasant, hare or even chicken.

1 onion	⅓ cup olive oil
1 carrot	Salt and pepper
1 stalk celery	3 chicken livers
2 bay leaves	½ cup dry Marsala wine
1 guinea fowl and its liver,	1 teaspoon flour
cleaned, washed and dried	2 teaspoons tomato paste
3 tablespoons butter	½ cup hot water

1. Clean and wash the onion, carrot and celery; chop fine. Break each bay leaf in half. Cut the fowl into 6 or 8 pieces.

2. Put butter and oil in a casserole, add guinea hen pieces, sprinkle with salt and pepper, brown on all sides over medium flame.

3. Add chopped vegetables and bay leaves, lower the flame and continue to simmer for a few minutes. Cut the fowl and chicken livers into small pieces, add to the casserole, then pour in the Marsala and stir. Cook, uncovered, until most of the liquid has evaporated.

4. Sprinkle the flour over the guinea hen, dilute the tomato paste in ½ cup of hot water and add to the casserole, stir in order to blend well, cover and cook on a low flame until the meat is tender. Remove pieces of fowl to a warm platter, put the sauce through a strainer, pour over the bird, and serve at once. Good with a simple *risotto* or with *polenta.*

173. TORDI CON UVA E GINEPRO
(*Thrush with Grapes and Juniper Berries*)

SERVES 4

The thrush is a much appreciated game bird because its meat is very aromatic. The reason for this is that it's not a carnivorous bird but one that eats only tasty berries. For all those who are ecologically minded and who will shudder at the thought of shooting this adorable creature, I would like to report something a hunter once told me. He said: "Why say poor thrush, or poor pheasant? They lead a normal, natural, free life and some die unexpectedly, just as men do. Don't you think chickens and pigs and lambs are more pathetic? They are raised in bondage, force-fed, and led to slaughter whenever it suits man, and yet everyone eats them and no one seems to feel as sorry for them as they do for the game that gets shot down." Gives you something to think about, doesn't it?

24 juniper berries
8 thrushes, plucked, cleaned, washed and dried
8 slices blanched bacon
2 tablespoons butter
⅓ cup Marsala wine
⅓ cup hot meat broth (see recipe No. 21)
¼ cup olive oil

3 cloves garlic, cleaned
½ cup black olives, slashed
5 leaves fresh sage or 1 teaspoon dried
3 tablespoons tomato sauce
1 cup grapes, washed and dried (use Moscato green if available)
Salt

1. Put 3 juniper berries into each bird, wrap 1 slice of bacon around it, secure with a toothpick.

2. Melt butter in large skillet, put in the birds, fry on all sides over medium flame. When birds are well-browned sprinkle with the Marsala wine, allow to evaporate, add broth, lower flame, and cook for another 10 to 15 minutes, until birds are tender.

3. Put oil, garlic, olives and sage into an attractive frying pan over medium flame. Allow garlic to brown, add the tomato sauce, stir, then add the cooked birds and their pan juices; surround with the grapes.

4. Lower the flame, sprinkle with salt, and cook for another 10 or 15 minutes, until all flavors have blended. The sauce should not be too liquid. Remove garlic cloves and serve at once, in the cooking utensil, with a good solid *polenta* on the side.

174. BECCACCE ARROSTO
(*Roast Woodcock*)

SERVES 4

According to game experts, the woodcock is one of the tastiest birds to serve roasted, so if you can get this delicacy, invite guests who know something about the subject; otherwise, it's a waste. On the other hand, if no woodcocks are available, this recipe is also good if made with squab—making allowance for the difference in size: two woodcocks equal one squab.

Ideally, this roast is served with its own *risotto* (see recipe No. 61), which is a rich dish made with plenty of butter, bacon and olive oil. Since squab meat is dry and compact, in my opinion the *risotto* is better with a squab base, because the richness of the *risotto* offsets the dryness of the meat to perfection. In Tuscany, however, the woodcock is by far more appreciated, because it's an authentic game bird, while squab is considered good, but of the domestic variety.

8 woodcocks or 4 squabs (10 and 5 if also making the risotto)

3 ounces prosciutto (*raw Italian ham*)

5 leaves fresh sage or 1 teaspoon dried

2 bay leaves

6 tablespoons butter

20 slices blanched bacon

Heavy wax paper

⅔ cup Chianti wine

⅓ cup grappa, *brandy or other* eau-de-vie

1. Clean the birds well, remove all insides, refrigerate for about 48 hours.

2. Chop the *prosciutto*, sage and bay leaves, add 2 tablespoons of butter, blend the mixture well and stuff the birds with it. Preheat the oven to 425° F. Wrap 2 slices of bacon around each bird and be sure to tuck them well under the wings and thighs.

3. Wrap each bird in a piece of heavy wax paper, put them in a baking dish and into the oven for about 20 minutes. Remove from the oven, unwrap, put back in the baking dish. Lower oven to 325° F.

4. Cover birds with remaining butter, douse them with the wine and *grappa*, put them back in the oven for another 15 minutes, or until most of the liquid has evaporated. If using squab, they may need 10 or 15 minutes more baking time. Serve hot, two woodcocks or one squab per person, with some of the pan juices. If serving with *risotto* put a tablespoon of baking juice on each portion of rice.

175. PICCIONE FARCITO DI VITELLA
(*Veal Stuffed Squab*)

SERVES 4

This is an 18th century recipe which is still valid. The squab is a savory bird and veal seems to render it more delicate.

2 large squabs	*1 white truffle, sliced, if*
2 slices of veal, as for a cutlet	*available*
Salt and pepper	*1 shotglass of sweet sherry or*
Butter, as needed	*Vin Santo*

1. Clean the squabs inside and out, rinse and dry. Clean the veal of all excess nerves and fat, pound well. Preheat the oven to 375° F.

2. Sprinkle veal slices with salt and pepper. Dot with butter and truffle slices, and roll up.

3. Stuff each bird with one of the veal rolls, sew the opening. Sprinkle birds with a little salt.

4. Put birds in a baking dish, dot with butter, bake for about 20 minutes. Pour the sherry or *Vin Santo* over them, continue to bake for another 15 minutes; take out of the oven, remove the thread, cut each bird and each veal roll in half, put on a warm platter, cover with the pan drippings and serve at once.

176. FAGIANO ARROSTO
(Roast Pheasant)

SERVES 5 OR 6

The pheasant is a dry bird and tastes much better when cooked with fatty substances. The female is better for roasting, because slightly fatter, the male is better suited for recipes that have a sauce.

1 large pheasant, female if possible	5 leaves fresh sage or 1 teaspoon dried
8 ounces prosciutto (Italian raw ham)	Salt
7 slices blanched bacon	Pepper

1. Clean the pheasant well, rinse and dry. Chop ½ of the *prosciutto* together with the bacon and sage. Preheat the oven to 350° F.

2. Stuff the bird with the mixture made in step 1, plus salt and fresh-ground pepper. Close opening with a skewer.

3. Wrap the bird in the remaining ham, tie with white string. Put in a baking dish and bake for about 45 minutes, or until cooked through. Baste once or twice with the pan juices. Remove from oven, unwrap, carve into 6 or 8 pieces.

4. Remove as much fat as possible from the gravy. Add ¼ cup of hot water to the pan juices, put on a low flame, scrape the bottom of the pan, stir well. Serve pieces of pheasant on a warm platter with its simple gravy poured over them. Surround with roasted or mashed potatoes.

177. FAGIANO CON FUNGHI E BESCIAMELLA
(*Pheasant with Mushrooms and Béchamel*)

SERVES 4 OR 5

2 ounces dried mushrooms
2 ounces cooked ham
⅓ cup olive oil
2 tablespoons chopped mint
    leaves or 2 teaspoons dried
    mint
2 cloves garlic
5 juniper berries
1 cleaned male pheasant, cut
    into 8 or 10 pieces
Salt

White pepper
Nutmeg, as needed
5 slices bacon
1 shotglass of brandy
4 ounces mozzarella cheese
2 tablespoons butter
2 tablespoons flour
1 bouillon cube dissolved in 1
    cup of hot water
¼ cup grated Parmesan cheese

1. Soak mushrooms in 1 cup of warm water for 30 minutes. Remove, wash carefully, cut into strips. Strain the water through several layers of cheesecloth and reserve. Chop the ham.

2. Put 3 tablespoons of oil, 1 tablespoon of chopped mint, the garlic and mushrooms in a large saucepan, simmer on medium flame for a few minutes. Add some of the strained mushroom water, stir, allow to cook until mushrooms are soft, about 20 minutes, adding more of the water if necessary. Remove the garlic. Take out 3 tablespoons of the cooked mushrooms and reserve. Preheat the oven to 425° F.

3. Crush the juniper berries. Sprinkle the pieces of pheasant with salt, a few twists of the white pepper grinder and a touch of nutmeg. Put the fowl in a baking dish, cover with the bacon, add the brandy and crushed juniper berries. Bake for about 20 minutes. Slice the mozzarella cheese.

4. Take the baking dish out of the oven and add all its contents to the saucepan containing the mushrooms. Put on a low flame, cover and cook until the meat is tender, at least 30 minutes.

5. Prepare a soft béchamel sauce with the butter, flour and bouillon. Add the chopped ham, the grated Parmesan, and the 3 tablespoons of reserved mushrooms. Stir well.

6. Take the pieces of pheasant out of the saucepan, then put the remaining contents of the saucepan into the baking dish in which the bird cooked. Settle the pieces of pheasant over this base, and cover

everything with the ham-béchamel-Parmesan sauce. Put a slice of mozzarella cheese over each piece of fowl, sprinkle everything with the remaining chopped mint, a little more nutmeg and white pepper, and put back into the oven for about 10 minutes, until the mozzarella has melted. Serve very hot, in the baking dish. This recipe is one way of taking the dryness out of the pheasant.

178. FAGIANO CON CREMA E TARTUFI
(*Pheasant with Truffles and Cream*)

SERVES 4 TO 6

This is a dish fit for a great occasion, but it requires a real pheasant and genuine white truffles.

2 whole white truffles
4 ounces very fat prosciutto
    (*Italian raw ham*)
1 pheasant, male or female,
    cleaned, washed and dried
Salt and fresh-ground pepper to
    taste
4 ounces sliced bacon, blanched

¼ cup olive oil
2 cloves garlic, cleaned
1 sprig fresh sage or ½ teaspoon
    dried
1 shotglass of brandy
1 cup beef broth, canned or
    homemade
½ cup heavy cream

1. Wash the truffles well under running water, using a little hard brush to remove all earth, then dry well. Put the *prosciutto* and one of the truffles through the meat grinder, mix well.

2. Stuff the pheasant with the *prosciutto*-truffle combination, close well. Sprinkle bird with salt and fresh-ground pepper, wrap the bacon around it—remember to tuck it in under the wings and thighs—tie with white string.

3. Put oil, garlic and sage into a casserole that's big enough to contain the bird, allow oil to get hot, then add the bird and fry on all sides.

4. Pour in the brandy, let it evaporate, then add some broth and cook, covered, on low flame, for another 30 to 40 minutes, or until the pheasant is done. Add additional broth if necessary to keep the pan from drying out.

5. Remove pheasant from casserole, untie it, carve into several pieces. Put pieces on a heated platter and keep warm.

6. Remove garlic and sage from the juices in the casserole, add cream, allow to get hot but not to boil; put through a sieve and pour over the pieces of pheasant. Serve at once, with very thin slices of the remaining truffle sprinkled over the bird. Slice truffle either with a truffle slicer or with a razor-sharp little knife; slices should be very, very thin.

Note: Canned white truffles can be obtained in specialty stores and they are almost as good as the fresh ones.

179. ARROSTO DI LEPRE CON SENAPE E BRANDY
(*Roast Hare with Mustard and Brandy*)

SERVES 4

This recipe is also good with rabbit, but it requires two saddles, since the rabbit is a smaller beast.

1 saddle of hare, weighing about 2 pounds	*Salt and pepper*
½ bottle dry red wine	*1 heaping tablespoon strong mustard*
1 onion, sliced	*1 stick (¼ pound) butter*
3 cloves garlic, cleaned and crushed	*8 slices white bread*
3 bay leaves	*⅓ cup brandy*

1. Cut the saddle into 2 pieces and keep them overnight in a marinade of the wine, sliced onion, crushed garlic cloves and the bay leaves broken into pieces.
2. Take the hare out of the marinade, dry, season with salt and fresh-ground pepper and cover with the mustard, spreading it as evenly as possible. Preheat the oven to 450° F. On top of the stove, melt ½ of the butter in a large baking dish and, as soon as it sizzles, put in the hare and brown well on all sides.
3. Put the 2 pieces of saddle into the oven—using the same baking dish used in step 2—and allow to bake for at least 1 hour, basting now and then with the marinating liquid.
4. Take about ⅔ of the remaining butter, melt in a frying pan

and fry the white bread. Be careful to use small amounts of butter for each slice rather than the whole amount at once, because bread absorbs hot butter, and, if it were all melted at once, the first slices fried would be very greasy and the last slices would be totally dry.

5. Cut the fried bread into triangles and line them up around the sides of a preheated platter, one overlapping the other. With a fork, check to see if the meat is tender—depending on the age of the animal it could take longer than one hour—and, when ready, take out of the baking dish and put on the center of the platter.

6. Take the baking dish out of the oven and set on a very low flame. Pour in the brandy, let it boil down to half the original amount, scrape the bottom of the baking dish in order to blend in any bits that may be stuck there. Remove from fire, add what's left of the butter, stir to incorporate, pour over the hare and serve at once.

180. LEPRE IN UMIDO CON SALSA DOLCE E FORTE
(*Stewed Hare with Sweet and Pungent Sauce*)

SERVES 6 TO 8

1 *hare, cleaned*	3 *sprigs fresh thyme or 1 tea-*
2 *onions*	*spoon dried*
1 *carrot*	3 *cloves*
A *handful of fresh basil or 1*	*Salt and pepper*
teaspoon dried	*Flour*
A *handful of parsley*	6 *tablespoons butter*
1 *bottle good Chianti*	1 *shotglass of Marsala*
2 *bay leaves*	3 *tablespoons wine vinegar*
7 *juniper berries*	*Sweet and Pungent Sauce*
1 *small piece of stick cinnamon*	*(recipe No. 79)*
or ¼ teaspoon powdered	

1. Cut the cleaned hare into pieces and put into a large bowl. Chop the onions coarse, slice the carrot, snip basil and parsley with scissors, add to bowl. Cover all with Chianti. Break up bay leaves, crush juniper berries and cinnamon and add to marinade. Add thyme and cloves. Mix well, add salt and pepper to taste, and refrigerate for 2 to 3 days, stirring twice each day.

2. Take the pieces of hare out of the marinade and drain. Put the

wine through a strainer, squeezing the vegetables to get as much flavor as possible into the liquid.

3. When meat is almost dry, dredge well with flour, and sprinkle with salt and pepper. Heat the butter in a frying pan, add the meat and brown all sides.

4. When all pieces are well browned, pour in the Marsala and the vinegar and continue cooking, uncovered, until they evaporate. Start adding the liquid from the marinade, lower the flame, mix thoroughly, scraping the bottom of the pan to loosen the burned flour. Continue cooking, covered, adding marinade liquid as needed. Much depends on the age of the animal, but on the average a medium-size hare needs about 2 hours of cooking time. It's done when the meat comes easily away from the bones.

5. Serve the hare with stewed rice or boiled potatoes and its own dark, velvety sauce. The sweet and pungent sauce should be served separately, as a relish.

181. LEPRE IN SALMI
(*Hare in Salmi*)

SERVES 6 TO 8

Hare is a savory, flavorful animal, but fairly tough. In order to make it *in salmi* it is recommended to marinate it first. For ingredients and procedure see recipe No. 172. Aftre step 1, put the pieces of hare into a marinade of dry red wine for 24 to 48 hours. For more aroma, add pieces of onion and garlic and a few bay leaves to the marinade. When ready to cook, remove the meat, dry it, and proceed from step 2.

182. ARROSTO DI CINGHIALE
(*Wild Boar Pot Roast*)

SERVES 6 TO 8

A pot roast of wild boar is not easy to make, because it's not easy to find and kill a young boar, such as will make a tender roast. In case you are lucky enough to come upon a good piece of rib roast or shoulder from such an animal, allow it to remain in your refrigerator for 3 to 4 days, then proceed with the marinating process. In case the animal is older it should "age" for 7 to 8 days, marinate for 3 to 4 days and be cooked as a stew rather than a roast.

When the meat comes out of the marinade it should be soft to the touch, otherwise the resulting roast will be too tough to eat.

About 4 pounds wild boar,
    preferably from the ribs or
    shoulder
2 quarts milk
Two 1 to 1½-inch pieces of
    lemon rind
1 onion
2 cloves garlic

1 carrot
1 stalk celery
½ cup olive oil
Salt and pepper
1 shotglass of cognac
½ cup dry red wine
2 cups beef broth

MARINADE
1 cup wine vinegar
1 quart dry red wine
A handful each of basil, sage
    and thyme
½ teaspoon powdered cinnamon
5 cloves
1 teaspoon fresh-ground black
    pepper

1 ounce saltpeter or potassium
    nitrate
4 tablespoons sea salt, if
    available, otherwise, plain
    salt

1. Put all ingredients for the marinade into a large bowl, stir well to melt the salt. Remove all hairs from the meat (use a razor if necessary), dip quickly in a pot of boiling water, then put into the marinade, which should cover it entirely. If not, add equal parts of vinegar, wine and water until it does. Cover well and allow to stand for 2 to 3 days, turning occasionally.

2. Remove from marinade and rinse well with warm running water. Put the milk and lemon rind into a casserole, heat to the boiling point, scald the meat in it for a few minutes, remove, dry with paper towels, cut into 2 or 3 pieces.

3. Clean, wash and chop the onion, garlic, carrot and celery. Put the oil and chopped vegetables into a casserole, add the pieces of wild boar, turn flame to medium and allow to brown on all sides. Stir the vegetables in order to avoid burning the onion. Sprinkle with salt and fresh-ground pepper.

4. When meat is well-browned, pour in the cognac, the wine and ½ of the broth. Lower the flame, cover and allow to cook for 1 hour.

5. Turn the meat, add remaining broth if necessary, and continue to cook until tender, for a total of 2 to 3 hours. If the gravy is too liquid allow to cook 10 to 15 minutes uncovered.

6. Remove meat, cut into slices. Put the gravy through a strainer, pour over the meat, and serve at once with the sauces in recipes No. 79 or No. 83.

183. STUFATO DI CINGHIALE
(*Wild Boar Stew*)

SERVES 4 TO 6

About 2 pounds wild boar, rib or shoulder
3 cloves garlic
2 sprigs fresh rosemary or 1 teaspoon dried
Flour, as needed

Salt and pepper
¼ cup olive oil
2 peeled Italian plum tomatoes
2 cups beef broth
1 cup dry red wine

1. Allow the meat to age for a few days and then marinate as in previous recipe.

2. Remove from marinade, rinse well with warm water, dry, cut into large cubes.

3. Clean and chop garlic, remove leaves from rosemary twig, discard the branch. Sprinkle the meat with flour, salt and fresh-ground pepper.

4. Put oil, chopped garlic, rosemary and meat into a casserole, allow meat to brown on all sides. Meanwhile, chop the tomatoes, discarding seeds and hard parts.

5. Add the tomatoes, ½ of the broth and ½ of the wine to the casserole, stir well, lower the flame. Scrape the bottom of the pan so that any residue will be incorporated into the sauce. Cover and allow to cook for at least 1 hour, stirring occasionally.

6. Add remaining broth and wine, stir, cook for another hour or 2, until the meat is tender. Gravy should be fairly thick; otherwise, adjust it one way or another. Serve hot, over noodles or *polenta*, with sweet and sour onions (recipes No. 192 and 193) or other winter vegetables.

184. CAPRIOLO IN UMIDO
(*Venison Stew*)

SERVES 4 OR 5

The *capriolo,* or roe deer, is a small European animal of the deer family and a very desirable hunter's trophy both for its hide and for its excellent meat. Other kinds of deer may be a bit tougher, but on the whole most venison, if marinated before cooking, is highly edible.

The marinating process used in Tuscany for deer is slightly different from the one used for hare or wild boar. The usual vegetables (onion, garlic, carrot, celery) are chopped and then they are wilted in a few tablespoons of olive oil. This mixture is then doused with a couple of cups of dry white wine plus one cup of strong, good wine vinegar and boiled for 3 to 4 minutes. Allow the liquid to cool, then put in the pieces of venison that you wish to marinate. Keep in this liquid for at least 48 hours, turning occasionally.

3 ounces bacon, sliced thick
4 ounces prosciutto (*raw Italian
    ham*)
*About 2 pounds good quality
    venison, rib or shoulder,
    marinated as described
    above*

Flour, as needed
Salt and pepper
6 tablespoons butter
1 cup dry red wine
1 teaspoon tomato paste
¼ cup hot water

1. Dice the bacon and *prosciutto.* Cut the drained venison into cubes no larger than 1-inch square; sprinkle with flour, salt and pepper.
2. Put ½ of the butter and the diced ham and bacon into a casserole, turn flame to medium, allow to heat through, add the meat.
3. When the meat has browned on all sides pour in the wine, stir well, lower the flame and cover.
4. Meanwhile, make a *roux* with the remaining butter and a tablespoon or 2 of flour. When the mixture is golden, add to the casserole, stir.
5. Dissolve the tomato paste in ¼ cup hot water, add to casserole. Continue to cook on low flame, covered, for at least 2 hours. Serve hot on toasted bread.

185. FRITTURA DI RANE
(*Fried Frogs' Legs*)

SERVES 4 OR 5

Frogs are eaten all over Italy, and Tuscany is no exception. There are several ways of preparing them, but fried frogs' legs is the best known recipe and probably the one most congenial to Anglo-Saxon palates. If the animal is fresh and cleaned properly, it tastes somewhat like delicate chicken breast. Frogs should be acquired from a very reliable source, because they are good only when extremely fresh. To clean the animal, chop off the head, remove the skin, the insides, and be sure to remove the little green sac of bile, because it's very bitter. The recipe below is for the small variety of frog—there is a new, giant frog that is also very good, but only 3 pairs of legs per person will be necessary.

About 40 pairs of frogs' legs,
    cleaned as described above
1 cup vinegar
1 cup water
1 onion
A handful of parsley

Salt
Flour, as needed
1 egg, beaten
Peanut oil for frying
1 lemon, cut into wedges

1. Put the cleaned frogs' legs into a marinade of 1 cup vinegar, 1 cup water, 1 onion chopped coarse, a handful of cleaned and chopped parsley leaves, and 1 teaspoon of salt. Allow to steep in the liquid for at least 2 hours.

2. Remove the meat from the marinade, drain, dry well. Roll in the flour and dip in the beaten egg. Meanwhile, heat about 1 cup of oil in a frying pan.

3. Fry the frogs' legs in the hot oil, a few at a time. Allow about 3 to 4 minutes for each batch, remove with a slotted spoon and drain on paper towels.

4. When all legs are fried, serve on a warm platter surrounded with lemon wedges.

186. CHIOCCIOLE ALLA MAREMMANA
(*Snails Maremma Style*)

SERVES 4 TO 6

The snail is one of those small animals eaten and appreciated in Italy but little known in the Northern world. The only exception: the French "escargot," which can easily be found in the United States in canned form, and which is nothing like the Italian *chiocciole* or *lumache*.

In Lombardy (Northern Italy) the thrifty peasants eat snails often, both because they are tasty and because they cost nothing but the effort of going into the fields and picking them. Furthermore, by picking the snails they save the cabbage crop, since snails literally invade the cabbage plants.

The region of Tuscany that boasts the best snails is the southern part, the Maremma, where it is said that all snails are good and plump. The best time to hunt for snails is the autumn. It is well to look for them in the fields or in the bushes, going out early in the morning, when the dew falls, or later in the day if it's right after a rainfall. Take with you a light bucket and a stick (for parting the foliage), and poke among the branches of low vegetation, behind stones and under leaves. If you have a cabbage patch, look into the heads and on the underside of each plant. Pick the adult specimens and put them into the bucket; check occasionally to make sure that none have worked their way up and out—snails are slow beasts, but persistent. And remember *not* to search for them in May, when they are full of eggs, or near oleander trees and bushes, where they are bitter and slightly poisonous.

Once you have between 60 and 80, go home and get a large box or container. Put a thick layer of bran or corn meal at the bottom, or a mixture of both. Make holes or leave a space for air (snails breathe), cover the box, and keep the snails in there for about a week. Some refined "gourmets" put mint leaves and catnip into the box, in order to get more aromatic snails. The above is a Tuscan method for cleansing the little animals; in Northern Italy they are purged with bread and vine leaves.

After a week of this bran and corn meal diet the snails are ready to be eaten. Take them out of the box and put them into lots of cold water, adding ½ cup of vinegar and a tablespoon of salt. They will release a great deal of foam. Change water, always adding vinegar and salt, and rinse as many times as necessary. They are ready when they no longer make foam, at which point you can proceed with the recipe below:

1 clove garlic
1 small onion
A handful of parsley
2 ounces canned tuna fish
2 anchovy fillets
⅔ cup olive oil
1 peperoncino (*Italian hot
      pepper, optional*)

*60 to 80 snails or escargots,
      purged and rinsed (see
      p. 202)*
Salt and pepper
⅔ cup dry white wine

1. Clean and rinse the garlic, onion and parsley. Chop parsley and garlic, slice the onion. Chop the tuna fish or put through a food mill, wash and clean the anchovies.

2. Put oil, chopped garlic, parsley and sliced onion into a large frying pan, fry on medium flame for a few minutes, add the anchovies and tuna fish, and the *peperoncino*, if used. Stir and cook for another minute or 2, then add the snails, salt and pepper and stir again.

3. When the snails are sizzling, add the white wine, cover, and cook on a low flame for at least 1 hour. Check the liquid level frequently, add a little water if necessary. Snails are tough and should be cooked for at least 1 hour, better if two.

4. Serve the snails hot, with their own bent little forks and gripper, and pour the sauce over them. Toasted bread rubbed with garlic is recommended.

VERDURE

(Vegetables)

187. ASPARAGI ALLA FIORENTINA
(Asparagus Florentine Style)

Asparagus is a very good vegetable but a rather expensive one. By cooking it this way, it becomes a complete second course and the meat can be omitted. The following dish, without the eggs, can be served as a regular vegetable.

> *1 pound fresh asparagus*
> *Salt*
> *6 tablespoons butter*
> *⅓ cup grated Parmesan cheese*
> *4 eggs*

1. Clean and wash the asparagus, tie in groups of 7 or 8, using white string or strong white thread. Boil in lightly salted water for about 12 minutes, or until soft.

2. Remove from water, drain well, untie. Put 4 tablespoons of the butter into a large frying pan, allow to melt, carefully ease in the asparagus in order to avoid breaking the tips. Simmer asparagus for a few minutes, then sprinkle lightly with salt and the cheese.

3. Meanwhile, using the remaining butter, fry the eggs sunny-side-up. Ease them out of their frying pan with a spatula, put on top of the asparagus and serve directly from the frying pan.

188. BROCCOLI ALLA FIORENTINA
(*Broccoli Florentine Style*)

SERVES 5 OR 6

In Tuscany this way of preparing broccoli is known as "florentine," but in other parts of Italy these are "broccoli aglio e olio."

> *1 pound young, tender broccoli*
> *3 cloves garlic*
> *Salt*
> *⅓ cup olive oil*
> *Pepper*

1. Clean and wash broccoli, discard hard parts, cut into pieces. Clean the garlic.

2. Boil the broccoli in 2 cups of lightly salted water for 10 minutes, or until tender but not too soft, drain.

3. Put oil and garlic into the saucepan, simmer until garlic is brown, remove garlic. Add drained broccoli, salt and pepper, stir and simmer for 10 more minutes on low flame. Serve hot.

189. CARCIOFI RITTI ALLA TOSCANA
(*Tuscan Standup Artichokes*)

SERVES 4

The difficulty with artichokes is in the cleaning. Especially with the thorny variety, it's important to do it carefully and well. Step 1 in this recipe will be useful for all other artichoke recipes.

8 *medium size fresh artichokes*	1 *small clove garlic, cleaned*
Juice of 1 lemon	*Salt and pepper*
A handful of parsley	⅓ *cup olive oil*
4 *slices bacon*	1 *cup water*

1. Break off, one by one, all the hard outer leaves of each artichoke. Stop when you get to the yellowish, soft inside leaves. With a small sharp knife, cut off the top of the artichoke, removing all thorns, if there are any left. Then, holding it in your left hand, pare the bottom of the artichoke by turning it slowly and cutting off the external hard part with your right hand. The bottom should be left in the shape of a shallow cone. With your fingers, open the artichoke at the center and, if you see any straw-like material (the choke), cut that out, too. Young artichokes don't have a choke and, except for the outer leaves, the whole bud is edible.

2. Put the lemon juice in a bowl of cold water. As soon as each artichoke is cleaned, put it into the acidulated water. When they're all done, take them out of the water, squeeze well, and stand them up, bottoms down, in a small casserole, preferably enamel or earthenware, and make sure that they fit in tightly. Using fingers, lightly open the top of each artichoke slightly.

3. Wash and clean the parsley. Chop it, together with the bacon and garlic. Sprinkle this mixture over the slightly opened artichoke tops. Add a little salt, some fresh-ground black pepper, then pour on the oil. Cover the casserole and put on medium-high flame.

4. After about 5 minutes, when bottoms of artichokes are browned, add 1 cup of water, cover again and cook on lower flame for about 20 minutes, or until artichokes are soft and most of the water has evaporated. Serve hot.

190. SFORMATO DI CARCIOFI
(*Artichoke Custard*)

SERVES 5 TO 6

Loosely translated, the Tuscan *sformato* can be called a "flan." It's a very good way of treating vegetables, by mixing them with béchamel (white sauce) and eggs and then cooking them in a double boiler. A *sformato* can be made with many vegetables: peas, broccoli, spinach, carrots, and so on. This one is my favorite, and can be used either as a refined vegetable dish, *contorno*, or as a light first course, but then it requires a sauce on the side. The sweetbreads render this recipe more delicate, but they can be omitted, in which case the quantity of artichokes should be increased accordingly.

*2 pounds fresh artichokes or 1
    pound frozen
Juice of 1 lemon
¼ pound butter
Salt and pepper*

*2 eggs
2 tablespoons grated Parmesan
    cheese
7 ounces veal sweetbreads
Bread crumbs*

WHITE SAUCE
*5 tablespoons butter
5 tablespoons flour*

*1½ cups milk
½ teaspoon salt*

1. Clean artichokes as in step 1 of recipe No. 189. Cut into quarters, remove choke, and put into a large bowl of cold water and lemon juice. When all artichokes are clean, drain. Cook slowly for about 15 minutes in about 3 tablespoons butter. The water that remains attached to the leaves should be sufficient to cook them through. If not, add a little water. Add salt and pepper to taste.

2. Meanwhile, make a white sauce with the ingredients listed above, as in recipe No. 76. It should be rather thick. When ready, remove from fire and allow to cool, then add the 2 eggs and grated Parmesan, stirring to blend well.

3. Wash and clean the sweetbreads, boil in water to cover for about 20 to 30 minutes, drain and chop into small pieces. Add to the white sauce, stir. Preheat oven to 325° F.

4. When artichokes are soft, remove from fire and let cool. Add to

white sauce mixture, stir to blend well. Butter the top of a large double boiler, sprinkle generously with dry bread crumbs. Fill with artichoke-white sauce mixture, even out top with a spatula, sprinkle with bread crumbs.

5. Put water in the bottom of the double boiler, bring to boiling point. Put the top into the bottom, let cook for about 45 minutes, never allowing the water to boil briskly. Transfer the top of the double boiler into the preheated oven and allow to bake for another 20 minutes. To check if the *sformato* is ready, stick a toothpick into the center. If it comes out dry, it's done.

6. Let cool for about 10 minutes, turn out onto a large platter. If served as a first course, pour a light tomato sauce over this *sformato*, see recipe No. 86. Or, try the sauce described in recipe No. 87.

191. CAVOLO SENESE
(*Sienese Cabbage*)

SERVES 4 TO 6

This cabbage recipe supposedly dates back to 1848, when Austrian troops were in Siena. Some say it also dates back to those meager winters when cabbage was the only vegetable available and giving it a new taste might have been just a way of making it more palatable.

1 *large cabbage*	1 *bay leaf*
Salt	3 *teaspoons sugar*
1 *onion*	2 *tablespoons flour*
5 *tablespoons butter or margarine*	*Juice of 1 lemon*

1. Wash and slice all cabbage leaves, sprinkle with salt, allow to stand for 1 hour. Clean and slice the onion.

2. Let the onion simmer slowly in 3 tablespoons of butter, *do not brown*. Squeeze out the cabbage, add to the simmering onion, cook for a few minutes. Add a ladle of hot water, the bay leaf, and sprinkle with 1 teaspoon of the sugar. Cover and cook on low flame for about 20 minutes.

3. Meanwhile, make a *roux* with the remaining butter and the flour. Add to the cooking cabbage, stir. In the same frying pan, melt the remaining teaspoons of sugar and allow to turn brown. Add lemon

juice, stir to combine, then add to the cabbage. Stir, cook for another few minutes, taste for seasoning, correct if necessary and serve hot. This is excellent with boiled or pot-roasted beef, but ideally suited as *contorno* to pork or game.

192. CIPOLLINE IN AGRO-DOLCE I
(*Sweet and Sour Onions I*)

SERVES 4 TO 6

This is a vegetable that can be considered a relish. It can be made in advance, it can be eaten in small quantities, and it's meant as a *contorno* for boiled or roasted meat. There are two versions of this recipe; my own preference is for the one that uses butter; the other makes a more abundant sauce.

11 ounces small yellow onions
Salt
4 tablespoons butter
Sugar, as needed
Wine vinegar, as needed

1. Clean the onions and boil for about 10 minutes in lightly salted water, drain.
2. Melt the butter in a large frying pan, add the onions, allow to simmer slowly and, when browned on both sides, sprinkle with 1 tablespoon of sugar and then add 2 tablespoons of vinegar. Stir carefully, cover and lower the flame to a minimum.
3. After about 5 minutes, uncover and carefully turn the onions. When the sauce bubbles, taste. The sweet and sour flavor should be balanced; if not, add more sugar, vinegar or water (always in small quantities) until the sauce seems right to you. Since much depends on the quality of the vinegar, it's difficult to know the exact proportions. The sauce should be dark and sticky, the onions dark on the outside but white on the inside. Serve hot or cold, with roasts, steaks or boiled meats.

193. CIPOLLINE IN AGRO-DOLCE II
(*Sweet and Sour Onions II*)

SERVES 4 TO 6

11 ounces small yellow onions
Salt
Vinegar, as needed.

⅔ cup water
Sugar, as needed
3 tablespoons flour

1. Clean the onions and boil for about 10 minutes in lightly salted water, drain. Put 2 tablespoons vinegar into ⅔ cup water.

2. Put 3 tablespoons of sugar in the bottom of a clean saucepan and allow to melt on a medium flame. When it's melted, add the flour and stir constantly until the mixture gets uniformly red. While continuing to stir, add the acidulated water, a little at a time. Make sure the sauce has no lumps in it.

3. Add the onions to the sauce, lower the flame and cook for another few minutes, shaking the pan frequently. To avoid damaging the onions, do not stir. Taste before serving and correct with additional sugar or vinegar if necessary. Serve as in previous recipe.

194. FAGIOLI AL FIASCO
(*Beans Cooked in a Flask*)

SERVES 6 TO 8

This is the classical Tuscan way of cooking beans, and I've written the recipe accordingly. But if you don't have a *fiasco* and genuine glowing embers it can be made with similar results in an earthenware casserole, on top of the stove, by keeping the flame very low and evaporation down to a minimum.

1¼ pounds dried white beans
    or 3 pounds fresh white
    beans
2 cloves garlic, crushed
5 leaves fresh sage or 1 teaspoon
    dried

½ cup olive oil
2 cups water
Salt and pepper

1. Shell fresh beans; if dried, soak overnight in warm water, then rinse before using.

2. Take a *fiasco* and remove its outer covering of straw. Fill with the beans, add the crushed garlic and the sage. Pour in the olive oil and 2 cups of water. Do not close the *fiasco* with a cork. Use straw or cloth: this allows the steam to evaporate slowly.

3. Place the *fiasco* on the embers of an outdoor grill or fireplace, making sure that it's standing firmly. If that isn't possible, then put it on a very low flame with an asbestos pad for protection.

4. Without touching the *fiasco*, allow beans to cook very slowly for about 3 hours. During this time the water will evaporate and the oil will be absorbed by the beans.

5. When the beans are cooked, remove them from the *fiasco* and sprinkle with salt and fresh-ground pepper; stir. They are very good hot, warm or cold. Personally, I like to add a drop of vinegar.

195. FAGIOLI ALL'UCCELLETTO
(*Beans in Tomato Sauce*)

SERVES 6 TO 8

This is another classical Tuscan preparation, but the name is hard to translate because *uccelletto* literally means "small bird," and I wasn't able to discover what kind of bird it's supposed to be. Basically, this is just a recipe for beans cooked *in umido*, which in Tuscany means a tasty stew.

1¼ *pounds dried white beans or*
    3 *pounds fresh white*
    toscanelli *or* cannellini *beans*
One 16-ounce can peeled Italian
    plum tomatoes
2 cloves garlic

⅓ *cup olive oil*
5 *leaves fresh sage or 1 teaspoon*
    dried
Salt and pepper
1 bouillon cube

1. Shell fresh beans; if dried, soak overnight in warm water, then rinse before using. Boil in water to cover for 40 minutes, drain. Chop the tomatoes, discarding seeds and hard parts.

2. Clean garlic and put in a large saucepan with the oil, sage, salt

and a little fresh-ground pepper. Simmer until the garlic turns brown, then add the beans, stir and allow to cook for a few minutes.

3. Add the tomatoes and bouillon cube, stir, cover and cook for another 15 minutes or until the sauce has thickened. Serve hot or warm with roasts and game.

196. FAGIOLI AL FORNO
(*Baked Beans*)

SERVES 4 TO 5

These beans require a covered earthenware casserole. If you own one, don't hesitate to prepare this tasty, easy dish.

2 pounds fresh white cannellini
    beans or 11 ounces dried
    white beans
2 pieces pork rind, each
    approximately 2 inches
    long and 1 inch wide

1 leek
5 peeled Italian plum tomatoes
2 cloves garlic
Salt and pepper

1. Shell beans if fresh, soak overnight in warm water if dried. Immerse pork rind in boiling water, remove, scrape off any bristles, cut into thin strips. Wash leek and slice into thin rounds. Chop tomatoes, discarding seeds and hard parts. Clean and crush garlic. Preheat oven to 375° F.

2. Put all ingredients into earthenware casserole, add salt to taste (about ½ teaspoon—beans are better undersalted) and a few twists of the pepper grinder. Add water to cover, plus 1 inch, stir. Cover tightly, put in preheated oven, bake for 2½ hours without uncovering. Serve hot.

197. FAGIOLINI TRIFOLATI
(*Sautéed String Beans*)

SERVES 4 OR 5

1 pound cleaned string beans

2 cloves garlic

3 tablespoons butter

2 tablespoons olive oil

Salt and pepper

2 tablespoons chopped parsley

1 bouillon cube

¾ cup hot water

1. Cut string beans in half. Clean garlic.

2. Put butter and oil in a large frying pan, allow to melt, add garlic and string beans, stir.

3. Cook on medium heat for a few minutes, add a little salt, freshground pepper and the chopped parsley, stir and cook for another few minutes, in total no more than 10.

4. Dissolve the bouillon cube in ¾ cup hot water, add to the string beans, stir, cover and cook on a low flame for another 20 to 30 minutes, or until most of the water is absorbed and the string beans are tender. If necessary, add more water while cooking, but be sure it's all evaporated at the end. There should be very little sauce. Serve with all meats; it's a very versatile vegetable.

198. FAGIOLINI IN UMIDO
(*Stewed String Beans*)

SERVES 5 TO 6

1 pound stringbeans, Blue Lake
    variety if possible

1 small onion

5 peeled Italian plum tomatoes
    or 5 tablespoons tomato
    sauce

Salt

½ teaspoon fennel seeds

¼ cup olive oil

1 bouillon cube

Pepper

1. Clean string beans and rinse. Clean and slice onion thin. Chop tomatoes, discarding seeds and hard parts.

2. Boil the string beans for 15 minutes in 3 cups lightly salted water, drain. Bruise the fennel seeds with a wooden mallet.

3. Put oil and onion in a saucepan, simmer for a few minutes, then

add the string beans, fennel seeds, bouillon cube, some fresh-ground pepper, and stir. Allow to cook for 5 minutes.

4. Add the tomatoes or tomato sauce, stir, lower the flame and cover. Cook for another 15 to 20 minutes, taste for seasoning, correct if necessary. If the sauce seems a little too thin (it should be rather tacky), cook uncovered for another few minutes. Serve hot, with any meat.

199. FINOCCHI SALTALI
(*Fennel Bulbs Sautéed*)

SERVES 4

4 large fennel bulbs
3 tablespoons butter or margarine
Salt
½ cup grated Parmesan or Swiss cheese

1. Clean and wash fennel. Cut into quarters and then cut each quarter into slices.

2. Heat butter in a frying pan, add slices of fennel, stir. Cook on medium flame for 15 to 20 minutes, stirring often to avoid sticking. About halfway through cooking time, sprinkle with salt and add a little water if necessary.

3. When the fennel is easily pierced with a fork, sprinkle with the grated cheese, and take to the table at once, preferably in the cooking utensil. Serve with dry meats such as roasts, steaks or boiled chicken. Also good with fish.

200. FUNGHI TRIFOLATI
(*Sautéed Mushrooms*)

SERVES 4 OR 5

1 pound good, fresh mushrooms,
   preferably porcini
2 tablespoons olive oil
3 tablespoons butter
2 cloves garlic

1 bouillon cube
Pepper
2 tablespoons chopped parsley
Salt

1. Clean mushrooms carefully with a small, sharp knife, rinse but do not wash much. Mushrooms absorb water and if they are soaked become waterlogged and lose flavor. Cut each of the larger mushrooms into quarters and then into slices. Slice the smaller ones without quartering.

2. Heat oil and butter in a frying pan, add the garlic, let it get brown, then add the mushrooms. Stir and cook for a few minutes on medium flame.

3. Add the bouillon cube, some fresh-ground pepper and the chopped parsley, stir again, cover and cook on a low flame for about 15 minutes.

4. Uncover, taste for seasoning, if necessary add a little salt or more pepper, remove the garlic and serve at once. In Tuscany this is the king of vegetables, the very best of *contorni*. Serve it with steak, roast beef or roast game.

201. FUNGHI IN UMIDO
(*Mushrooms in Tomato Sauce*)

SERVES 4 TO 5

Mushrooms can be served with anything. They are excellent as a vegetable, but they are also good as a meat substitute, and this recipe makes very good sauce for *polenta*.

1 *pound fresh, good quality mushrooms*	A *handful of* nepitella (*see note on recipe No.* 122)
3 *cloves garlic*	1/3 *cup olive oil*
3 *peeled Italian plum tomatoes or 3 tablespoons tomato sauce*	1 *bouillon cube*
	Juice of 1/2 *lemon* (*optional*)
	Pepper

1. Clean mushrooms well; wash carefully, removing all sand; cut into thin slices. Clean garlic. Chop tomatoes, removing seeds and hard parts. Wash *nepitella*, remove hard stalks.

2. Put oil, garlic and *nepitella* into a large frying pan, allow to simmer until garlic is brown, then remove both garlic and *nepitella* and add mushrooms and bouillon cube. Stir, lower the flame and allow to

cook for about 10 to 15 minutes, adding very little water if necessary to keep the pan from drying out.

3. Add the tomatoes, lemon juice, and a little fresh-ground pepper. Stir, cook for another 10 minutes, serve hot.

202. LENTICCHIE I
(*Lentils I*)

SERVES 4

Lentils are a winter favorite. They are eaten with sausages, with pork, with roasts or boiled meats. On January 1st, lentils are served in every home because to eat them the first day of the year brings luck. Following are two recipes, one with tomato and one without. Don't worry if any are left over, they taste even better reheated.

5 ounces dried lentils
1 small stalk celery
A few leaves of parsley
1 bay leaf
1 small onion
1 slice prosciutto (*Italian raw ham*)

2 tablespoons butter
1 bouillon cube
⅔ cup hot water
Salt

1. Soak lentils overnight. Make a *bouquet garni* with the cleaned and washed celery, parsley, bay leaf and ½ of the onion. Rinse the soaked lentils, cover with water, add the *bouquet garni* and cook for 45 minutes, or until soft.

2. Chop the remaining ½ onion and the *prosciutto*. Drain the lentils, remove the *bouquet garni*. Put the butter in a frying pan, add the chopped onion and ham, allow to simmer for a few minutes, add the lentils, stir, cover and lower the flame.

3. Dissolve the bouillon cube in ⅔ cup hot water. Add to the frying pan, stir. Cook, uncovered, for about 30 minutes, or until the sauce is thick. Taste for seasoning, add a little salt if necessary. Serve hot.

Note: A *bouquet garni* is made by tying together the vegetables used, usually celery, parsley, bay leaf and basil, sometimes onion. It is best to use a piece of white string or a strong white thread.

203. LENTICCHIE II
(*Lentils II*)

SERVES 4

5 ounces dried lentils
1 small carrot
½ stalk celery
1 small onion
¼ cup olive oil

1 bouillon cube
1 cup hot water
Salt and pepper
1 tablespoon tomato paste

1. Soak lentils overnight in warm water. Clean and wash carrot, celery and onion, chop fine.

2. Drain lentils, rinse, cover with water and cook for about 45 minutes or until soft. Drain.

3. Put oil and chopped vegetables in a saucepan, cook on medium flame for a few minutes, then add the lentils, salt and pepper to taste, stir, cook on low flame for another 5 to 10 minutes.

4. Dissolve the tomato paste and bouillon cube in 1 cup hot water, add to the lentils, stir, cover and cook on low flame for another 45 minutes, or until the lentils are very soft. If 45 minutes is not enough, cook longer, but be sure to add more water. Lentils are good when very soft. Serve with winter roasts, pork or game.

204. FRIGO DI PATATE, CIPOLLE E ZUCCHINI
(*Fried Potatoes, Onions and Zucchini Squash*)

SERVES 4

The name of this dish is misleading because it isn't just fried but also baked. At any rate, it's delicious, and in our house the portion below is just enough for three.

1 pound Maine or firm yellow
    potatoes
2 large onions
3 large zucchini squash
⅓ cup olive oil

10 leaves fresh basil or 1
    teaspoon dried
⅔ cup pomarola (*see recipe No.
    86*)
Salt and pepper

1. Peel potatoes, wash, cut into fairly thick slices. Clean and slice onions. Wash zucchini, cut off ends, cut into rounds.

2. Put most of the oil into a frying pan, add the onions, allow to wilt on medium flame. Add potatoes and cook for another 10 minutes, stirring often to avoid browning the onions too much. Preheat the oven to 350° F.

3. Add zucchini, stir and cook for another few minutes, until the zucchini have wilted somewhat. Chop the basil leaves.

4. With the remaining oil grease a baking dish, then pour the contents of the frying pan into it. Add the *pomarola*, sprinkle with a teaspoon of salt, some fresh-ground pepper and the chopped basil. Bake for about 20 to 25 minutes, serve hot.

205. INSALATA DI PATATE SAPORITA
(*Spicy Potato Salad*)

SERVES 4 TO 6

2 *pounds good quality Maine or firm yellow potatoes*
2 *eggs, hard-boiled*
1 *stalk celery*
A *handful of parsley*
5 *leaves fresh basil or 1 teaspoon dried*
3 *small sour gherkins*

2 *tablespoons capers*
3 *anchovy fillets*
3 *small onions*
1 *green pepper*
Wine *vinegar, as needed*
Olive *oil, as needed*
Salt *and pepper*

1. Boil the potatoes in their skins for 30 minutes, allow to cool slightly, then peel and slice. Chop the eggs. Wash and clean the celery, parsley and basil, dry and chop. Chop gherkins, capers and anchovies.

2. Clean the onions and the green pepper, slice, cover with wine vinegar, boil for 5 minutes, drain.

3. Put all ingredients in a bowl, season with olive oil, salt, fresh-ground black pepper and vinegar, used sparingly. Toss well and taste. If necessary, add more oil, vinegar, salt or pepper.

206. PATATE CONDITE ALLA TOSCANA
(*Tuscan Potato Salad*)

SERVES 4 TO 6

2 pounds good quality Maine or
    firm yellow potatoes
1 small onion
1 clove garlic
1 egg, hard-boiled
½ cup grated Pecorino or
    Parmesan cheese

½ cup cottage or ricotta *cheese*
Olive oil, as needed
Wine vinegar, as needed
Salt and pepper

1. Boil the potatoes in their skins, allow to cool, peel and slice. Meanwhile, clean and chop the onion and garlic, chop the egg.

2. Put the chopped vegetables and egg in a bowl, add the *Pecorino* (it's spicier than Permesan, but if unavailable Parmesan is equally good), the cottage cheese or *ricotta*, 5 tablespoons of oil and 5 teaspoons of vinegar, salt and pepper to taste.

3. Stir well to blend all ingredients, and note that this sauce should be on the liquid side. If it is not liquid enough, add more olive oil and, proportionately, more vinegar.

4. Add the potatoes, toss. This salad is very good with roasts or boiled meats.

207. POLPETTE DI PATATE AL FORNO
(*Baked Potato Croquettes*)

SERVES 4 TO 6

This is one recipe where the Parmesan cheese can be bought already grated.

2 pounds potatoes
2 cloves garlic
A handful of parsley
½ cup grated Parmesan cheese

3 eggs
Salt and white pepper
Olive oil, as needed

1. Wash potatoes and cook in lightly salted water for about 25 minutes or until tender. Drain, peel and mash with a fork—in other words, not completely, like a purée, but partially, leaving a few lumps. Preheat the oven to 400° F.

2. Clean and wash garlic and parsley, chop fine. Put potatoes, Parmesan, eggs, chopped garlic and parsley into a large bowl, add a little salt and some fresh-ground white pepper and stir until well blended.

3. Shape into croquettes about the size of an egg. Pour about 3 tablespoons of oil into a baking dish, distribute it evenly over the bottom and line up the croquettes in it. Put into the hot oven, bake for about 20 minutes and serve hot or warm.

208. STAMPO DI RICOTTA E PATATE
(*Ricotta and Potato Pie*)

SERVES 4 OR 5

1 *pound potatoes*
1¼ *cups* ricotta *cheese*
3 *whole eggs plus* 1 *egg white*
   beaten stiff
Salt

1 *teaspoon potato flour or corn*
   starch (*optional*)
Butter, as needed
Bread crumbs

1. Peel and boil the potatoes and, when cooked, drain the water and put the potatoes back on the flame to dry, tossing constantly. Mash and let cool. Preheat the oven to 350° F.

2. Mix cold mashed potatoes with *ricotta*, 3 whole eggs, the beaten egg white, and salt to taste. If mixture is too loose, add corn starch or potato flour. Blend well.

3. Butter well the bottom and sides of a small, deep pyrex dish and sprinkle with fine bread crumbs. Pour *ricotta* and potato mixture into it, smooth top with a spatula, and bake for about 20 minutes, or until the top is golden brown and a toothpick inserted into the center comes out dry.

4. Serve medium hot, with pot roasts, *scaloppine*, or with recipe No. 85 as a light first course.

209. PEPERONATA
(*Pepper Stew*)

SERVES 4 OR 5

1 *large or 2 medium-sized onions*
3 *large sweet peppers, green or*
  yellow
3 *large Maine or firm yellow*
  potatoes
⅓ *cup olive oil*

One *16-ounce can peeled Italian*
  plum tomatoes
1 *bouillon cube*
Pepper
Salt

1. Clean the onion and slice thin. Clean and wash the peppers, remove seeds and inside membrane, cut into strips, lengthwise. Peel and dice potatoes.

2. Put oil and sliced onion in saucepan, let simmer for a few minutes, being careful not to brown the onions. Add peppers, cover and lower flame, cook for about 10 minutes.

3. Add tomatoes, opening each one with your hands and discarding seeds and hard pieces. Stir well, cook covered for another 10 or 15 minutes, add potatoes, bouillon cube and a little fresh-ground pepper. Cover and continue to cook. After 10 minutes check the liquid level. Peppers and tomatoes make liquid, potatoes absorb it. If the flame is kept low and the pan is covered the liquid should be sufficient to cook the potatoes; if some liquid has evaporated and the *peperonata* gets too thick, add a little hot water and stir. This eliminates sticking. Cook for 30 minutes after the potatoes have been added, taste for seasoning, add salt if necessary, serve hot.

210. PINZIMONIO
(*Olive Oil Dip*)

The simplest, most sophisticated dip for raw vegetables. Raw artichokes, fennel, celery, radishes, etc. are all suitable for dipping in this Tuscan sauce which is nothing but excellent olive oil, a touch of fresh-ground pepper and salt. By putting a knife or a small piece of bread under a dish one creates a slightly inclined plane. Pour a few tablespoons of olive oil into the bottom of this inclined plane, add the other ingredients

—personally I like to add a few drops of lemon juice, but Tuscans frown on that—and stir everything with the piece of raw vegetable you're dipping.

There is one other vegetable that, in my opinion, is ideal for the *pinzimonio*. But it has to be cooked first. And in order to be really perfect, it has to be fresh. The vegetable I mean is asparagus. Clean, wash and boil until tender in lightly salted water. To avoid breaking the tips, tie asparagus together in groups of 7 or 8. Remove from water, allow to drain well, serve lukewarm. Make a *pinzimonio* at the bottom of a plate and dip.

Note: When having *pinzimonio* with asparagus I sometimes add the yolk of a hard-boiled egg to the dip, crush it with a fork and incorporate it into the oil, lemon, salt and pepper. Try it, it's sheer heaven!

211. PISELLI ALLA TOSCANA
(*Peas Tuscan Style*)

SERVES 4 TO 5

1 clove garlic
5 slices blanched bacon
¼ cup olive oil
1 pound shelled fresh, frozen or
    canned peas

Salt
1 tablespoon chopped parsley
Sugar, as needed

1. Clean garlic and slice thin. Chop the bacon.
2. Put oil, bacon and garlic into a large frying pan, simmer on medium flame until the garlic is light brown, add peas, salt to taste, add parsley, stir.
3. Cook on low flame until peas are tender. Young, tender peas will cook quickly without any water; older, tougher peas will take longer to cook and may require a ladle of hot water to prevent them from sticking.
4. When ready sprinkle with 1 teaspoon of sugar, stir. Allow to cook for another minute or 2, serve hot with white or red meats, grilled or roasted.

Note: Remember that canned peas have to be thoroughly drained and require much less cooking time than fresh or frozen peas.

212. PISELLI AL BURRO E PROSCIUTTO
(*Peas with Butter and Ham*)

SERVES 4 TO 5

For this dish, it's essential that the peas be tiny, tender and young; preferably the first peas of spring. If using canned or frozen peas, use the smallest you can find.

1 *pound shelled fresh, frozen or canned peas*
1 *small white onion*
2 *slices* prosciutto (*Italian raw ham*) *or 4 slices blanched bacon*

4 *tablespoons butter*
Sugar, as needed
Salt and white pepper

1. Put fresh or frozen peas in a bowl of water. Clean the onion and chop fine. Chop the *prosciutto* or bacon.
2. Put the butter, chopped ham or bacon and onion in an earthenware casserole or enameled saucepan. Add 1 teaspoon sugar, a little salt and some fresh-ground white pepper. Drain the peas, allowing some of the water to remain clinging to them. Add to the casserole, stir, cover, and put on a medium flame.
3. Allow to cook for 10 minutes, uncover, taste. Correct seasoning if necessary. Depending on the quality of the peas, they may need from 10 to 20 minutes of cooking time. If there is too much liquid, cook uncovered for a few minutes longer. The final consistency should be creamy, not soupy. Serve hot, with steaks, pot roasts or roasts.

213. SFORMATO DI PISELLI
(*Pea Custard*)

SERVES 4 TO 6

This is an old Tuscan recipe that slightly resembles the new *cuisine minceur*. But in those days nobody worried about an additional inch on the waistline, so a little butter and a little flour are used here. This dish is very delicate both in taste and appearance. Serve with tender, pink

roast beef and creamy mashed potatoes and your table will be a study
in pastel colors.

1 *small white onion*	*Salt and white pepper*
2 *ounces* prosciutto (*Italian raw*	2 *tablespoons flour*
ham)	1 *cup good chicken broth*
Butter, as needed	2 *eggs*
1 *tablespoon parsley, chopped*	2 *tablespoons grated Parmesan*
fine	*cheese*
1¼ *pounds shelled peas, fresh,*	*Bread crumbs, as needed*
frozen or canned	

1. Clean the onion and chop fine. Chop the *prosciutto*, both the
lean parts and the fat.

2. Put 2 tablespoons butter, the chopped onion, ham and parsley
into a frying pan. Simmer for a few minutes, add the peas, sprinkle
with a little salt and fresh-ground white pepper, cover and allow to
cook on low flame until peas are done. Frozen peas will cook faster than
fresh; canned peas cook fastest of all.

3. Take about ⅓ of the cooked peas and purée them: use either a
food mill or a blender. Preheat oven to 325° F.

4. Make a béchamel with 2 tablespoons butter, the flour and the
chicken broth. Add the puréed peas, the whole peas with their pan
juices, the eggs, the Parmesan and stir well. Pour into a baking dish that
has been buttered well and sprinkled with bread crumbs, and bake for
about 20 to 25 minutes, or until the *sformato* has set. Unmold on a
warm platter and serve at once.

214. SPINACI ALLA FIORENTINA
(*Spinach Florentine*)

SERVES 4 OR 5

The name of this dish is almost redundant, since in terms of international gastronomy to say "florentine" is to say "spinach." Actually,
spinach made this way is eaten all over Tuscany, and many recipes in
this book are florentine and do not contain spinach. I've given this
recipe its local name because many cooks may be familiar with it and
now will know that in Tuscany it's called "spinach florentine." Further-

more, it's a dish eaten here often, and holds its own proudly in this collection of Tuscan specialties. Finally, it happens to be one of my personal favorites, the perfect vegetable to serve with veal, chicken, pork, eggs or mashed potatoes.

12 ounces cleaned fresh or
    frozen spinach
2 cloves garlic
Butter, as needed

Salt and white pepper
1½ cups milk
5 tablespoons flour
½ cup grated Parmesan cheese

1. If fresh, wash spinach well and cook for 10 minutes without adding extra water. If frozen, follow directions on package. When ready, drain, let cool, squeeze out remaining water, chop.

2. Put cleaned garlic and 2 tablespoons butter in frying pan, let garlic brown over high heat, remove it, add chopped spinach, lower the flame, stir, let remaining water evaporate. Add salt to taste and a few twists of the white pepper grinder. Preheat the oven to 400° F.

3. Meanwhile, heat the milk, but do not let it boil. In a saucepan melt 5 tablespoons butter, add the flour, stir well and, as soon as it's incorporated, add the milk. Lower the flame, stir, allow to thicken. As soon as the béchamel is ready, add just a touch of salt and the grated Parmesan.

4. Incorporate half of this white sauce into the chopped spinach. Mix well in order to get a homogeneous mixture. Put into a buttered baking dish, smooth out the surface with a spatula, cover with the remaining béchamel. Put into the oven for 8 to 10 minutes, just enough to give the top a touch of color; remove and serve hot directly from the baking dish.

215. TORTA DI PORRI E PATATE
(*Leek and Potato Pie*)

SERVES 4 TO 6

2 pounds potatoes
2 pounds leeks
6 tablespoons olive oil
⅔ cup flour
2 anchovy fillets
2 tablespoons capers

2 tablespoons black olives,
    pitted and chopped
Salt and pepper
3 tablespoons grated Parmesan
    cheese

1. Peel the potatoes, wash, dice and boil in salted water. When ready, drain, mash and reserve. Meanwhile, clean and wash the leeks, slice into rounds. Heat 5 tablespoons of olive oil in a large frying pan, add the leeks, simmer on medium flame for about 10 minutes, stirring often to avoid sticking. When ready the leeks should be cooked but not browned. Remove from flame and reserve.

2. When the mashed potatoes are cool, add the flour and work into a dough. With the remaining oil, grease a round pyrex dish. Separate the dough into 2 pieces, one slightly larger than the other, and line the pyrex with the larger piece, using your hands to spread it out as evenly as possible. Preheat the oven to 400° F.

3. Cut the anchovies into 4 or 5 pieces each. Add capers, olives and anchovies to the cooked leeks, stir, taste for seasoning, add salt or pepper if necessary (for my taste a little pepper is enough; there is salt in both the anchovies and olives).

4. Transfer this mixture to the pyrex dish lined with dough, sprinkle with the grated Parmesan cheese. With the remaining dough, make a round and cover the pyrex dish, pinching the edges in order to close the pie. Make a few holes near the center of the top crust so that the steam can escape while cooking.

5. Bake for about 25 minutes or until golden brown, serve at once.

216. TORTINO DI ZUCCHINI ALLA FIORENTINA
(*Florentine Zucchini Casserole*)

SERVES 4 OR 5

The basic difference between the Tuscan *tortino* (which I've called "casserole" but which literally translates as "small pie" or "pielet") and an omelet, is that the omelet is done in a frying pan on top of the stove, while the *tortino* is a baked dish. As a result of the oven heat, the casserole is lighter, softer on the surface, and can be used as a meat substitute or as a light first course, while an omelet, at least in Tuscany, is usually an appetizer or part of a light supper. The vegetable base for a *tortino* can be anything: artichokes, eggplant, spinach (boiled, drained, squeezed and chopped) or even potatoes.

A *small handful of parsley*   8 *eggs*
4 *large or 8 small zucchini*   *Salt*
    squash   6 *tablespoons milk*
Flour, as needed   1 *teaspoon oregano*
Peanut or corn oil, as needed

1. Clean and wash parsley, dry and chop fine. Wash zucchini, cut off ends, slice into thin, even rounds. Dust lightly with flour. Preheat the oven to 400° F.

2. Put a little oil in a frying pan, when hot fry the zucchini rounds on both sides. Take out fried rounds with slotted spoon and drain on absorbent paper. When the oil has been absorbed put the fried zucchini into an oiled baking dish.

3. Break eggs into a bowl, add salt to taste, the milk, chopped parsley and oregano. Beat together with a fork. When the mixture is well blended pour into the baking dish, covering the fried zucchini rounds. Bake for about 20 minutes, or until the eggs set. Serve at once.

217. VERDURE PRIMAVERA
(*Spring Vegetables*)

SERVES 4 OR 5

2 *carrots*   4 *tablespoons olive oil*
2 *potatoes*   *Salt and pepper*
2 *zucchini squash*   ½ *cup peas*
1 *clove garlic*   1 *bouillon cube*
2 *peeled Italian plum tomatoes*

1. Clean, wash and dice the carrots, potatoes and zucchini. Clean garlic and chop fine. Chop the tomatoes, discarding seeds and hard parts.

2. Put oil and garlic into a saucepan, simmer on medium flame. After 2 minutes add the diced vegetables, except the tomatoes, a little salt and pepper, and the peas, stir and continue to cook for another 5 minutes.

3. Add the tomatoes and bouillon cube, stir, cover and cook for another 20 to 30 minutes, or until the carrots are cooked through. If necessary, add a ladle or 2 of hot water to prevent sticking. Taste for seasoning, correct if necessary. Serve hot, with roasts or grilled meats.

218. SCARPACCIA
(*Zucchini and Onion Pizza*)

SERVES 6 OR 7

The *scarpaccia* is a sort of *pizza* made with zucchini squash and onions. It's characteristic of the city where I live, Camaiore. No one knows where the name comes from; literally and liberally translated, it means "big old shoe," and some claim that it's meant to imply that this *pizza* should be as flat as possible, like the sole of a very old pair of shoes. Other places in Tuscany don't seem to know it, and I include it in this collection because it's very good, and quick and easy to make. Here it's made in spring, when the zucchini are small and full of flowers. It can be made without flowers, but the zucchini should always be small—the large ones have too much water.

1 *pound small zucchini squash* *with flowers*	¼ *cup grated Parmesan cheese*
3 *scallions or 1 large onion*	*Salt and pepper*
About 1 cup water	*Flour, as needed*
2 *eggs*	½ *cup olive oil*

1. Preheat the oven to 375° F. Wash the zucchini squash, cut off the ends, slice into thin rounds, cut up the flowers with a pair of scissors. Clean the onions and chop fine.

2. Put cut vegetables into a bowl, add about 1 cup of water, the eggs, the grated Parmesan, 1 teaspoon salt, a few twists of the pepper grinder, and enough flour to give the mixture the consistency of pancake batter.

3. Pour ¼ cup of the oil into a large baking dish, distribute it evenly over the bottom, pour in the zucchini and onion mixture to a depth of about ½-inch. If there is more, use an additional baking dish, but do not make the *scarpaccia* any higher. Spread the mixture evenly with a spatula. Pour the rest of the oil over it.

4. Bake for about 30 minutes or until the top is golden brown and the bottom is crisp.

Note: This tasty *pizza* can be used both as a vegetable and as an appetizer, and it is equally good hot or cold.

219. ZUCCHINI CON ORIGANO
(*Zucchini Squash with Oregano*)

SERVES 4

Origano or oregano is not frequently used in Tuscan cooking. It seems to have entered Italian cooking in general at a late date. The first mention we find of it is in the 16th century when it was used to give a pleasant aroma to pork sausages and anchovies.

Nowadays, it has acquired lasting fame as the herb that gets sprinkled on *pizza*. In this recipe the indication is for oregano seeds, not for the leaves, but in case you can't get the seeds the little dried leaves will do just as well, provided they are reasonably fresh and still full of their spicy perfume.

> *1 pound young, firm zucchini squash*
> *¼ cup olive oil*
> *Salt and pepper*
> *1 teaspoon dried or fresh oregano, seeds or leaves*

1. Wash the zucchini, chop off both ends and cut into rounds.

2. Put the oil into a frying pan, add the zucchini, stir and cook on a high flame for a few minutes, stirring often.

3. Sprinkle with salt and fresh-ground pepper, lower the flame and cook for another 10 minutes, remembering to stir now and then. Sprinkle with the oregano and serve at once.

PANE E DOLCI
(*Breads and Sweets*)

220. PANE TOSCANO
(*Tuscan Bread*)

Spaghetti is the staple food of Southern Italy; rice is the basis of Northern Italian cooking; handmade egg noodle dough served in various ways is typical of Bologna and its fat region, the Emilia-Romagna; bread is all of these for Tuscany. Many country homes have a *forno a legna*, wood-burning oven, which is lit on Saturday, in order to provide fresh home-baked bread for Sunday, and not-so-fresh but always very edible bread for the rest of the week.

One of the most striking characteristics of Tuscan bread is the almost complete absence of salt. Now that I'm used to it, the presence of salt in bread actually bothers me. Saltless bread is good because of its neutral taste and practical because it does not attract water and therefore has a tendency to dry rather than get moldy.

In one of the "canti" of the *Divine Comedy*, Dante complains that the "bread of exile is bitter and salty." Some critics have attached a realistic meaning to the comment and claim that the great poet just missed his saltless Tuscan bread.

To make bread, any bread, is both very simple and very difficult. In the case of Tuscan bread the ingredients are just three, flour, water and yeast: the secret of success or failure is in the hands of the baker. If you've never made bread before, don't start with this recipe. Ask a friend with experience to make it for you, and watch. The quantities below make two good-sized loaves.

2 ounces brewer's yeast, very fresh
Lukewarm water, as needed (about 60° F.)
About 2 pounds whole wheat flour or 1¾ pounds white and ¼ pound
*   bran flour, mixed*

1. Put the yeast in a cup of warm water, break it up until it dissolves, add enough flour to make a soft dough. Keep in a warm place, allow to rise.

2. Put the flour on a large wood or marble surface, make a hole in the center. Start pouring water into this hole, working flour toward center, where the water is. When the flour has absorbed enough water add the yeast dough and work it in. Do it slowly, working with your hands to blend well. If necessary, add more water or more flour.

3. When dough is smooth, knead it for 5 to 10 minutes, lifting the ball of dough and hitting it on the table. It's ready when it will stand away from both your hands and the table.

4. Sprinkle a large bowl with flour and put the ball of dough into it. Cover with a linen cloth and allow to stand at room temperature for at least 30 minutes. The dough should at this point have doubled its size. Preheat the oven to 350° F.

5. Remove dough from bowl onto the flour-sprinkled surface, knead it again for 5 to 10 minutes. Shape into 2 loaves and put them on a baking sheet. Allow to stand in a warm place for another 15 or 20 minutes, or until the loaves double their size again.

6. Bake for about 30 minutes or until the bread is golden brown. Remove from the oven and allow to cool. Keeps well for at least 5 days.

221. SCHIACCIATA O FOCACCIA
(*Flat Bread*)

SERVES 4 TO 8

This flat, salty bread is usually eaten with ham, warm, in small quantities, as a mid-morning snack. In Lucca they make it very flat and crisp, in Florence and Pisa a little softer. Children love it.

> *Olive oil*
> *1 to 1½ cups bread dough (see previous recipe)*
> *Salt*

1. Spread a thin layer of olive oil on a baking sheet. Preheat the oven to 400° F.
2. Work the bread dough into a flat sheet about ½-inch thick, put on the oiled baking sheet, squeeze down with your hands, making it as even as possible.
3. Press the dough here and there, making little wells. Sprinkle with salt and with a little more olive oil and bake for about 10 minutes or until golden brown. Serve hot or warm—it can be eaten cold, but it's only half as good.

222. BISCOTTINI DI PRATO
(*Prato Biscuits*)

MAKES ABOUT 2 POUNDS

The word "biscuit" or "biscotto" tells us that this popular cookie is twice cooked. In fact "bis," twice or again; "cuit" or "cotto," cooked. The *biscottini di Prato* are an excellent example of bis-cooking, because in their final form they are hard and dry, and if stored in a tightly closed jar will keep for months. Tuscans dip their *biscottini* in Vin Santo in order to soften them a bit before eating—they are equally good dipped in hot tea or coffee.

½ *pound almonds*
About 2 pounds flour
8 eggs
About 2 pounds powdered sugar
1 teaspoon ammonium
        carbonate (if not available,
        use baking soda)

Salt
Butter, as needed

1. Scald the almonds in boiling water, peel, dry in a hot oven and chop coarse.
2. Sift most of the flour onto a large board or wooden table, make a well, add the eggs, the sugar, the ammonium carbonate and a pinch of salt. Preheat the oven to 375° F.
3. Work the ingredients together with your hands until they are well blended, add chopped almonds, work again until the dough is completely uniform.
4. Break up into balls the size of a large fist and roll them into sticks about ¾-inch wide. Place sticks on a buttered and floured baking sheet and bake for about 10 minutes.
5. Remove from oven and slice the sticks diagonally, into slices the thickness of a finger. Put them back into the hot oven and bake for another 20 to 30 minutes, until very dry.
6. Remove from oven, allow to cool, store in a tightly covered tin or jar.

223. BUCCELLATO DI LUCCA
(*"Danish" Luccan Style*)

SERVES 8 TO 10

This sweet bread has very ancient origins, the word comes from the Latin "buccellatum," which indicated a Roman military bread, destined to be cut into slices called "buccellae" which were then toasted and became biscuits. *Buccella* is the diminutive of *bucca*, mouth, and literally means "morsel."

This bread has existed in Lucca since mediaeval times, when "buccellatus" indicated a sweet bread that the vassal gave his feudal lord. Later it became popular as a confirmation gift, and the godparents gave big wheels of it to their godchildren. It was so popular that in 1578 the city of Lucca, finding itself in need of money for some urgent public works, levied a tax on the commerce of *buccellato,* a tax which remained until 1606.

1 *pound flour*
¾ *cup sugar*
⅔ *cup milk*
Grated rind of 1 orange
1 *whole egg plus 1 egg white*
5 *tablespoons butter, just melted*

½ *ounce brewer's yeast, dissolved in a little warm water*
1 *ounce raisins (optional)*
1 *ounce candied fruit, cubed (optional)*

1. Sift the flour into a mound, add the sugar, milk, orange rind, whole egg, butter and yeast. Mix everything well and knead briefly, adding additional flour if dough sticks to your hands.

2. If desired, add raisins and candied fruit—personally, I like the "poor" version of this sweet bread better.

3. Make a large doughnut with the dough, put on a buttered and floured baking sheet, cover with a towel and allow to stand for 2 to 3 hours in a warm place. Preheat the oven to 350° F.

4. When the dough has doubled in size, brush with the egg white and bake for 30 to 40 minutes. Serve warm or cold and, if any is left over, slice, and toast the slices.

224. BOMBOLONI
(*Doughnuts Tuscan Style*)

MAKES ABOUT 50

⅔ *cup milk*
½ *ounce brewer's yeast*
Flour, as needed
1 *pound mealy potatoes*
Sugar, as needed

1 *egg*
1 *tablespoon butter*
1 *teaspoon grated lemon rind*
Peanut oil or shortening for frying

1. Heat up a few tablespoons of milk, dissolve the yeast in it, add a little flour to make a soft dough.

2. Sift about 2 cups of flour, make a mound, put the yeast dough into a hole in the center of the mound. Allow the yeast to rise.

3. Meanwhile, peel wash and cook the potatoes, mash and allow to cool. Add to the yeast dough, then add 3 tablespoons of sugar, the egg, butter, lemon rind and the remaining milk.

4. Mix all ingredients together on a board. Knead the resulting dough for a few minutes, then divide into balls about the size of a small egg. Put in a warm place and allow to rise, covered.

5. Heat the oil or shortening and fry the balls of dough until golden brown. Do not fry more than 3 at one time. Remove with a slotted spoon, sprinkle with sugar, serve warm.

Note: If a doughnut shape is desired, press the center of the dough balls with your finger just before frying. Make sure the hole goes through to the other side.

225. LA TORTA DELLE QUATTRO TAZZE
(*Four-Cup Cake*)

SERVES 8

1 *cup sifted flour*
1 *cup corn meal*
1 *cup sugar*
1 *cup milk*

2 *teaspoons sifted baking powder*
Butter, as needed

1. Put all ingredients except butter into a bowl and mix well. Preheat oven to 375° F.

2. Pour the batter into a well-buttered, round cake pan.

3. Bake for 30 or 40 minutes. Stick a toothpick into the center; if it comes out dry, the cake is ready. Serve warm or cold.

226. TORTA DI NOCI E CAFFÈ
(*Coffee and Walnut Cake*)

SERVES 6 TO 8

½ cup butter
1 pound walnuts
2 cups flour
2 eggs

1½ cups sugar
⅔ cup very strong or Italian
    espresso coffee
1 tablespoon baking powder

1. Take the butter out of the refrigerator. Crack the walnuts, remove meats, put them through a nut grinder. The result should be 2 cups of fine, powdered walnuts—if more, save for other use. Butter a spring-form cake pan and sprinkle with flour. Preheat oven to 400° F.

2. Sift flour and baking powder together. Put it in a bowl, add eggs, sugar and butter. Work well with a spoon or spatula. Add powdered walnuts and cold coffee. Mix thoroughly, making sure ingredients are well blended.

3. Pour mixture into buttered cake form, put into the oven, bake for 30 to 45 minutes, until a toothpick stuck into the center comes out dry.

227. TORTA DI CACHI
(*Persimmon Cake*)

SERVES 8 OR 10

An old-fashioned cake made by mixing fresh fruit with dried fruit. If you have a persimmon tree and lots of its soft jelly-like fruits ripen at the same time, this cake is a pleasant way of using them.

½ cup chopped almonds
¾ cup chopped walnuts
⅓ cup chopped peanuts
1½ tablespoons chopped pinoli
    nuts
3 cups persimmon pulp, mashed

½ cup sugar
3 cups flour
1 teaspoon baking powder
1 teaspoon grated lemon or
    orange rind
Butter, as needed

1. Mix the almonds, walnuts, peanuts and *pinoli* with the persimmon pulp. Preheat the oven to 350° F.

2. Add the sugar, 3 cups of flour, the baking powder and grated citrus fruit rind, stir and blend thoroughly.

3. Butter a cake pan, sprinkle it with flour, pour in the batter and bake for about 40 minutes, or until toothpick stuck in the center comes out dry. Serve cold.

228. TORTA COI PINOLI
(*Pinoli Pie*)

SERVES 6 TO 8

This is a pie that is simple to make and hearty to eat. In our home we serve it with *Vin Santo*, but it's very good with sweet sherry, coffee or tea.

½ cup butter	1 ounce cleaned pinoli nuts
2 cups flour	2 cups milk
1 cup sugar	Salt
3 eggs	3½ ounces semolina
Marsala, Vin Santo or sweet	3 drops vanilla extract
sherry, if needed	Confectioners' sugar, as needed

1. Reserve 1 tablespoon of butter and make pie dough with the remaining butter, the flour, ½ cup of sugar and 1 egg. If the dough is too dry, add 1 or 2 tablespoons of wine. Make a ball and allow to stand while you prepare the filling. Chop *pinoli* nuts coarse.

2. Put milk in a saucepan, add remaining sugar, a pinch of salt, and the reserved tablespoon of butter; bring to the boiling point. With left hand pour in the *semolina* slowly, while stirring constantly with the right.

3. Cook on low flame for at least 15 minutes, stirring often in order to avoid lumping. Remove and allow to cool slightly, add the remaining 2 eggs, the vanilla and the *pinoli* nuts; stir well. Preheat the oven to 400° F.

4. Line a large pie plate with half the dough and pour in the *semolina* filling. Cover the pie with a lattice of the remaining dough and bake for about 30 minutes or until the crust is golden brown. Allow to cool and sprinkle with confectioners' sugar before serving.

229. TORTA DI BERNARDONE
(*Bernardone Cake*)

SERVES 6 TO 8

This cake is made with apples and pears in winter and with cherries or peaches in summer. A recipe similar to this is well known all over Tuscany, but I got this particular one from a restaurant that is run by three sisters, Silvia, Maria Grazia and Lia. They inherited a roadside bar from their father and, with the help of two industrious husbands, transformed it into a sophisticated *trattoria*. The food they serve is hearty and very Tuscan: *crostini* and other local *antipasti*, bean broth with homemade *pasta*, marvelous *tortelli* and excellent *pappardelle*, grilled meats and all the seasonal Tuscan vegetables, always served with their own virgin olive oil. At the end of such a substantial meal, it's a pleasure and a delight to eat the light, soft, fruity cake described in the recipe below. This is the winter version; in summer it can be made with 5 large peaches or 2 cups of pitted cherries instead of the apples and pears.

2 pears, peeled, cored and
    quartered
2 apples, peeled, cored and
    quartered
6 tablespoons butter
1½ cups sugar

3 eggs
2 cups flour, sifted with 2
    teaspoons baking powder
⅓ cup liqueur, anise, cherry or
    other
3 drops vanilla extract

1. Cut each of the pear and apple quarters into 3 or 4 thinner slices. Butter a large cake pan or 2 small ones (using about 1 teaspoon butter per pan); melt remaining butter on a very low flame. Preheat oven to 350° F.

2. Using a wooden spoon, beat together the sugar and eggs. Add the sifted flour and baking powder, stir well; then add the melted butter, stir well again; then add the liqueur. The mixture should be smooth and well blended.

3. Add the vanilla extract, stir, then pour the batter into the buttered cake pan and cover with the apple and pear slices. The surface should be entirely covered with fruit.

4. Put the cake in preheated oven and bake for 30 minutes, without opening the oven door. Check by sticking a toothpick in the center. If it comes out dry the cake is ready; otherwise, bake for another 10

minutes. Since this is a very liquid batter and the fruit releases juices as well, depending on the oven, the center of this cake may remain soft and pudding-like, but this does not alter its excellent flavor. Serve warm or cold.

230. TORTA GARFAGNANA
(*Garfagnana Cake*)

SERVES 8 OR 10

This tasty cake is made in the Garfagnana region as a fit ending for the big meal served on St. Peter's day. St. Peter is the beloved patron saint of this mountain region.

½ cup sweet almonds	3 eggs
¾ cup butter	1 shotglass of cherry brandy
2⅔ cups flour	⅔ cup milk
1 cup sugar	1 tablespoon cream of tartar
1 tablespoon aniseed	1 teaspoon baking soda
Grated peel of ½ lemon	

1. Drop almonds into boiling water for 1 minute, drain, peel. Dry with a white linen cloth, then chop fine.
2. Use about 1 teaspoon of the butter to grease a cake pan, sprinkle with flour. Melt the remaining butter on very low flame, allow to cool. Preheat oven to 375° F.
3. Put remaining flour, sugar, chopped almonds, aniseed and grated lemon rind in a large bowl, mix well. Make a hole in the center of this dry mixture, break eggs into it, add cooled butter and cherry brandy. Work everything together until mixture is smooth.
3. Warm the milk, add cream of tartar and baking soda. When it foams up add to the bowl, stir in order to blend well, pour into the prepared cake pan, put into the oven and bake for about 60 minutes or until a toothpick stuck into the center comes out dry. Remove from oven, serve warm or cold.

231. MANTOVANA
(*Cake Mantova Style*)

SERVES 6 TO 8

1 whole egg plus 3 yolks
1 cup sugar
1¾ cups flour
¾ cup butter, melted in a
    double boiler

1 teaspoon vanilla extract
½ teaspoon baking powder
½ cup almonds, peeled and cut
    into matchsticks

1. Put the whole egg and yolks into a large bowl, beat as for scrambled eggs. Preheat the oven to 375° F.

2. Add all other ingredients except almonds, blend well.

3. Butter a cake pan, sprinkle with flour, pour in the mixture, which should be rather liquid.

4. Sprinkle the almond matchsticks over the top, put into the oven, bake for 35 to 40 minutes, or until a toothpick stuck into the center comes out dry. Serve cold.

232. CROSTATA ALLA CREMA
(*Cream Pie*)

SERVES 6

DOUGH
6 tablespoons softened butter
3 cups sifted flour
¾ cup sugar
3 egg yolks

Pinch of salt
Pinch of baking soda
Grated rind of 1 lemon

CREAM FILLING
⅓ cup sugar
3 egg yolks
½ cup sifted flour

2 cups milk
Rind of 1 lemon
1 egg, lightly beaten

1. To make dough cut the softened butter into small pieces. Working quickly and with light fingers, combine butter with all other dough ingredients and make a ball. Cover and chill for about 1 hour.

2. Meanwhile, start the cream filling by stirring sugar into the egg yolks with a wooden spoon, then slowly add flour and milk. Make sure the resulting mixture is smooth. Add lemon rind.

3. Put cream mixture in a saucepan and, on a low flame, stir constantly until the cream coats the spoon and does not taste of flour. Preheat oven to 425° F.

4. Set cream aside to cool, discard lemon rind. Put about ⅔ of the dough on floured pastry board and roll out with a floured rolling pin, starting from center. Roll into a round about ⅙-inch thick and about 11 to 12 inches in diameter.

5. Grease a 9-inch spring-form pan and dust with flour. Fold the rolled-out dough into quarters, put it into the baking pan and unfold gently, fitting the dough into the corners and up the side of the pan. Pour in the cream filling, smooth out with a spatula. Make a lattice with the remaining dough and place over the cream filling. Brush with beaten egg.

6. Bake for about 30 minutes, reducing the oven to 350° F. for the last 15. The crust should be golden. Serve warm or cold.

CASTAGNE

In the Middle Ages, during periods of famine, *castagne*, chestnuts, in all forms, were a staple food. In the Tuscan mountains habit and memories of those days still prevail, and chestnuts are dried and reduced to flour now, even as they were a long time ago. The resulting product is called *farina dolce*, sweet flour, and it was once an important part of the winter diet of the marble workers in the Garfagnana mountains. They used it as a base for a cheap and nourishing gruel, *polenta di castagne*, which was eaten, whenever possible, with *biroldo*, a Tuscan pork sausage made with the ears, cartilage, fat and blood of the animal and spiced with pepper, nutmeg, cloves and coriander. Some manufacturers add raisins. These two substantial dishes were naturally washed down with plenty of good local wine.

Chestnut flour is still in use today. In Florence they make a good flat cake out of it, called *castagnaccio*, which is covered with *pinoli* nuts and scented with rosemary leaves, and then eaten with creamy *ricotta* cheese.

233. CASTAGNACCIO
(*Chestnut Flour Cake*)

SERVES 6 TO 8

2 tablespoons raisins
4 cups chestnut flour
6 tablespoons olive oil
3 tablespoons sugar
½ teaspoon salt
2 cups water

Butter, as needed
Bread crumbs, as needed
1 sprig fresh rosemary, or ½
    teaspoon dried
2 tablespoons pinoli *nuts*

1. Preheat oven to 400° F. Cover raisins with warm water. Sift the flour into a large bowl, add olive oil, sugar and salt. Stir well, then slowly add the water, always mixing with a wooden spoon. The result should be a semi-liquid batter.

2. Butter a cake pan, sprinkle it with bread crumbs. Drain the raisins. Remove the rosemary leaves from sprig and chop them coarse. Pour the batter into the cake pan, sprinkle with *pinoli* nuts, raisins and rosemary.

3. Bake for 40 to 50 minutes, until a light crust is formed on top and a toothpick stuck into the middle comes out dry. Serve hot or cold.

234. NECCI
(*Chestnut Flour Crêpes*)

SERVES 4 OR MORE

This simple dish presupposes the use of special gadgets, called *testi* or *ferri da cialde*. These are two iron dishes, each with a handle, which are brought together when the dough is put in the center and put on the fire. *Necci* are good wrapped around a tablespoonful of fresh *ricotta* cheese.

About 3 cups chestnut flour
Salt
Peanut oil

1. Work the flour with enough salted water to make a dough which should have the consistency of pancake dough.

2. Dip a pastry brush in the oil and grease the *testi* (Tuscans traditionally use twigs of rosemary instead of the brush), then put 2 or 3 tablespoons of the dough on one side, close the gadget, put into the embers or on the fire.

3. Turn after 1 minute, remove, continue to grease and cook until all dough is used. *Necci* should be eaten warm, as they come off the fire.

Note: The same dough can be fried in hot shortening and served sprinkled with sugar. It is then called *frittelle di farina dolce*.

SIENESE SWEETS

The three recipes that follow are from Siena, and seem to confirm the theory that, in the Middle Ages, this city was a caravan stopover. Trade routes from the Orient existed by land as well as by sea, and the caravans, coming as they did at reasonably regular intervals, rested and replenished their food stores at the same regular places. Many Italian cities, forming an oblique line that goes across the country from Southeast to Northwest, still retain signs of these visits, and historians have difficulty proving whether the visits were occasional or the city was actually a caravan resting place—it should be noted that in those days, when a caravan stopped somewhere, it wasn't simply an overnight stay, but a ten to fifteen day rest.

Siena is centrally located on the Italian peninsula, and its people have always been good merchants. It is therefore quite possible that the city was one of the resting places for the caravans which, loaded with silks, jewels and spices, were working their way north. The decidedly Oriental flavor of the sweets described below can be used as additional evidence for the thesis that the Arabs were at home in Siena during the Middle Ages.

Another theory has it that these recipes were brought back by the Crusaders, which only reconfirms their Oriental origin. All of the above notwithstanding, these sweets, as made now and, I daresay, for the last hundred years, have been modified by popular usage. Even if they retain the Oriental tendency for overspicing and oversweetening, they are no longer entirely Arab, but simply Sienese.

235. RICCIARELLI DI SIENA

MAKES ABOUT 50

3½ cups shelled almonds
2 cups sugar
2 egg whites

Confectioners' sugar, as needed
½ teaspoon vanilla extract
About 50 large white wafers*

1. Preheat the oven to 250° F. Drop the almonds into boiling water for 1 minute, drain and peel. Put them on a baking sheet and into the oven for 10 minutes, or until dry.

2. Measure the almonds again; there should be 3 cups. Put through a nut grinder, or if you don't have this gadget, through a coffee grinder. It is important to reduce the almonds to a powder without allowing their oil to ooze out.

3. Add the sugar, mix well, put through a sieve. If any pieces of almond remain, grind again. The resulting mixture of ground almonds and sugar must be fine and uniform.

4. Put egg whites into a bowl, beat a little with a fork. *Do not whip.* Add to the almond sugar mixture, then add ¾ cup of the confectioners' sugar and the vanilla. Blend well to obtain a soft, smooth paste.

5. Sprinkle table with confectioners' sugar, then put a tablespoon of the mixture on it and flatten it out with your hand. You should obtain a longish diamond about 3 inches thick and 1½ inches wide. Work with the flat side of a wide knife, always dipped in the confectioners' sugar.

6. Continue until all *ricciarelli* are made, then place each one on a wafer and place wafers on one or more baking sheets. Leave overnight.

7. Next morning preheat the oven to about 200° F., or on the lowest setting you have, put in the *ricciarelli* for about 15 minutes in order to dry them. They should emerge soft and white. Trim off any excess wafer, allow to cool, sprinkle generously with confectioners' sugar, serve or store.

* May be purchased at wholesale bakery suppliers.

236. CAVALLUCCI DI SIENA

MAKES ABOUT 30

1½ cups sugar
⅔ cup water
1 cup cleaned walnuts, chopped
Flour, as needed
⅓ cup candied orange, chopped

1 teaspoon powdered cinnamon
and cloves combined
2 teaspoons powdered anise
Butter, as needed

1. Put sugar into a saucepan, add ⅔ cup water. Cook on medium flame until the syrup, when taken between two fingers, makes a thread.

2. Remove syrup from flame, add walnuts, 3 cups flour, candied orange and spices. Mix carefully but thoroughly. Preheat the oven to 275° F.

3. Flour part of the kitchen table—wood, stone or plastic top— and pour the mixture onto it. Pat it down with your hands, then even it with a spatula. It should be ½-inch thick and as even as possible. Butter a baking sheet and sprinkle with flour.

4. Cut the flattened mixture into diamonds, about 1½ inches per side. Raise carefully with a narrow metal spatula or wide knife and place each one on the baking sheet, leaving at least 2 inches between them. Bake for 45 minutes, checking once or twice in order to avoid browning. The resulting cookie should be white and not too hard.

237. PANFORTE DI SIENA
(*Spice Cake Siena Style*)

SERVES 6 TO 10

This is a very spicy cake, usually eaten in small quantities. Put in a cookie box, it keeps for at least one month.

1½ cups peeled almonds,
    chopped
1 cup cleaned walnuts, chopped
2 cups candied watermelon,
    chopped
4 tablespoons candied orange,
    chopped
Flour, as needed

¼ teaspoon powdered coriander
½ teaspoon powdered cloves
    and nutmeg combined
1¾ teaspoons powdered
    cinnamon
1½ cups sugar
10 to 12 large white wafers*

1. Put the chopped almonds, walnuts and candied fruit on a large floured board. Sprinkle with the powdered coriander, cloves and nutmeg, and with ¾ teaspoon of the powdered cinnamon. Add ¾ cup sifted flour, mix well.

2. Put the sugar in a small container with a thick bottom, in old days there was a special copper pan for this operation. Put on a medium flame and let the sugar melt. Keep stirring until the thick syrup makes a little ball between your fingers, then remove from fire.

3. Pour syrup onto the nuts–candied fruit–flour mixture. Using your hands, blend everything well. Make a round, flat patty, about 1-inch thick. Preheat the oven to 300° F.

4. Cover a baking sheet with the wafers, put the patty on these wafers. Mix 2 tablespoons of flour with the remaining teaspoon of cinnamon and sprinkle the mixture over the *panforte*.

5. Bake for about 30 minutes, or until dry. Remove from baking sheet, cut off excess wafer with kitchen shears and brush off excess flour and cinnamon with a baker's brush. Serve when cold, cut into small squares.

* May be purchased at wholesale bakery suppliers.

LUCCAN PIES

Lucca, one of the more interesting Tuscan provinces, has several characteristic breads and sweets. Among them are a series of *torte*, pies, with fillings that can be either sweet, as in recipe No. 240, or salt-and-peppery, as in the case of recipe No. 241.

There are several dough recipes, both sweet and non-sweet. I give one for each type. The fillings are many, but I will list only two for each type—your imagination, and the ingredients you happen to have at hand, can provide you with others.

238. SFOGLIA PER TORTA DOLCE
(*Sweet Dough*)

FOR ONE PIE

1⅓ cups flour
⅓ cup sugar
1 egg
6 tablespoons plus 1 teaspoon butter, softened

1. Work all ingredients together until the resulting dough is smooth.
2. Make a ball with the dough and hit it several times against the table: this procedure improves the consistency. Allow to rest for about 30 minutes.
3. Roll out into a large circle and line a pie plate with it. With what is left over, make a lattice top to cover the filling.

239. SFOGLIA PER TORTA COI BECCHI
(*Non-Sweet Dough*)

FOR ONE PIE

2½ cups flour
1 egg
Salt
⅓ cup olive oil

1. Work together flour, egg, a pinch of salt and about ⅓ cup olive oil. Add a little water if necessary.

2. When the dough is smooth, make it into a ball and hit it on the table several times. Allow to rest for 30 minutes.

3. Roll out into a disk no more than ½-inch thick. Cut out a circle and line a pie plate with it. Let remaining dough hang over the edge of the plate. When filling is inside cut the edge of the dough into 2-inch lengths, and pinch each piece with your fingers. This will form little peaks around the pie which justify its name: *Torta coi becchi*, pie with beaks.

240. TORTA DI RISO CON CANDITI
(*Rice Pie with Candied Fruit*)

SERVES 6 TO 8

2 cups milk
1 cup water
6 to 8 tablespoons sugar
1 heaping cup short-grained rice
⅓ cup raisins
1 egg
3 tablespoons candied fruit, diced

3 tablespoons pinoli *nuts*
2 to 3 drops vanilla extract
3 tablespoons cognac or other liqueur
1 portion sweet dough (recipe No. 238)

1. Put milk, water and sugar into a casserole, bring to the boiling point, add rice, lower flame and cook for about 15 minutes, until all liquid is absorbed and rice is soft. Allow to cool. Meanwhile, steep raisins in a cup of hot water. Preheat the oven to 400° F.

2. Drain the raisins; add them plus all other ingredients to the cooked rice, mix thoroughly, fill the dough shell, cover with lattice top.

3. Bake for about 40 minutes, allow to cool slightly. Serve either warm or cold.

241. TORTA PEPATA
(*Peppery Pie*)

SERVES 6 TO 8

1 *heaping cup short-grained rice*
About 6 ounces Swiss chard,
    boiled, drained and
    chopped
3 *tablespoons chopped parsley*
3 *eggs*
⅓ *cup grated Parmesan or*
    Pecorino *cheese*

Salt and pepper
Nutmeg
Powdered cinnamon (*optional*)
3 *ounces* ricotta *cheese*
    (*optional*)
1 *portion non-sweet dough*
    (*recipe No. 239*)

1. Boil rice for 20 minutes in lightly salted water, drain, allow to cool. Preheat oven to 375° F.

2. Mix rice, Swiss chard, parsley, eggs, grated cheese, salt and at least 1 teaspoon fresh-ground black pepper. Add a touch of nutmeg, a pinch of cinnamon and the *ricotta*, if desired.

3. Blend well. Line the pie plate with dough, put in filling, make the peaks around the edge (see recipe No. 239). Bake for about 40 minutes or until the crust is golden brown. Remove from oven, cool slightly, serve warm or cold with plenty of good, young, dry red wine.

242. TORTA RUSTICA CON ERBE
(*Sweet Rustic Pie with Greens*)

SERVES 6 TO 8

2 *pounds Swiss chard*
5 *tablespoons sugar*
3 *tablespoons powdered cocoa*
¼ *cup chopped almonds*

2 *eggs*
1 *shotglass of sweet liqueur*
1 *portion sweet dough* (*see*
    recipe No. 238)

1. Wash the Swiss chard, cook for 10 minutes in boiling water, drain. Allow to cool, squeeze out all excess water, chop fine.

2. Put chopped greens in a large bowl, add sugar, chocolate, almonds, eggs and liqueur, blend well. Preheat the oven to 400° F.

3. Line a pie plate with ⅔ of the dough, put in the filling, make a

lattice top with remaining dough, cover the pie with it and bake for about 1 hour, or until crust is golden and filling is cooked through. Serve warm or cold.

243. TORTA COI BECCHI
(*Pie with Beaks*)

SERVES 6 OR 8

1 pound stale white bread
Milk, as needed
3 tablespoons raisins
1 pound Swiss chard, boiled,
    drained and chopped
3 tablespoons pinoli nuts,
    chopped
1 egg

⅓ cup grated Pecorino *or*
    Parmesan *cheese*
Salt and pepper
2 tablespoons chopped parsley
1 teaspoon fresh thyme leaves
    or ⅔ teaspoon dried
1 portion non-sweet dough
    (recipe No. 239)

1. Soak the bread in milk to cover, remove and squeeze out excess milk. Soak raisins in warm water for 15 minutes, drain.

2. Mix chopped chard, soaked bread, raisins, *pinoli* nuts, egg, grated cheese, salt and fresh-ground pepper, parsley and thyme. Be sure everything is well blended. Add a little milk if resulting mixture seems too dry. Preheat oven to 375° F.

3. Line a pie plate with dough, pour in mixture, proceed as in step 3 of recipe No. 239.

244. ZUCCOTTO

SERVES 5 TO 6

The name of this excellent, rich Florentine dessert comes from *zucca*, pumpkin, because it has the shape of half a pumpkin. In order to make it you need a bowl that has a 1½-quart capacity and a very round shape.

About 10 to 12 ounces sponge
  cake
2 tablespoons butter
¾ cup sugar
2 tablespoons powdered cocoa
5 tablespoons water
1 pint heavy cream
5 tablespoons confectioners' sugar

3 ounces bitter chocolate, broken
  into bits
2 ounces candied cherries, cut
  in half
1 shotglass of brandy
1 shotglass of sweet liqueur
1 shotglass of rum

1. Cut the sponge cake into layers about ½-inch thick, remove crust. Make 1 round piece for the bottom of the mold, then cut as many rectangular slices as possible.

2. Put butter, sugar, cocoa and 5 tablespoons water into a small saucepan. Cook over low heat for 2 to 3 minutes, stirring often, until it becomes a chocolate syrup. Remove from fire and allow to cool.

3. Put cream and confectioners' sugar in a mixing bowl, whip until stiff. Add about ⅓ of the whipped cream to the chocolate syrup, stir well to blend. Add the chocolate bits and candied cherries to the remaining ⅔ of the whipped cream, mix well.

4. Line bottom of the bowl with the round of sponge cake. Mix brandy, liqueur and rum, pour some onto the round. Then line the sides of the bowl with some of the sponge cake rectangles and dampen them with the mixed liqueur.

5. Pour in the chocolate and cream mixture, even out with a spatula, then pour in the cream and candied fruit and even that out. Cover with remaining sponge cake squares, previously soaked in remaining alcoholic mixture, then cover the *zuccotto* with a sheet of wax paper and put into the refrigerator.

6. After at least 5 hours remove, unmold, slice and serve. Some put this creamy dessert into the freezer for an hour; personally, I prefer the taste of it when the flavors run together rather than when they solidify. It's good either way.

CONSERVE
(*Preserves*)

245. ARISTA DI MAIALE SOTT'OLIO
(*Loin of Pork in Oil*)

SERVES 6 OR 7

2 pounds loin of pork
Salt and pepper
Olive oil, as needed
2 tablespoons chopped onion

2 cloves garlic, crushed
2 cups dry white wine
4 bay leaves

1. Bone the loin of pork, sprinkle generously with salt and pepper.
2. Put 3 tablespoons of oil in a casserole, add the onion and garlic, allow to cook for 2 minutes over medium flame, add the meat.
3. When meat is browned on all sides pour in the wine, stir in order to scrape up any bits that may have got stuck at the bottom of the pan, cook uncovered until all wine has evaporated.

4. Lower the flame, add a ladleful of water, continue to cook until the meat is ready, about 45 minutes. Remove meat from casserole and allow to cool.

5. Put meat into a large, sterilized glass container with a glass or plastic top, arrange the bay leaves around it, pour in olive oil to cover, put on the lid and store in cool, dark place. Keep for about 3 months. This pork roast can be served cold or warmed up.

246. CARCIOFINI SOTT'OLIO
(*Artichokes Stored in Oil*)

MAKES 2 TO 4 JARS

This recipe is made with young, tender artichokes which in Tuscany are available at the end of May. It can be made with larger artichokes or even with the frozen ones available on the U.S. market, but the result is not as delicate.

> *100 small, tender artichokes*
> *1 quart good wine vinegar*
> *Bay leaves*
> *Olive oil, as needed*

1. Clean the artichokes of their hard, outer leaves and drop into a container of cold water acidulated with vinegar.

2. Put vinegar into an enameled or pyrex casserole, bring to the boiling point.

3. Drop in about 30 of the cleaned artichokes, allow to boil again, keep in boiling vinegar for 5 minutes.

4. Remove with a slotted spoon and put into a sieve which has been lined with a clean linen cloth.

5. Repeat twice until all artichokes are cooked and have been put into the sieve. Fold the linen cloth over them and keep covered for several hours, until they are as dry as possible.

6. Line up artichokes in sterilized glass jars with plastic or glass tops (no rubber), fitting them as close together as possible. Slip 1 or 2 bay leaves into each jar. Cover with olive oil, cover jar, store in a cool place. Keeps from 6 to 12 months.

Note: Vegetables in oil should be checked after a few days. Often the oil level drops and more oil has to be added. Vegetables should be completely covered with oil, otherwise the ones at the top may develop mold.

247. FUNGHI SOTT'OLIO
(*Mushrooms Stored in Oil*)

MAKES 2 TO 4 JARS

About 100 small, hard porcini mushrooms
1 quart good wine vinegar
Bay leaves, as needed
Olive oil, as needed

1. Clean the mushrooms well with a small, sharp knife, wipe with damp cloth.

2. Put vinegar into an enameled or pyrex casserole, bring to the boiling point.

3. Drop in about 20 or 30 mushrooms, allow to boil again, keep in boiling vinegar for 5 minutes.

4. Remove with slotted spoon and put into a sieve which has been lined with a clean linen cloth.

5. Repeat until all mushrooms are cooked and have been put into the sieve, then fold the linen cloth over them. Keep covered for several hours, until all outside liquid has been absorbed.

6. Line up cooked mushrooms in sterilized glass jars with glass or plastic (not rubber) lids, fitting them as close as possible. Slip 2 bay leaves into each jar, then pour in olive oil to cover. Store in a cool place, check after 5 or 6 days. If oil level has dropped, add more oil. Store in cool, dark place. Keeps for 6 to 12 months.

248. MELANZANE GRIGLIATE SOTT'OLIO
(*Grilled Eggplant in Oil*)

MAKES 3 TO 4 JARS

12 medium eggplants of the round variety
Salt
Peanut oil, as needed
Sterilized glass jars with glass or plastic tops, no rubber
Whole black peppercorns

1. Wash eggplants, dry, then cut into slices about ⅙-inch thick. Put on an inclined plane and sprinkle with salt. Allow to stand for about 2 hours, rinse with cold water, dry.

2. Grease each slice with a pastry brush dipped in oil. Put a heavy iron grill or saucepan on the fire; when it's hot put a few slices of eggplant on it, allow to cook for 1 or 2 minutes, turn with a spatula.

3. Turn each slice 3 or 4 times, in order to be sure each one is cooked through. When done, remove and put on a platter. Continue until all slices are cooked, always piling them one on top of the other.

4. Pour more oil on the pile of slices, sprinkle with a little salt, wait until the oil is absorbed. Meanwhile, pour a thin layer of oil into a jar, then fill with grilled eggplant slices, adding a few peppercorns. Add more oil until there is a layer of pure oil on top. Cover the jar, store in a cool, dark place. Keeps for at least 6 months. When serving, add a few drops of vinegar, salt and fresh-ground pepper.

249. MOSTARDA TOSCANA
(*Tuscan Mustard*)

MAKES 4 OR 5 JARS

This is an old recipe for a fruity mustard that goes very well with boiled or grilled meat. Our own word for "mustard" comes from this spicy marmalade, because it was made with "must," *mosto,* which is nothing but grape juice in its fresh form, before it becomes wine.

4 pounds sweet white grapes,
  washed
2 pounds mealy apples
2 large pears
2 cups Vin Santo *or sweet sherry*

4 tablespoons dry mustard
½ cup candied citrus fruit
  (lemon, orange, grapefruit,
  cedar)
Powdered cinnamon, as needed

1. Press the grapes by putting them through a food mill, allow to sit for 2 days, then squeeze out all liquid and discard pits and other solids.

2. Peel apples and pears, cut into slices, put in a casserole, add all but 5 tablespoons of the *Vin Santo* or sweet sherry. Cook until the wine has been absorbed, then add the grape juice.

3. Continue to cook on slow flame until the mixture reaches the consistency of a thick marmalade, remove from fire, allow to cool. Meanwhile, heat the 5 remaining tablespoons of wine and dissolve the mustard in it. Add this to the fruit and juice mixture. Stir, then add the candied citrus fruit and stir again.

4. Fill sterilized glass jars almost to the top, sprinkle with powdered cinnamon. Cover and store in a cool, dark place. Serve with boiled meats, roasts and steaks.

250. ODORI TRITATI E SALATI SOTT'OLIO
(*Chopped Vegetables Preserved in Salt and Oil*)

MAKES 1 OR 2 JARS

This is a practical solution for campers or sailors who want to eat well. A jar of these vegetables mixed with salt and oil is an excellent base for all Tuscan sauces or stews. Also practical for busy cooks. Vary the proportions of the various ingredients to suit your taste; add garlic if you like it.

> *2 pounds onions, carrots, celery, parsley and basil, mixed*
> *10 tablespoons salt*
> *Olive oil, as needed*

1. Clean and wash all vegetables, drain well, allow to dry on a linen cloth for at least 6 hours.

2. Put all vegetables through a grinder or chop fine, add the salt, combine well.

3. Put vegetable-salt mixture into sterilized glass jars with glass or plastic (not rubber) lids, cover with olive oil. Cover the jars and store in cool, dark place. Keeps for about 6 months.

251. OLIVE IN SALAMOIA
(*Olives in Brine*)

MAKES 2 TO 3 JARS

2 pounds fresh ripe black Tuscan olives
½ cup salt
2 quarts boiling water
1 small stick cinnamon
1 teaspoon whole cloves

1. Wash the olives, put in a large glass container, cover with cold water, cover the container. Allow to stand for 40 days.

2. Drain the olives, rinse well, discard any that float or look damaged. Put them back into the container, cover with cold water, check after 48 hours. If the water has colored, even slightly, drain olives, rinse and cover with cold water again. Continue to do this until water remains completely clear. Four or five changes of water should be sufficient.

3. Melt the salt in 2 quarts of boiling water, allow to cool. Put drained, rinsed olives into several smaller jars, cover with cold salted water, add a few small pieces of cinnamon and a few cloves to each jar, cover. Allow to stand for at least 60 days before using. Keeps 12 months.

252. OLIVE MARINATE ALLA TOSCANA
(*Tuscan Marinated Olives*)

MAKES 2 TO 3 JARS

2 pounds fresh ripe black Tuscan
  olives
3 cups dry white wine
5 cloves garlic
3 whole peperoncini (*Italian
  hot peppers*)

2 sprigs fresh rosemary or 1
  tablespoon dried
Olive oil, as needed
3 tablespoons salt

1. Wash olives, put in a pan with 3 cups water and the wine, allow to boil for about 20 minutes, until soft; drain the olives and discard the liquid.

2. Clean and wash garlic, wash red peppers, remove rosemary leaves from twig. Mix these three ingredients and chop fine.

3. Put drained olives into a large bowl, add ⅔ cup olive oil, salt and chopped garlic, rosemary and peppers. Toss well, add more oil if necessary to coat olives.

4. Put seasoned olives into jars, cover, store in a cool place. Use after 20 or 30 days. Keeps for about 6 months.

Note: This recipe is also excellent if olives are baked in the oven for 15 to 20 minutes rather than boiled.

253. POMAROLA CONSERVATA SOTTO VUOTO I
(*Canned Tomato Sauce I*)

MAKES 2 QUARTS

About 4 pounds ripe, firm Italian plum tomatoes
Four 1-pint sterilized glass jars with rubber sealing tops

1. Wash and dry tomatoes, cut in half, put in a large casserole, cover, cook on medium flame for 15 minutes.

2. Put all tomatoes through a food mill and the resulting purée into the jars. Close jars according to manufacturer's instructions.

3. Put the jars into a large container or canning pan, cover with water, bring to the boiling point and allow to cook slowly for 45 minutes.

4. Turn off flame and allow water to cool naturally. Remove jars, dry them, test to be sure they are properly sealed. Store in dark, cool place. Keeps about 12 months.

254. POMAROLA CON ODORI CONSERVATA
SOTTO VUOTO II
(*Canned Tomato Sauce II*)

MAKES 2 QUARTS

Same as previous recipe, plus 2 carrots and 2 onions. In step 1, clean and wash carrots and onions, chop coarse and add to the tomatoes.

This sauce has the flavor of the tomato sauce in recipe No. 86. When in need of a quick sauce for *pasta* just open a jar, add butter or olive oil and a bouillon cube, cook for 10 minutes and serve.

255. PELATI SOTTO VUOTO
(*Canned Peeled Plum Tomatoes*)

MAKES 2 QUARTS

About 4 pounds ripe, firm Italian plum tomatoes
Four 1-pint sterilized glass jars with rubber sealing tops

1. Wash the tomatoes. Put a large pot full of water on the stove, bring to the boiling point.

2. Drop a few tomatoes into the boiling water, leave for less than 1 minute, remove, peel and put in a sieve.

3. Repeat with remaining tomatoes, then fill the jars with peeled tomatoes and close according to manufacturer's instructions.

4. Repeat steps 3 and 4 of recipe No. 253.

INDEX

Born in Poland and educated in Rio de Janeiro and New York City, Wilma Pezzini has lived in the Tuscan village of Camaiore for more than ten years. Her book results from the casual suggestion of a satisfied dinner guest.